New Jersey Electrical Contractor Exam Information Sheet

Prerequisites:

The applicant must be at least 21 years old and hold a high school diploma or equivalency certificate. Five years experience are needed in the installation, alteration, or repair of wiring for electric light, heat or power in compliance with the National Electrical Code. A four-year approved apprenticeship program may substitute for four of these years. Alternatively, a bachelor's degree in electrical engineering may substitute for three of these years.

Application Process:

Fill out the Application for Examination at the Board website (below). Include the $100 application fee. When your application is approved, you will receive the Examination Eligibility Notice by mail.

Exam Details:

There are three computer-based multiple-choice exams that must be taken on the same day (1st time applicants):

Examination	Time (minutes)	Number of Questions	Fee
Electrical Contracting	260	100	$78
Business and Law	130	50	$43
Alarm Systems	165	50	$43

The testing center provides copies of 2014 NFPA 70 National Electrical Code. The candidate may bring their own tabbed and highlighted copy of NASCLA Contrators Guide to Business, Law, and Project Management, New Jersey.

70% of the questions must be correct on each section in order to pass. If one of the sections is failed, the applicant must wait six months before retesting that section.

Reciprocity:

None

Contact Information:

New Jersey Office of the Attorney General
Division of Consumer Affairs
Board of Examiners of Electrical Contractors
124 Halsey Street, 6th Floor, P.O. Box 45006
Newark, New Jersey 07101
(973) 504-6410
http://www.njconsumeraffairs.gov/elec/Pages/default.aspx

Copyright © 2016
All rights reserved.
Printed in the United States of America

First Edition

The contents of this book are the property of Brown Technical Publications, Inc. All rights reserved. No part of this book covered by the copyright hereon may be reproduced, transmitted, stored or used in any form or by any means, graphic, electronic or mechanical, including, but not limited to, photocopying, recording, scanning, digitizing, Web distribution, information networks or by any information storage and retrieval systems, except as permitted under Section 107 or 108 of the 1976 United States Copyright Act, without the prior written permission of the publisher.

While every precaution has been taken in preparation of this book, the author and publisher assumes no responsibility for errors or omissions. Neither is any liability assumed from the use of the information contained herein. The reader is expressly warned to consider and adopt all safety precautions and to avoid all potential hazards. The publisher and author make no representations or warranties of any kind, nor are any such representations implied with respect to the material set forth here. The publisher and author shall not be liable for any special, consequently, or exemplary damages resulting, in whole or part, from the reader's use of, or reliance upon, this material.

National Electrical Code® and the NEC® are registered Trademarks of the National Fire Protection Association, Inc., Quincy, MA

Author: Ray Holder

TABLE OF CONTENTS

INTRODUCTION..	4
USEFUL FORMULAS...	11
POWER FORMULAS..	12
OHMS LAW...	12
POWER FACTOR FORMULAS...	13
VOLTAGE DROP..	14
COMMONLY USED NEC® TABLES & ARTICLES................	15
UNIT 1 – BASIC ELECTRICAL FORMULAS........................	16
UNIT 2 – BRANCH CIRCUITS..	28
UNIT 3 – COOKING EQUIPT. & APPL. DEMAND LOADS.....	41
UNIT 4 – CONDUCTOR AMPACITY & SIZING....................	52
UNIT 5 – BOX AND RACEWAY SIZING...............................	64
UNIT 6 – VOLTAGE DROP CALCULATIONS......................	78
UNIT 7 – AC MOTOR CALCULATIONS...............................	88
UNIT 8 – ONE FAMILY DWELLING SERVICE CALCULATIONS...............	96
UNIT 9 – MULTI-FAMILY DWELLING SERVICE CALCULATIONS............	114
UNIT 10 – COMMERCIAL LOAD CALCULATIONS..............	133
EXAM 1...	158
EXAM 2...	164
EXAM 3...	171
EXAM 4...	178
EXAM 5...	184
EXAM 6...	191
EXAM 7...	197
EXAM 8...	203
EXAM 9...	209
EXAM 10...	216
EXAM 11...	222
EXAM 12...	229
FINAL EXAM 1...	236
FINAL EXAM 2...	260

Copyright© 2016

ANSWER KEY EXAM 1	**284**
ANSWER KEY EXAM 2	**286**
ANSWER KEY EXAM 3	**289**
ANSWER KEY EXAM 4	**292**
ANSWER KEY EXAM 5	**294**
ANSWER KEY EXAM 6	**296**
ANSWER KEY EXAM 7	**298**
ANSWER KEY EXAM 8	**300**
ANSWER KEY EXAM 9	**302**
ANSWER KEY EXAM 10	**304**
ANSWER KEY EXAM 11	**306**
ANSWER KEY EXAM 12	**308**
ANSWER KEY FINAL EXAM 1	**310**
ANSWER KEY FINAL EXAM 2	**318**
GLOSSARY	**324**
APPENDIX A	**343**
APPENDIX B	**348**

INTRODUCTION

HOW TO PREPARE FOR THE EXAM

Congratulations on purchasing this book! You have taken the first step towards successfully passing your Master Electrician's Licensing Exam. You have in your hands the best self-study guide available for master electrician's exam preparation. This book will not make you a competent electrician, nor teach you the electrical trade, but it will give you an idea of the type of questions asked on most electrician's licensing exams and how to answer them correctly. This book covers practically all the subjects you will likely be tested on, including: branch circuits and feeders, motors and motor controls, transformers, hazardous locations, special occupancies, conductors, box and raceway fill, services, and the ever present electrical calculations, plus much more.

Most electrician's licensing exams consists of multiple-choice questions therefore, these are the types of questions shown in this exam preparation guide. The exam questions you may encounter may be, fill in the blank, complete a sentence, select a correct choice, or complete a math calculation. In this self-study guide you will find simulated exams, with questions much like the actual test questions. These questions are an example of the many questions the author and his students come upon when taking numerous licensing exams in recent years.

Begin your exam preparation with two important points in mind.
   * Opportunities in life will arise - be prepared for them.
   * The more you LEARN - the more you EARN.

Attempting to take an exam without preparation is a complete waste of time. Don't make that mistake. Attend classes at your local community college. Attend seminars, electrical code updates, and company sponsored programs. Many major electrical suppliers and local unions sponsor classes of this type at no cost. Take advantage of them.

Become familiar with the National Electrical Code®; the Code has a LANGUAGE all its own. Understanding this language will help you to better interpret the NEC®. Do not become intimidated by its length. Become thoroughly familiar with the definitions in Chapter One; if you don't, the remainder of the NEC® will be difficult to comprehend. Remember, on the job we use different "lingo" and phrases compared to the way the NEC® is written and to the way many test questions are expressed.

Copyright© 2016

HOW TO STUDY

Before beginning to study, get into the right frame of mind, and relax. Study in a quiet place that is conducive to learning. If such a place is not available, go to your local library. It is important that you have the right atmosphere in which to study.

It is much better to study many short lengths of time than attempt to study fewer, longer lengths of time. Try to study a little while, say about an hour, every evening. You will need the support and understanding of your family to set aside this much needed time.

As you study this exam preparation book, the NEC® and other references, always highlight the important points. This makes it easier to locate Code references when taking the exam.

Use a straight edge, such as a six-inch ruler when using the NEC® tables and charts. A very common mistake is to get on the wrong line when using these tables; when that happens, the result is an incorrect answer.

Use tabs on the major sections of your NEC®, so they are faster and easier to locate when taking the exam. The national average allowed per question is less than three minutes, you cannot waste time.

WHAT TO STUDY

A common reason for one to be unsuccessful when attempting to pass electrical exams is not knowing what to study. Approximately forty percent of most exams are known as "core" questions. These type of questions are reflected in this exam preparation book.

The subject matter covered in most electrical license examinations is:

* Grounding and bonding
* Overcurrent protection
* Wiring methods and installation
* Boxes and fittings
* Services and equipment
* Motors
* Special occupancies
* Load calculations
* Lighting
* Appliances
* Box and raceway fill
* Hazardous locations

Become very familiar with questions on the above. Knowing what to study is a major step toward passing your exam.

HELPFUL HINTS ON TAKING THE EXAM

* **Complete the easy questions first.** On most tests, all questions are valued the same. If you become too frustrated on any one question, it may reflect upon your entire test.

* **Keep track of time.** Do not spend too much time on one question. If a question is difficult for you, mark the answer sheet the answer you think is correct and place a check (✓) by that question in the examination booklet. Then go on to the next question; if you have time after finishing the rest of the exam, you can go back to the questions you have checked. If you simply do not know the answer to a question, take a guess. Choose the answer that is most familiar to you. In most cases, the answer is B or C.

* **Only change answers if you know you are right.** - Usually, your first answer is your best answer.

* **Relax** - Do not get uptight and stressed out when testing.

* **Tab your Code Book.** - References are easier and faster to find.

* **Use a straightedge.** - Prevent getting on the wrong line when referring to the tables in the NEC®.

* **Get a good nights rest before the exam.** - Do not attempt to drive several hours to an exam site; be rested and alert.

* **Understand the question.** - One key word in a question can make a difference in what the question is asking. Underlining key words will help you to understand the meaning of the question.

* **Use a dependable calculator.** - Use a solar-powered calculator that has a battery back-up. Since many test sites are not well lighted, this type of calculator will prepare you for such a situation. If possible, bring along a spare calculator.

* **Show up at least 30 minutes prior to your exam time.** – Be sure to allow yourself time for traffic, etc. when planning your route to the exam location.

TYPICAL REGULATIONS AT THE PLACE OF EXAMINATION

Most licensing agencies outsource their examinations to a testing agency that is a separate entity from the licensing agency. After you get approval from the licensing agency to take the exam, contact the testing agency for their regulations. To ensure that all examinees are examined under equally favorable conditions, the following regulations and procedures are observed at most examination sites:

* Each examinee must present proper photo identification, preferably your driver's license before you will be permitted to take the examination.

* No cameras, notes, tape recorders, pagers, or cellular phones are allowed in the examination room.

* No one will be permitted to work beyond the established time limits.

* Examinees are not permitted any reference material EXCEPT the National Electrical Code®.

* Examinees will be permitted to use noiseless calculators during the examination. Calculators which provide programmable ability or pre-programmed calculators are prohibited.

* Permission of an examination proctor must be obtained before leaving the room while the examination is in progress.

* Each examinee is assigned to a seat specifically designated by name and/or number when admitted to the examination room.

TYPICAL EXAMINATION QUESTIONS

EXAMPLE 1

An equipment grounding conductor of a branch circuit shall be identified by which of the following colors?

A. gray
B. white
C. black
D. green

Here you are asked to select from the listed colors the one that is to be used to identify the equipment grounding conductor of a branch circuit. Since Section 250.119 of the NEC® requires that green or green with yellow stripes be the color of insulation used on a grounding conductor (when it is not bare), the answer is **D**.

EXAMPLE 2

A circuit leading to a gasoline dispensing pump must have a disconnecting means _____.

A. only in the grounded conductors
B. only in the ungrounded conductors
C. operating independently in all conductors
D. that simultaneously disconnects both the grounded and ungrounded conductors supplying the dispensing pump

Here the "question" is in the form of an incomplete statement. Your task is to select the choice that best completes the statement. In this case, you should have selected **D** since Section 514.11(A) of the NEC® specifies that such a circuit shall be provided with a means to disconnect simultaneously from the source of supply all conductors of a circuit, including the grounded conductor.

Copyright© 2016

EXAMPLE 3

A building or other structure served shall be supplied by only one service EXCEPT one where the capacity requirements are in excess of _____.

A. 800 amperes at a supply voltage of 1000 volts or less
B. 1000 amperes at a supply voltage of 1000 volts or less
C. 1500 amperes at a supply voltage of 1000 volts or less
D. 2000 amperes at a supply voltage of 1000 volts or less

Again, the "question" is in the form of an incomplete statement and your task is to select the choice that best completes the statement. In this case, you are to find an exception. You have to select the condition that has to be met when supplying a building or structure by more than one service. You should have selected **D** because Section 230.2(C)(1) requires the conditions listed in **D** but does not require or permit the conditions listed in A, B, or C.

EXAMPLE 4

Disregarding exceptions, the MINIMUM size overhead service-drop conductors shall be _____ AWG copper.

A. 6
B. 8
C. 12
D. 14

Here the "question" is in the form of fill in the blank and your task is to select the choice that best completes the statement. In this case, exceptions are not applicable. You have to select the minimum size conductor required for overhead service-drop conductors. You should have selected **B** because Section 230.23(B) specifies that the conductors shall not be smaller than 8 AWG copper.

HOW TO USE THIS BOOK

Practice exams numbers 1-12 contained in this book consists of 25 questions each. The time allotted for each of these practice exams is 75 minutes or 3 minutes per question. After taking the first 12 exams try the final exams. The two final exams are 100 questions in length; the allotted time for each final exam is 5 hours. Using this time limit as a standard, you should be able to complete an actual examination in the allotted time.
You will seldom find trick questions in this exam prep guide, but many will require careful reading. Certain words such as, shall, shall not, should and should not, can make a difference in the correct answer. When a question contains verbiage such as, in general, generally, the general rule is, disregarding exceptions, etc., this means exceptions are not to be taken into consideration.

To get the most out of this book you should answer every question and highlight your NEC® for future reference. If you have difficulty with a question and cannot come up with the answer that is familiar to you, put a check mark next to the question and come back to it after completing the remainder of the questions. Review your answers with the **ANSWER KEY** located in the back of this book. This will help you identify your strengths and weaknesses. When you discover you are weaker in some areas than others, you will know that further study is necessary in those areas.

Do only one practice exam contained in this book during an allotted study period. This way you do not get burned out and fatigued trying to study for too long a period of time. This also helps you develop good study habits. **GOOD LUCK!**

ABOUT THE AUTHOR

H. Ray Holder has worked in the electrical industry for over fifty years as an apprentice, journeyman, master, field engineer, estimator, business manager, contractor, inspector, consultant, and instructor.

Mr. Holder is a graduate of Texas State University and holds a Bachelor of Science Degree in Occupational Education. He also holds a lifetime teaching certificate from the Texas Education Agency, in the field of Vocational Education.

He is a certified instructor of electrical trades. His classes are presented in a simplified, easy-to-understand format for electricians.

He has taught over 35,000 students at Austin Community College, and the University of Texas at Austin, Texas, Odessa College, at Odessa, Texas, Howard College at San Angelo, Texas, Technical-Vocational Institute of Albuquerque, New Mexico, and in the public school systems in Ft. Worth and San Antonio, Texas. He is currently the Director of Education for Electrical Seminars, Inc.

Mr. Holder is a former member of the National Fire Protection Association, International Association of Electrical Inspectors, and retired member of the International Brotherhood of Electrical Workers.

USEFUL FORMULAS

To Find	Single Phase	Three Phase	Direct Current
Amperes when kVA is known	$\dfrac{kVA \times 1{,}000}{E}$	$\dfrac{kVA \times 1{,}000}{E \times 1.732}$	not applicable
Amperes when horsepower is known	$\dfrac{HP \times 746}{E \times \%Eff. \times PF.}$	$\dfrac{HP \times 746}{E \times 1.732 \times \%Eff. \times PF.}$	$\dfrac{HP \times 746}{E \times \%Eff.}$
Amperes when Kilowatts are known	$\dfrac{kW \times 1{,}000}{E \times PF.}$	$\dfrac{kW \times 1{,}000}{E \times 1.732 \times PF.}$	$\dfrac{kW \times 1{,}000}{E}$
Kilowatts	$\dfrac{I \times E \times PF.}{1{,}000}$	$\dfrac{I \times E \times 1.732 \times PF.}{1{,}000}$	$\dfrac{I \times E}{1{,}000}$
Kilovolt Amperes	$\dfrac{I \times E}{1{,}000}$	$\dfrac{I \times E \times 1.732}{1{,}000}$	not applicable
Horsepower	$\dfrac{I \times E \times \%Eff. \times PF.}{746}$	$\dfrac{I \times E \times 1.732 \times \%Eff. \times PF.}{746}$	$\dfrac{I \times E \times \%Eff.}{746}$
Watts	$E \times I \times PF.$	$E \times I \times 1.732 \times PF.$	$E \times I$

I = Amperes
E = Volt
kW = Kilowatts
kVA = Kilovolt-Amperes

HP = Horsepower
%Eff. = Percent Efficiency
PF. = Power Factor

Power – "Pie" Circle Formulas

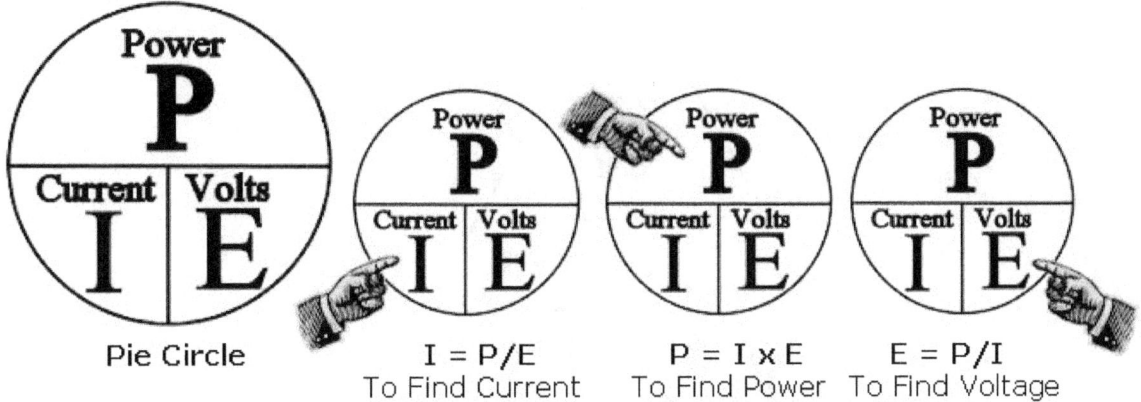

Ohms Law Circle Formulas

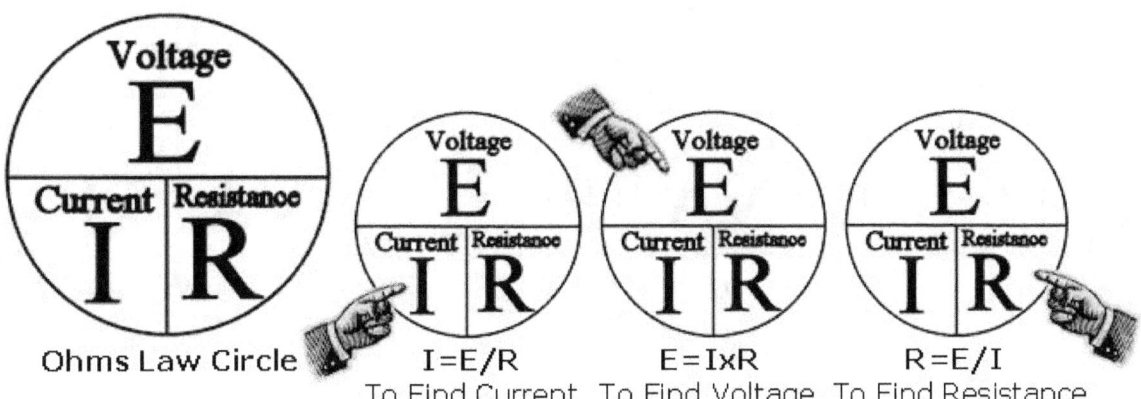

Power Factor Triangle Formulas

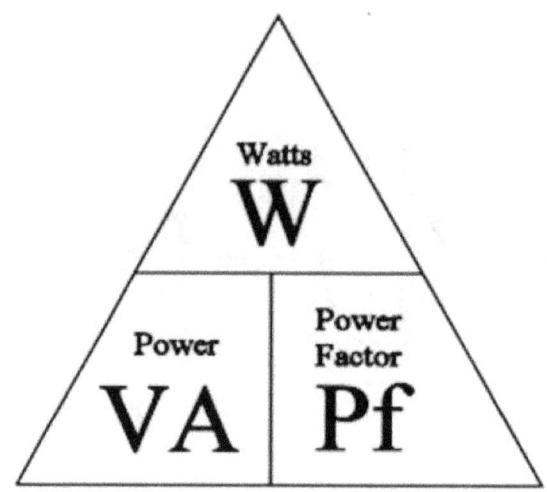

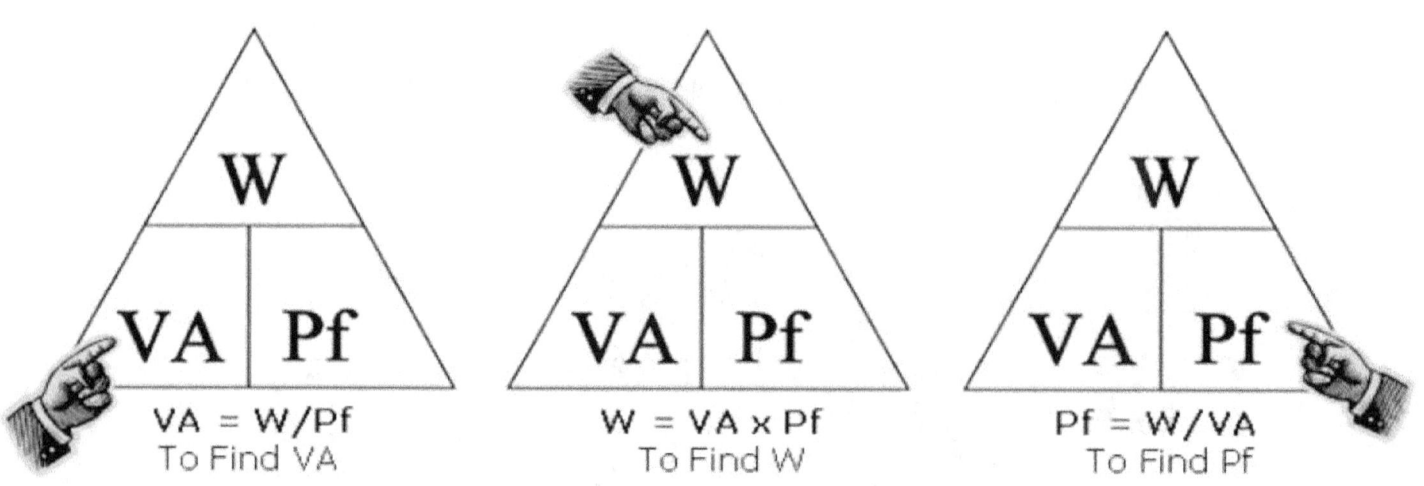

VOLTAGE DROP FORMULAS

Formula Definitions:

VD = Volts dropped from a circuit.

2 = Multiplying factor for single-phase circuits. The 2 represents the conductor length in a single-phase circuit.

1.732 = Multiplying factor for three-phase circuits. The square root of 3 represents the conductor length in a three-phase circuit. The only difference between the single-phase and three-phase formulas is that "1.732" has replaced "2".

K = Approximate resistivity of the conductor per mil foot. A mil foot is a wire 1 foot long and one mil in diameter. The approximate K value for copper wire is **12.9** ohms and for aluminum wire is **21.2** ohms per mil foot.

I = Current or amperage draw of the load.

D = The distance from the source voltage to the load.

CM = Circular mil area of the conductor. (Chapter 9, Table 8)

*NOTE – When determining wire size, distance or current, VD is the actual volts that can be dropped from the circuit. The recommended percentage for a branch-circuit is 3%. Example: 3% of 120 volts is 3.6 volts. DO NOT enter 3% in the VD position.

To find voltage drop in a single-phase circuit.

$$VD = \frac{2 \times K \times I \times D}{CM}$$

To find wire size in a single-phase circuit.

$$CM = \frac{2 \times K \times I \times D}{VD}$$

To find distance in a single-phase circuit.

$$D = \frac{CM \times VD}{2 \times K \times I}$$

To find MAXIMUM current in amperes in a single-phase circuit.

$$I = \frac{CM \times VD}{2 \times K \times D}$$

Commonly used NEC® Tables and Articles:

Tbl. 110.26(A)(1)	Working Spaces About Electrical Equipment of 600 Volts or Less
Tbl. 110.28	Enclosure Selection
210.8	GFCI Protection
210.12	AFCI Protection
Tbl. 210.21(B)(3)	Receptacle Ratings
Tbl. 210.24	Branch-Circuit Requirements
Tbl. 220.12	General Lighting Loads by Occupancy
Tbl. 220.42	Lighting Load Demand Factors
Tbl. 220.55	Demand Factors for Household Cooking Appliances
Tbl. 220.56	Demand Factors for Commercial Kitchen Equipment
Tbl. 220.84	Optional Calculation-Demand Factors for Multi-Family Dwellings
240.6(A)	Standard Ampere Ratings of Overcurrent Protection Devices
Tbl. 250.66	Grounding Electrode Conductor
Tbl. 250.122	Equipment Grounding Conductors
Tbl. 300.5	Burial Depth of Conductors and Cables
Tbl. 310.15(B)(2)(a)	Ambient Temperature Correction Factors for Conductors
Tbl. 310.15(B)(3)(a)	Adjustment Factors for More Than 3 Wires in Raceway
Tbl. 310.15(B)(2)(c)	Temperature Adjustment for Rooftop Conductors and Conduits
Tbl. 310.15(B)(16)	Allowable Ampacities of Conductors in Raceways
Tbl. 310.15(B)(17)	Allowable Ampacities of Single Conductors in Free Air
Tbl. 310.104(A)	Conductor Applications and Insulations
430.32	Overload Sizing for Motors
Tbl. 430.52	Motor Overcurrent Protection
Tbl. 430.248	Single-Phase Motors Full-Load Current Ratings
Tbl. 430.250	Three-Phase Motors Full-Load Current Ratings
Tbl. 450.3(A)	Overcurrent Protection for Transformers Over 600 Volts
Tbl. 450.4(A)	Overcurrent Protection for Transformers of 600 Volts or Less
Chpt. 9, Tbl. 4	Dimensions and Percent Area of Conduit and Tubing
Chpt. 9, Tbl. 5	Dimensions of Insulated Conductors
Chpt. 9, Tbl. 8	Conductor Properties
Annex C	Conduit and Tubing Fill for Conductors of the Same Size
Annex D	Calculation Examples

BASIC ELECTRICAL FORMULAS

Upon successfully completing this unit of study, the student will be familiar with the concepts and application of Ohm's Law, power formulas and power factor.

 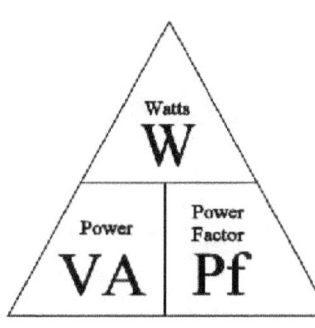 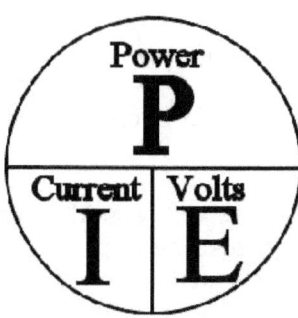

UNIT 1

BASIC ELECTRICAL FORMULAS

PIE CIRCLE FORMULAS

RELATED INFORMATION:

- The **PIE** formula circle illustrates the relationship between **power, current and voltage**.

- Power may be expressed as true power such as, **watts, kilowatts, kW** or **horsepower**; power may also be expressed in terms as apparent power such as, **volt-amps, VA, kilo volt-amps** or **kVA**.

- The letter "**P**" represents power.

- The letter "**I**" represents current.

- The letter "**E**" represents voltage.

- The letter "**k**" is the abbreviation of kilo or one thousand (1,000).

- One **kW** equals 1,000 watts.

- One **kVA** equals 1,000 volt-amps.

- One **horsepower** equals 746 watts.

➢ Formulas used to determine the available power for a single-phase circuit, load or an electrical system are:

P = I x E

P = current x volts

P = volts x amps

P = VA

P = kVA

kW = current x volts
      1,000

kVA = current x volts
       1,000

EXAMPLE – Determine the available power, in VA, for a 100 ampere, 240 volt, single-phase circuit.

    A. 2,400 VA
    B. 24,000 VA
    C. 240,000 VA
    D. 2.40 VA

    ANSWER – (B)   24,000 VA

    VA = I x E
    VA = 100 amperes x 240 volts = 24,000 VA

EXAMPLE – Determine the apparent power, in kVA, for a 150 ampere, 120/240 Volt, single-phase electrical system.

    A. 36 kVA
    B. 3.60 kVA
    C. 360 kVA
    D. 3,600 kVA

    ANSWER – (A) 36 kVA

    kVA = I x E
          1,000

    kVA = 150 amps x 240 volts = 36,000 = 36 kVA
                 1,000   1,000

➤ Formulas used to determine the available power for three-phase circuits, loads or electrical systems are:

P = I x E x 1.732

P = current x volts x 1.732

P = volts x 1.732 x amps

P = VA x 1.732

kW = current x volts x 1.732
            1,000

kVA = current x volts x 1.732
             1,000

EXAMPLE – Determine the available power, in VA, for a 100 ampere 208Y/120 volt, three-phase circuit.

    A. 3,603 VA
    B. 36,026 VA
    C. 360,260 VA
    D. 20,800 VA

    ANSWER – (B)36,026 VA

    VA = I x E x 1.732
    VA = 100 amps x 208 volts x 1.732 = 36,026 VA

*Note – In this situation we are to use 208 volts and multiply by 1.732 (the square root of 3), because we are to balance the load in the three current-carrying conductors.

EXAMPLE – A load that draws 50 amperes when connected to a 208Y/120 volt, three-phase source has a kW rating of _____.

    A. 18 kW
    B. 1.8 kW
    C. 180 kW
    D. 1,800 kW

    ANSWER – (A)18 kW

    kW = current x volts x 1.732
                1,000
    kW = 50 x 208 x 1.732 = 18,013 = 18 kW
              1,000   1,000

- Current may be expressed in terms such as **amps**, **amperes**, **full-load current**, **FLC**, **full-load amps**, **FLA**, **load in amps** or **amperes**, **amperage**, **amperage draw** or **line load**.

- The letter "I" represents the intensity of the current.

- Formulas used to determine the current in a single-phase circuit, load or an electrical system are:

$$I = \frac{P}{E}$$

$$I = \frac{power}{voltage}$$

$$I = \frac{watts}{volts}$$

$$I = \frac{kW \times 1{,}000}{volts}$$

$$I = \frac{VA}{volts}$$

$$I = \frac{kVA \times 1{,}000}{volts}$$

EXAMPLE – Determine the current, in amperes, for a 120 volt, single-phase branch circuit that has only six (6) 100 watt incandescent luminaries (lighting fixtures) connected.

       A. 5 amperes
       B. 15 amperes
       C. 20 amperes
       D. 2 amperes

ANSWER – (A)   5 amperes

$$I = \frac{watts}{volts} \quad I = \frac{600}{120} = 5 \text{ amperes}$$

EXAMPLE – Determine the current, in amperes, of a 2.4 kW load connected to a 240 volt, single-phase source.

    A. .01 ampere
    B. 1 ampere
    C. 100 amperes
    D. 10 amperes

ANSWER – (D)   10 amperes

$$I = \frac{2.4 \text{ kW} \times 1,000}{240} = \frac{2,400}{240} = 10 \text{ amperes}$$

➢ Formulas used to determine the current in a three (3)-phase circuit, load, or an electrical system are:

$$I = \frac{P}{E \times 1.732}$$

$$I = \frac{\text{power}}{\text{volts} \times 1.732}$$

$$I = \frac{\text{watts}}{\text{volts} \times 1.732}$$

$$I = \frac{\text{kW} \times 1,000}{\text{volts} \times 1.732}$$

$$I = \frac{\text{VA}}{\text{volts} \times 1.732}$$

$$I = \frac{\text{kVA} \times 1,000}{\text{volts} \times 1.732}$$

EXAMPLE – A 36,026 VA load connected to a 208Y/120-volt, three-phase circuit will draw _____ of current per phase.

    A. 10 amperes
    B. 173 amperes
    C. 250 amperes
    D. 100 amperes

ANSWER – (D)   100 amperes

$$I = \frac{\text{VA}}{E \times 1.732}$$

$$I = \frac{36,026 \text{ VA}}{208 \text{ volts} \times 1.732} = \frac{36,026}{360.25} = 100 \text{ amperes}$$

EXAMPLE – A balanced 60 kVA load connected to a 480Y/277-volt three-phase electrical system will have a full-load current draw of _____ per phase.

   A. 72 amperes
   B. 125 amperes
   C. 720 amperes
   D. 80 amperes

   ANSWER – (A) 72 amperes

$$I = \frac{kVA \times 1{,}000}{volts \times 1.732}$$

$$I = \frac{60\ kVA \times 1{,}000}{480\ volts \times 1.732} = \frac{60{,}000}{831.36} = 72\ amperes$$

POWER FACTOR

RELATED INFORMATION:

- **Power factor (PF)** is the ratio between true power expressed as **watts**, **kilo watts** or **kW** and the apparent power expressed as **volt-amps**, **VA** or **kVA**.

- Power factor is expressed as a percent that does not exceed 100 percent or a decimal.

- True power, is expressed as **watts**, a unit of work, **kW** or **kilowatts**; this condition occurs in AC circuits or loads that contain only resistance. This is why electric ranges, ovens, cooktops, dryers and water heaters are all rated in **watts** or **kW**. The current and the voltage will be "in-phase", meaning that the voltage and the current will reach their peak and zero values at the same time. This is what we call unity or a power factor of 100 percent.

- True power (**watts**) equals apparent power (**VA**) in an electrical circuit or load containing only resistance.

- True power (**watts**) is less than apparent power (**VA**) in a circuit or load containing inductance or capacitance, such as motors, transformers, HID and fluorescent lighting.

- The true power (**watts**) of a single-phase circuit or load that contains inductance or capacitance can be calculated by the use of the following formula:

   Watts = volts x amperes x power factor

EXAMPLE – What is the true power, in watts, of a 10 ampere load supplied with 120 volts, having a power factor of 80 percent?

    A. 1,000 watts
    B. 1,200 watts
    C. 2,400 watts
    D. 960 watts

    ANSWER – (D)   960 watts

Watts = volts x amperes x power factor
Watts = 120 volts x 10 amps x .8 = 960 watts

➤ The true power (watts) of a three-phase circuit or load that contains inductance or capacitance can be calculated by the use of the following formula:

Watts = volts x 1.732 x amperes x power factor

EXAMPLE – Determine the true power (watts) of a 7.5 ampere load with a power factor of 87 percent supplied from a three-phase, 208-volt source.

    A. 1,375 watts
    B. 2,350 watts
    C. 2,700 watts
    D. 3,132 watts

    ANSWER – (B) 2,350 watts

Watts = volts x 1.732 x amperes x power factor
Watts = 208 volts x 1.732 x 7.5 amps x .87 = 2,350 watts

➤ In most **ac circuits** containing inductance or capacitance a phase shift exists, the current is **"out-of-phase"** with the voltage; the current and the voltage do not reach their peak and zero values at the same time. Apparent power (VA) is usually more than the power in watts when this condition occurs. Apparent power is calculated without considering the phase shift that may be present between total voltage and current in the circuit.

➤ Formulas used to determine the power factor are:

Power factor = $\dfrac{\text{watts}}{\text{VA}}$

Power factor = $\dfrac{\text{watts}}{\text{volt amps}}$

Power factor = $\dfrac{\text{kW x 1,000}}{\text{volt amps}}$

EXAMPLE - The power factor of a 5 kW load drawing 30 amperes of current when connected to a 208-volt, single-phase source is _____.

A. 92 percent
B. 46 percent
C. 80 percent
D. 83 percent

ANSWER – (C) 80 percent

$$PF = \frac{kW \times 1{,}000}{volt \times amperes}$$

$$PF = \frac{5\ kW \times 1{,}000}{208\ volts \times 30\ amps} = \frac{5{,}000}{6{,}240} = .80 \text{ or } 80\%$$

- Formulas used to determine the current of a single-phase electrical load or system when the voltage and power factor are known are:

$$I = \frac{watts}{volts \times PF}$$

$$I = \frac{kw \times 1{,}000}{volts \times PF}$$

EXAMPLE – A 300 watt industrial type HID luminaire (lighting fixture) has a power factor of 85 percent and is connected to a 120 volt branch circuit. The luminaire will draw _____ of current.

A. 2.94 amperes
B. 2.50 amperes
C. 3.25 amperes
D. 2.13 amperes

ANSWER – (A) 2.94 amperes

$$I = \frac{watts}{volts \times PF}$$

$$I = \frac{300\ watts}{120\ volts \times .85} = \frac{300}{102} = 2.94 \text{ amperes}$$

> Formulas used to determine the current of a three-phase load or system when the voltage and the power factor are known are:

$$I = \frac{watts}{volts \times 1.732 \times PF}$$

$$I = \frac{kw \times 1,000}{volts \times 1.732 \times PF}$$

EXAMPLE - A 5 kW load having a power factor of 90 percent will draw _____ when connected to a 208Y/120 volt, three-phase electrical system.

    A. 37.47 amperes
    B. 13.88 amperes
    C. 17.87 amperes
    D. 15.42 amperes

ANSWER – (D)   15.42 amperes

$$I = \frac{kW \times 1,000}{volts \times 1.732 \times PF}$$

$$I = \frac{5 \text{ kW} \times 1,000}{208 \text{ volts} \times 1.732 \times .9} = \frac{5,000}{324.2} = 15.42 \text{ amperes}$$

OHM'S LAW CIRCLE FORMULAS

RELATED INFORMATION:

> The Ohm's Law circle formula illustrates the relationship between **voltage**, **current** and **resistance**.

> The letter "**E**" represents electromotive force, or voltage.

> The letter "**I**" represents the intensity of the current.

> The letter "**R**" represents the friction opposite the flow of electrons in a conductor and is known as resistance; the unit of measurement is the ohm.

> In an alternating current circuit, factors that oppose current flow are conductor resistance, capacitive reactance, and inductive reactance. This total opposition to current flow is known as impedance and is also measured in ohms; the letter "**Z**" represents the impedance and may be substituted for the letter "**R**".

➢ The formula used to determine the current flow in an electrical circuit or load when the resistance and voltage are known is:

$$I = \frac{E}{R}$$

$$I = \frac{volts}{resistance}$$

EXAMPLE – A 120 volt circuit supplies an incandescent luminaire (lighting fixture) with a resistance of 200 ohms. Determine the current flow, in amperes, of the circuit.

    A. 6.00 amperes
    B. 0.60 amperes
    C. 3.00 amperes
    D. 1.60 amperes

        ANSWER – (B)0.60 amperes

$$I = \frac{volts}{resistance} = \frac{120 \text{ volts}}{200 \text{ ohms}} = 0.60 \text{ amperes}$$

➢ The formula used to determine the voltage or voltage drop in an electrical circuit when the current and resistance are known is:

$$E = I \times R$$

$$E = current \times resistance$$

EXAMPLE – Determine the voltage drop of two size 10 AWG copper conductors that supply a 16 ampere load located 100 feet from the voltage source.
Given: The total resistance of the two conductors is 0.25 ohms.

    A. 2.00 volts
    B. 0.40 volts
    C. 4.00 volts
    D. 40.00 volts

        ANSWER – (C)4.00 volts

$$E = I \times R$$
$$E = 16 \text{ amperes} \times .25 \text{ ohms} = 4 \text{ volts}$$

➢ The formula used to determine the resistance in an electrical circuit or load when the voltage and current are known is:

$$R = \frac{E}{I}$$

$$R = \frac{voltage}{current}$$

EXAMPLE – Determine the resistance of the heating elements of an electric baseboard heater that draws 8 amperes when supplied from a 120 volt source.

    A. 0.07 ohms
    B. 960 ohms
    C. 15 ohms
    D. 150 ohms

ANSWER – (C)15 ohms

$$R = \frac{volts}{current} = \frac{120 \text{ volts}}{8 \text{ amperes}} = 15 \text{ ohms}$$

UNIT 2

BRANCH CIRCUITS

Upon successfully completing this unit of study, the student will be familiar with the concept of sizing, rating and overcurrent protection of branch circuits as well as calculating the number required.

of CIRCUITS = $\dfrac{\text{LOAD VA}}{\text{CIRCUIT VA}}$

UNIT 2

BRANCH CIRCUITS

RELATED INFORMATION:

- The definition of a **branch circuit** is the circuit conductors between the final overcurrent device (circuit breaker or fuse) protecting the circuit and the outlet(s). **[Article 100]** In other words, that portion of a wiring system that is beyond the final overcurrent device protecting the circuit and the outlet(s).

- The rating of a **branch circuit** is determined by the maximum ampere rating of the overcurrent protective device (circuit breaker or fuse) and **NOT** by the size of the conductors used for the branch-circuit. **[210.3]**

- In general, branch-circuit conductors shall have an allowable ampacity (current-carrying capacity) of **NOT** less than **125%** of the **continuous** load, plus **100%** of the **non-continuous** load to be served. **[210.19(A)(1)(a)]**

EXAMPLE – When a single branch-circuit serves a continuous load of 20 amperes and a non-continuous load of 10 amperes, the branch-circuit conductors are required to have an allowable current-carrying capacity of at least _____.

    A. 30.00 amperes
    B. 37.50 amperes
    C. 35.00 amperes
    D. 32.50 amperes

    ANSWER – (C) 35.00 amperes

    20 amperes x 1.25 = 25 amperes
    10 amperes x 1.00 = <u>10 amperes</u>
                  TOTAL = 35 amperes

- The definition of a **continuous** load is a load where the maximum current is expected to continue for **3 hours** or more. **[Article 100]**

- Examples of **continuous** loads are lighting loads for commercial and industrial occupancies that are expected to be operated for at least three (3) hours.

- Examples of **non-continuous** loads are general-purpose receptacle outlets provided for commercial, industrial, and residential occupancies and general-purpose lighting loads for residential occupancies.

- In general, overcurrent devices protecting branch-circuits shall have a rating of not less than **125%** of the **continuous** load to be served plus **100%** of the **non-continuous** load to be served. **[210.20(A)]** In other words, overcurrent devices protecting branch circuits are not to be loaded more than **80%** of their rated value when protecting **continuous** loads.

    EXAMPLE - When a 100 ampere rated circuit breaker is used to protect a branch circuit serving a continuous load, the load shall not exceed _____.

    A. 80 amperes
    B. 100 amperes
    C. 125 amperes
    D. 115 amperes

    ANSWER – (A) 80 amperes

    100 amperes x .80 = 80 amperes

- Note the exception to **210.20(A)**. If the overcurrent device protecting the circuit is **listed** for **continuous operation**, it shall be permitted to have a rating of **100%** of the continuous load(s) to be served. **Be advised**, circuit breakers are **NOT** listed for continuous operation, unless they have a rating of at least **400 amperes** or more.

- In general, branch-circuit loads shall be calculated as shown in **220.12, 220.14,** and **220.16 [220.10]**

- In general, lighting loads are to be supplied by 15-and 20-ampere rated branch-circuits. **[210.23(A)]**

- Lighting loads for specific occupancies shall be based on the unit load per square foot depending on the type of occupancy as given on **Table 220.12**. **[220.12]**

    Table 220.12 General Lighting Loads by Occupancy

Type of Occupancy	UNIT LOAD	
	Volt-Amperes per Square Meter	**Volt-Amperes per Square Foot**
Armories and auditoriums	11	1
Banks	39[b]	3½[b]
Barber shops and beauty parlors	33	3
Churches	11	1
Clubs	22	2
Court rooms	22	2
Dwelling units[a]	33	3
Garages – commercial (storage)	6	½
Hospitals	22	2
Hotels and motels, including apartment houses without provision for cooking by tenants[a]	22	2
Industrial commercial (loft) buildings	22	2
Lodge rooms	17	1½
Office buildings	39[b]	3½[b]
Restaurants	22	2
Schools	33	3
Stores	33	3
Warehouses (storage)	3	¼
In any of the preceding occupancies except one-family dwellings and individual dwelling units of two-family and multifamily dwellings:		
Assembly halls and auditoriums	11	1
Halls, corridors, closets, stairways	6	½
Storage spaces	3	¼

ᵃSee 220.14(J)   ᵇSee 220.14(K)

> General lighting loads are to be calculated from the outside dimensions of the building. **[220.12]**

> To determine the area, in square feet, of a building, simply multiply the length of the building times the width of the building.

   EXAMPLE -   A building has outside dimensions of 100 feet in length and 75 feet in width. The building has a total area of _____.

   A. 750 square feet
   B. 175 square feet
   C. 7,500 square feet
   D. 1,750 square feet

   ANSWER -   (C)   7,500 sq. ft.

   100 ft. x 75 ft. = 7,500 sq. ft.

> When calculating the area, in square feet, of a multi-story building, multiply the length of the building by the width of the building by the number of stories.

EXAMPLE -   A three (3) story building having outside dimensions of 100 feet by 75 feet has a total area of _____.

   A. 2,225 square feet
   B. 7,500 square feet
   C. 15,000 square feet
   D. 22,500 square feet

   ANSWER -   (D)   22,500 sq. ft.

   100 ft. x 75 ft. x 3 (stories) = 22,500 sq. ft.

> When calculating lighting loads for **dwelling units** do **NOT** include open porches, garages or unfinished spaces not adaptable for future use. **[220.12]**

> Remember, in general, lighting loads for habitable spaces of dwelling units and guest rooms of hotels and motels are **not considered** as continuous use. But lighting loads of commercial and industrial occupancies **are considered** as continuous use.

➢ The formula used to determine the minimum number of general lighting branch-circuits required for a dwelling unit is:

Number of Circuits = $\dfrac{\text{load VA}}{\text{circuit VA}}$

EXAMPLE – A dwelling unit having 2,000 sq. ft. of habitable space is required to have at least _____ 15-ampere, 120-volt general-purpose lighting branch-circuits.

A. two
B. three
C. four
D. five

ANSWER - (C) four

$\dfrac{2{,}000 \text{ sq. ft.} \times 3 \text{ VA}}{120 \text{ volts} \times 15 \text{ amperes}} = \dfrac{6{,}000 \text{ VA}}{1{,}800 \text{ VA}} = 3.3 = 4 \text{ circuits}$

➢ When calculating branch-circuits, when your calculation is more than a whole number, ex. 3.3, you must go to the next whole number. In other words, you cannot install part of a circuit or circuit breaker.

➢ Apartment dwellings without provisions for cooking by tenants are to be calculated at the same value, **2 VA** per square foot, as hotels and motels when determining the minimum of general lighting branch-circuits required for the living units. **[Table 220.12]**

EXAMPLE - An apartment complex, without cooking facilities provided for the tenants, having 12,000 sq. ft. of living area, is required to have at least _____ 20 ampere, 120-volt general lighting branch-circuits, or at least _____ 15 ampere, 120-volt general lighting branch-circuits.

A. ten – ten
B. fourteen – fourteen
C. ten – thirteen
D. ten – fourteen

ANSWER – (D)   ten – fourteen

$\dfrac{12{,}000 \text{ sq. ft.} \times 2 \text{ VA}}{120 \text{ volts} \times \mathbf{20} \text{ amperes}} = \dfrac{24{,}000 \text{ VA}}{2{,}400 \text{ VA}} = 10 \text{ circuits}$

$\dfrac{12{,}000 \text{ sq. ft.} \times 2 \text{ VA}}{120 \text{ volts} \times \mathbf{15} \text{ amperes}} = \dfrac{24{,}000 \text{ VA}}{1{,}800 \text{ VA}} = 13.3 = 14 \text{ circuits}$

- A formula used to determine the minimum number of required general lighting branch-circuits for an office building, store, bank, restaurant, etc. is :

  Number of Circuits = $\dfrac{\text{load VA} \times \mathbf{125\%}}{\text{circuit VA}}$

  EXAMPLE - A 10,000 sq. ft. restaurant is required to be provided with at least _____ 20-ampere, 120-volt general lighting branch-circuits.

  A. eight
  B. nine
  C. ten
  D. eleven

  ANSWER -   (D)   eleven

  $\dfrac{10{,}000 \times 2 \text{ VA} \times \mathbf{125\%}}{120 \text{ volts} \times 20 \text{ amps}} = \dfrac{25{,}000 \text{ VA}}{2{,}400 \text{ VA}} = 10.4 = 11 \text{ circuits}$

- Because the circuit breakers protecting the branch-circuits are not permitted to be loaded to more than **80 percent** of their rated value, **[210.20(A)]** we can also use this formula:

  number of circuits = $\dfrac{\text{load VA}}{\text{circuit VA} \times \mathbf{80\%}}$

  number of circuits = $\dfrac{10{,}000 \times 2 \text{ VA}}{120 \times 20 \times \mathbf{80\%}} = \dfrac{20{,}000 \text{ VA}}{1{,}920 \text{ VA}} = 10.4 = 11 \text{ circuits}$

- Notice that **Table 220.12** reflects minimum requirements for general lighting loads. Many commercial, particularly mercantile, occupancies have luminaries (lighting fixtures) installed for display, specialty, enhancement or accent lighting in addition to the general lighting. These loads are required to be included when calculating lighting loads.

EXAMPLE - A 15,000 sq. ft. retail store has 10,000 VA of accent lighting in addition to the general lighting. How many 120-volt, 20-ampere branch-circuits are required for the accent and general lighting loads?

A. 30
B. 24
C. 36
D. 32

ANSWER -   (A)   30 circuits

General ltg. circuits = $\dfrac{15{,}000 \times 3 \text{ VA}}{120 \times 20 \times 80\%} = \dfrac{45{,}000}{1{,}920} = 23.4 = 24$

Accent ltg. circuits = $\dfrac{10{,}000 \text{ VA}}{120 \times 20 \times 80\%} = \dfrac{10{,}000}{1{,}920} = 5.2 = 6$

24 + 6 = 30 circuits total

➢ When reviewing **Table 220.12** notice the subscript **(b)** opposite of banks and office buildings which refers you to **220.14(K)**. This article indicates when the number of general-purpose receptacle outlets to be installed in the building has not yet been determined, **one VA** per square foot is to be added to the calculation for the outlets. The NEC initiated this requirement because it is common practice for banks and office buildings to have future tenant spaces and the actual number of general-purpose receptacle outlets to be installed have not been determined prior to complete construction of the building.

➢ For non-dwelling units, receptacle outlets are to be calculated at a value of not less than **180 volt-amperes** for each single or duplex receptacle. **[220.14(I)]**

➢ The formula used to determine the maximum number of receptacle outlets permitted on a branch-circuit is:

Number of Receptacles = $\dfrac{\text{circuit VA}}{180 \text{ VA}}$

EXAMPLE - No more than _____ duplex receptacle outlets installed in a commercial establishment may be supplied from a single 20-ampere rated, 120-volt branch-circuit.

A. ten
B. twelve
C. thirteen
D. fourteen

ANSWER -   (C)   thirteen

$$\frac{120 \text{ volts} \times 20 \text{ amperes}}{180 \text{ VA}} = \frac{2,400}{180} = 13.3 = 13 \text{ receptacles}$$

➢ When determining the minimum number of required branch-circuits for general-purpose receptacle outlets when the specific number of receptacle outlets to be installed in a commercial building is known, this formula may be used:

$$\text{number of circuits} = \frac{180 \text{ VA} \times \text{number of receptacles}}{\text{circuit VA}}$$

EXAMPLE - You are to install one hundred (100) duplex receptacle outlets in an existing office building. How many 20-ampere, 120-volt, branch-circuits will need to be added to supply the additional receptacles?

A. twelve
B. ten
C. seven
D. eight

ANSWER -   (D)   eight

$$\frac{180 \text{ VA} \times 100}{120 \text{ volts} \times 20 \text{ amps}} = \frac{18,000}{2,400} = 7.5 = 8 \text{ circuits}$$

➢ Article **220.14(G)** indicates two methods are permitted when calculating branch-circuits for show window lighting.
  (1) 180 VA per receptacle outlet in compliance with **210.62**, which requires one receptacle per twelve linear feet of the show window.
  (2) 200 volt-amps per linear foot of the show window.

The linear foot calculation method is the most commonly used method. The following formula may be used:

$$\text{number of circuits} = \frac{200 \text{ VA} \times \text{linear ft.} \times \mathbf{125\%}}{\text{circuit VA}}$$

EXAMPLE - A department store is to have seventy five (75) linear feet of show window space. Using the linear foot method of calculation, how many 20-ampere, 120-volt branch-circuits must be provided for the show window lighting?

A. eight
B. seven
C. six
D. five

ANSWER -   (A)   eight

$$\frac{200 \text{ VA} \times 75 \text{ ft.} \times \mathbf{125\%}}{20 \text{ amps} \times 120 \text{ volts}} = \frac{18{,}750}{2{,}400} = 7.8 = 8 \text{ circuits}$$

➢ When calculating the number of required branch-circuits for multioutlet assemblies installed in commercial, industrial and educational locations, the calculation is to be based on the use of the supplied cord-connected equipment that is expected to be used at the same time. **[220.14(H)]**

➢ When calculating the required branch-circuits for fixed multioutlet assemblies where the cord-connected appliances are **unlikely** to be used simultaneously, you can use the following formula:

$$\text{number of circuits} = \frac{(\text{linear ft.}/5) \times 180 \text{ VA}}{\text{circuit VA}}$$

EXAMPLE - A small cabinet makers shop is to install fifty (50) feet of multioutlet assembly where the appliances to be used are unlikely to be operated simultaneously. Where 20-ampere, 120-volt branch-circuits are used to supply the assembly, what is the minimum required?

A. one
B. two
C. three
D. four

ANSWER -   (A)   one

$$\frac{(50/5) \times 180}{120 \text{ volts} \times 20 \text{ amps}} = \frac{(10) \times 180}{2{,}400} = \frac{1{,}800}{2{,}400} = .75 \text{ or } 1 \text{ circuit}$$

➤ When calculating the branch-circuits required for fixed multioutlet assemblies where the cord-connected appliances are **likely** to be used simultaneously, the following formula may be used:

number of circuits = $\dfrac{\text{linear ft.} \times 180 \text{ VA}}{\text{circuit VA}}$

EXAMPLE - Seventy five (75) feet of fixed multioutlet assembly is to be wall-mounted in a retail outlet displaying television sets where most of the TV sets are operating simultaneously. How many 20-ampere, 120-volt branch-circuits are needed to supply this installation?

A. two
B. five
C. six
D. seven

ANSWER -   (C)   six

$\dfrac{75 \text{ ft.} \times 180 \text{ VA}}{120 \text{ volts} \times 20 \text{ amps}} = \dfrac{13{,}500}{2{,}400} = 5.6 = 6 \text{ circuits}$

➤ The definition of an individual branch-circuit is a branch-circuit that supplies only one utilization equipment. Examples of individual branch circuits would be branch-circuits supplying electric water heaters, dryers, ranges, cooktops, air conditioners, etc. **[Article 100]**

➤ For **other than** individual branch-circuits the rating of the circuits shall be 15, 20, 30, 40 and 50 amperes. **[210.3] Individual** branch circuits may also have ratings of the same size, in addition they may have ratings of 25, 35, 45 and 60 amperes or more. See **Article 240.6(A)** for the standard size ampere ratings of fuses and circuit breakers.

➤ When selecting ampere ratings of overcurrent protective devices, if the conductors being protected are **NOT** part of a multi-outlet branch circuit supplying receptacles for cord-and-plug-connected portable loads and the ampacity of the conductors do not correspond with the standard ampere rating of a fuse or circuit breaker and the next higher standard rating selected does **not exceed 800 amperes**, the next higher standard overcurrent device shall be permitted to be used. **[240.4(B)(1),(2)&(3)]**

➤ When selecting overcurrent protective devices where the overcurrent device is rated **over 800 amperes**, if the ampacity of the conductors do not correspond with the standard rating of a fuse or a circuit breaker you must go **down** to the next standard size fuse or circuit breaker. **[240.4(C)]**

- The overcurrent protection for small conductors, sizes 14 AWG through 10 AWG, shall be as listed in **240.4(D)**. Do not get overcurrent confused with ampacity.

- When sizing branch-circuits and overcurrent protection for appliances such as water heaters and cooktops, they are to be sized per **Article 422**. Branch-circuits for household cooking appliances shall be permitted to be in accordance with **Table 220.55**, which will be discussed later. **[422.10(A)]**

- Fixed storage-type water heaters with a capacity of 120 gallons or less shall be considered a continuous load when sizing branch-circuits. **[422.13]**

EXAMPLE - The branch-circuit conductors supplying a 5 kW, 240-volt, single-phase water heater, are required to have an ampacity of at least _____.

A. 15.0 amperes
B. 20.8 amperes
C. 26.0 amperes
D. 31.2 amperes

ANSWER -   (C)   26.0 amperes

$I = \dfrac{5 \text{ kW} \times 1{,}000}{240 \text{ volts}} = \dfrac{5{,}000}{240} = 20.8 \times \mathbf{125\%} = 26.04$ amperes

*NOTE - To solve this problem you should refer to **422.13** and **422.10(A)**.

EXAMPLE - The MAXIMUM size circuit breaker that may be used to protect a 5 kW, 240-volt, single-phase electric water heater has a rating of _____.

A. 20 amperes
B. 25 amperes
C. 30 amperes
D. 35 amperes

ANSWER -   (D)   35 amperes

$I = \dfrac{5{,}000}{240} = 20.8$ amps $\times\ 150\% = 31.2$ amperes

*NOTE - The next standard size circuit breaker has a rating of 35 amperes. To solve this problem you should refer to **422.11(E)(3)** and **240.6(A)**.

➢ When sizing branch-circuits and overcurrent protection for fixed electric space-heating equipment, they are to be sized in compliance with **Article 424**.

➢ Fixed electric space-heating equipment shall be considered as **continuous loads**. **[424.3(B)]**

EXAMPLE - The branch-circuit conductors supplying a 15 kW, 240 volt, single-phase fixed electric space-heater, are required to have an ampacity of at least _____.

A. 42 amperes
B. 52 amperes
C. 63 amperes
D. 78 amperes

ANSWER -   (D)   78 amperes

$$I = \frac{15 \times 1{,}000}{240} = \frac{15{,}000}{240} = 62.5 \times \mathbf{125\%} = 78 \text{ amperes}$$

➢ The following formula may be used to determine the minimum number of a required branch-circuits to supply fixed electric space-heating equipment:

$$\text{number of circuits} = \frac{\text{load VA} \times \mathbf{125\%}}{\text{circuit VA}}$$

EXAMPLE - What is the minimum number of 20-ampere, 240-volt branch-circuits required for twelve (12) baseboard heaters, each rated 1,250 watts at 240-volts, single-phase?

A. three
B. four
C. six
D. eight

ANSWER – (B) four

$$\frac{1{,}250 \times 12 \times \mathbf{125\%}}{240 \text{ volts} \times 20 \text{ amps}} = \frac{18{,}750}{4{,}800} = 3.9 = 4 \text{ circuits}$$

UNIT 3

COOKING EQUIPMENT & APPLIANCE DEMAND LOADS

Upon successfully completing this study unit, the student will be familiar with the concept of calculating demand loads for household cooking equipment and appliances.

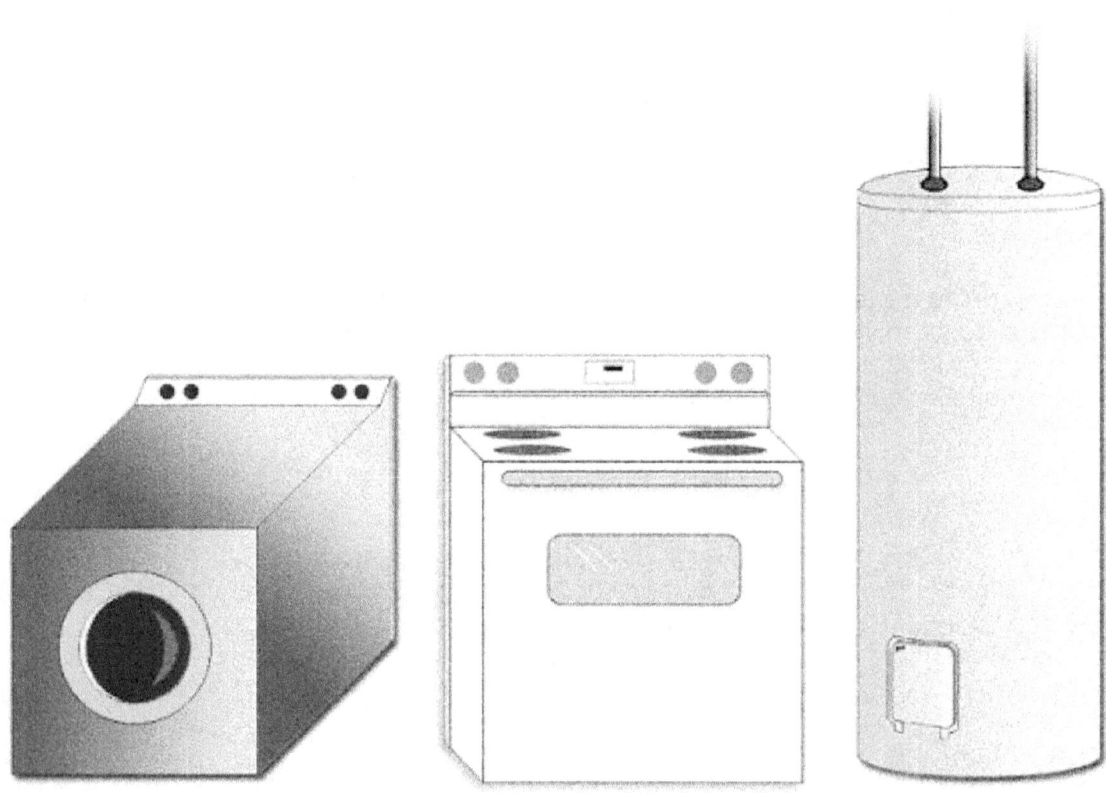

Unit 3

COOKING EQUIPMENT & APPLIANCE DEMAND LOADS

RELATED INFORMATION:

- The definition of **demand factor** is the ratio of the maximum demand of a system, or part of a system, to the total connected load of a system or the part of the system under consideration. **[Article 100]**

- The **demand load** of an electrical system or an electrical appliance is the MAXIMUM load of the system or appliance that may be required at a given time. In other words, **demand factors** are applied because all of the electrical loads are not used at the same time; all of the luminaires (lighting fixtures) will not be on at the same time, neither will all the receptacle outlets and appliances be fully loaded at the same time.

- A good example of this concept would be an electric range having a **connected load** rating of **12 kW**. The range-top has four heating elements, the oven has one heating element, another heating element is required for the broiler, and accessories such as timers and lights are included in the total connected load. Therefore, we can apply **demand factors** as shown in **Table 220.55** which reflects a **demand load** of **8 kW**, because we would not be using all of the heating elements and the accessories at their **MAXIMUM** value at any given time.

- **Table 220.55** and it's related notes are to be used to apply **demand factors** for household electric ranges, wall-mounted ovens, counter-mounted cooking units, and other household cooking appliances over **1¾ kW** rating. This table is to be used when applying **demand factors** when sizing services, feeders and branch circuits for dwelling units and instructional programs for educational institutions.

Table 220.55 Demand Factors and Loads for Household Electric Ranges, Wall-Mounted Ovens, Counter-Mounted Cooking Units, and Other Household Cooking Appliances over 1¾ kW Rating (Column C to be used in all cases except as otherwise permitted in Note 3).

Demand Factor (Percent) (See Notes)

Number of Appliances	Column A (Less than 3½ kW Rating)	Column B (3½ kW to 8¾ kW Rating)	Column C Maximum Demand (kW) (See Notes) (Not over 12 kW Rating)
1	80	80	8
2	75	65	11
3	70	55	14
4	66	50	17
5	62	45	20
6	59	43	21
7	56	40	22
8	53	36	23
9	51	35	24
10	49	34	25
11	47	32	26
12	45	32	27
13	43	32	28
14	41	32	29
15	40	32	30
16	39	28	31
17	38	28	32
18	37	28	33
19	36	28	34
20	35	28	35
21	34	26	36
22	33	26	37
23	32	26	38
24	31	26	39
25	30	26	40
26-30	30	24	15 kW + 1 kW for each range
31-40	30	22	
41-50	30	20	25 kW + ¾ kW for each range
51-60	30	18	
61 and over	30	16	

1. Over 12 kW through 27 kW ranges all of same rating. For ranges individually rated more than 12 kW but not more than 27 kW, the maximum demand in Column C shall be increased 5 percent for each additional kilowatt of rating or major fraction thereof by which the rating of individual ranges exceeds 12 kW.
2. Over 8¾ kW through 27 kW ranges of unequal ratings. For ranges individually rated more than 8¾ kW and of different ratings, but none exceeding 27 kW, an average value of rating shall be calculated by adding together the ratings of all ranges to obtain the total connected load (using 12 kW for any range rated less than 12 kW) and dividing by the total number of ranges. Then the maximum demand in Column C shall be increased 5 percent for each kilowatt or major fraction thereof by which this average value exceeds 12 kW.
3. Over 1¾ kW through 8¾ kW. In lieu of the method provided in Column C, it shall be permissible to add the nameplate ratings of all household cooking appliances rated more than 1¾ kW but not more than 8¾ kW and multiply the sum by the demand factors specified in Column A and Column B for the given number of appliances. Where the rating of cooking appliances falls under both Column A and Column B, the demand factors for each column shall be applied to the appliances for that column, and the results added together.
4. Branch-Circuit Load. It shall be permissible to calculate the branch-circuit load for one range in accordance with Table 220.55. The branch-circuit load for one wall-mounted oven or one counter-mounted cooking unit shall be the nameplate rating of the appliance. The branch-circuit load for a counter-mounted cooking unit and not more than two wall-mounted ovens, all supplied from a single branch circuit and located in the same room, shall be calculated by adding the nameplate rating of the individual appliances and treating this total as equivalent to one range.
5. This table also applies to household cooking appliances rated over 1¾ kW and used in instructional programs.

➢ Take notice that household electric ranges having a rating of **8.75 kW** or **more** are required to be supplied by at least a **40 ampere** rated branch circuit. **[210.19(A)(3)]** Also, **note 4** to **Table 220.55** states the branch circuit load for **one** wall-mounted oven or **one** counter-mounted cooking unit shall be the **nameplate rating** of the appliance. Therefore, demand factors are **not** to be applied when sizing branch circuits for these single cooking units.

➢ **Table 220.55** is separated into four columns. The first column shows the number of appliances. **Column A** is to be used when determining demand factors of cooking equipment of **less than 3½ kW rating** and is expressed in **percent**. **Column B** is used for equipment rated **3½ to 8¾ kW** and is also expressed in **percent**. **Column C** lists applicable demand factors for equipment rated **not over 12 kW** and is expressed in **kW**. When applying demand factors be sure you are in the correct column and on the right line, because the maximum demand changes in relationship with the number of appliances.

➢ As per **note 3**, When the rating of cooking appliances fall under **both** Column A and B, the demand factors for each column shall be applied for that column and the results added together.

    EXAMPLE – A small residential duplex has a 3 kW counter-mounted cooktop and a 4 kW wall-mounted oven installed in each unit. Determine the demand load, in kW, to be added to the ungrounded service-entrance conductors for the cooking equipment.

    A. 9.7 kW
    B. 14.0 kW
    C. 11.2 kW
    D. 10.5 kW

    ANSWER -   (A)   9.7 kW

    Col. A – 3 kW + 3 kW = 6 kW x **75%** = 4.5 kW
    Col. B – 4 kW + 4 kW = 8 kW x **65%** = 5.2 kW
                           TOTAL = 9.7 kW demand

➢ When a single range having a rating of **3½ kW to 8¾ kW** is used as cooking equipment for households, we may use the demand factors shown in **Column B** when sizing branch-circuits, (**note 4**) feeders and service-entrance conductors.

EXAMPLE – What is the demand load, in kW, for the branch-circuit conductors supplying an 8 kW residential electric range?

A. 8.0 kW
B. 6.4 kW
C. 6.0 kW
D. 7.2 kW

ANSWER –   (B)   6.4 kW

8 kW x 80% = 6.4 kW demand load

➤ Column C is to be used when applying demand factors for electric ranges of **not over 12 kW** rating.

EXAMPLE - Determine the demand load, in kW, to be added to the ungrounded service-entrance conductors for a 9.6 kW residential electric range.

A. 9.6 kW
B. 8.0 kW
C. 10.0 kW
D. 12.0 kW

ANSWER -   (B)   8.0 kW

Column C of Table 220.55 shows a demand of **8 kW** for one range not over 12 kW rating.

➤ When we have multiple ranges of **equal ratings** up to **12 kW** we are to also use **Column C**.

EXAMPLE - A ten (10) unit apartment complex is to have a 10 kW electric range installed in each unit. When sizing the ungrounded service-entrance conductors, the total demand load for the multiple ranges is _____.

A. 30 kW
B. 80 kW
C. 25 kW
D. 100 kW

ANSWER -   (C)   25 kW

Column C of Table 220.55 shows a demand of 25 kW for ten ranges of not over 12 kW rating.

➢ When applying maximum demand factors for ranges all of the **same rating over 12 kW through 27 kW**, we are to apply **note 1 and Column C** of **Table 220.55**, which states we are to increase the Column C demand value by **5%** for each kW that exceeds 12 kW.

    EXAMPLE - What is the branch-circuit demand load, in amperes, for one 16 kW, 240 volt, single-phase residential electric range?

      A. 33 amperes
      B. 50 amperes
      C. 40 amperes
      D. 67 amperes

        ANSWER – (C) 40 amperes

        16 kW – 12 kW = 4 kW x 5% = 20% increase in Column C
        Col. C demand (1 range) = 8 kW x 120% = 9.6 kW demand

$$I = \frac{9.6 \text{ kW} \times 1{,}000}{240 \text{ volts}} = \frac{9{,}600}{240} = 40 \text{ amperes}$$

➢ When applying demand factors for **multiple ranges**, all having the **same** nameplate rating of **more than 12 kW**, but **not more than 27 kW**, we are to also apply **note 1 and Column C** of **Table 220.55**.

    EXAMPLE - A four (4) unit residential town house has a 14 kW electric range installed in each unit. What is the demand load for the ranges, in kW, to be added to the ungrounded service-entrance conductors when sizing the service?

      A. 56.0 kW
      B. 44.8 kW
      C. 28.0 kW
      D. 18.7 kW

        ANSWER -   (D)   18.7 kW

        14 kW – 12 kW = 2 kW x 5% = 10% increase in Column C
        Col. C demand (4 ranges) = 17 kW x 110% = 18.7 kW

➢ When applying maximum demand factors of ranges having **unequal ratings** of **8¾ kW through 27 kW** we are to apply **note 2 and Column C** of **Table 220.55**.

EXAMPLE - The vocational education department of a high school is to have three (3) electric ranges installed in a classroom; one 10 kW, one 11 kW and one 12 kW. The ranges are to be supplied by a 208 volt, single-phase feeder from a sub-panel. What is the demand load, in amperes, on the ungrounded feeder conductors?

A. 58 amperes
B. 67 amperes
C. 136 amperes
D. 142 amperes

ANSWER - (B) 67 amperes

In this situation you simply refer to Column C, which shows demand of 14 kW for three ranges, because not any of the ranges have a nameplate rating above 12 kW.

$$I = \frac{14 \text{ kW} \times 1,000}{208 \text{ volts}} = \frac{14,000}{208} = 67.3 \text{ amperes}$$

> When calculating demand factors for ranges of **unequal ratings** of **8¾ through 27 kW**, when the nameplate rating of any **range less than 12 kW** you are to use **12 kW** as a **minimum** and add the ratings together and divide by the number of ranges to obtain the average, then apply the same steps as per **note 1**. **[Note 2, Table 220.55]**

EXAMPLE - Refer to the previous example. Another classroom in the high school is to install two electric ranges, one 16 kW and one 11 kW. Determine the demand load, in amperes, on the 208 volt, single-phase ungrounded feeder conductors.

A. 67 amperes
B. 76 amperes
C. 58 amperes
D. 63 amperes

ANSWER – (C)58 amperes

$$12 \text{ kW (minimum)} + 16 \text{ kW} = \frac{28 \text{ kW}}{2 \text{ (ranges)}} = 14 \text{ kW average}$$

14 kW – 12 kW = 2 kW x **5%** = **10%** increase in Column C
Col. C demand (2 ranges) = 11 kW x **110%** = 12.1 kW demand

$$I = \frac{12.1 \text{ kW} \times 1,000}{208 \text{ volts}} = \frac{12,100}{208} = 58 \text{ amperes}$$

➤ **Note 4** of **Table 220.55** addresses **branch-circuits**; it states it is permissible to calculate the branch-circuit load for one range in accordance with **Table 220.55**, as we have shown. As mentioned before, the branch-circuit load for **one wall-mounted oven** or **one counter-mounted cooking unit** shall be the **nameplate rating** of the appliance. When sizing branch-circuit loads for a **single branch-circuit** supplying a counter-mounted cooking unit and not more than two (2) wall-mounted ovens, it is permissible to add the nameplate ratings of the appliances together and treat the result as one range.

EXAMPLE - A 240-volt, single-phase branch-circuit (home run) is to supply one (1) 6 kW rated counter-mounted cooking unit and two (2) wall-mounted 4 kW rated ovens in a residential kitchen. What is the demand load, in amperes, on the branch-circuit for the appliances?

    A. 22 amperes
    B. 27 amperes
    C. 33 amperes
    D. 37 amperes

    ANSWER -   (D)   37 amperes

    6 kW + 4 kW + 4 kW = 14 kW connected load
    14 kW – 12 kW = 2 kW x 5% = **10%** increase in Column C
    Col. C demand (1 range) = 8 kW x 110% = 8.8 kW demand load

$$I = \frac{8.8 \text{ kW} \times 1{,}000}{240 \text{ volts}} = \frac{8{,}800}{240} = 36.6 \text{ amperes}$$

➤ **Section 220.61(B)(1)** permits an additional demand factor of **70 percent** for the **neutral** (grounded) conductor, for a feeder or service supplying household electric ranges, wall-mounted ovens, counter mounted cooking units, and electric dryers after apply the applicable demand factors of **Table 220.55** for ranges and **Table 220.54** for dryers.

EXAMPLE - A four (4) unit apartment house is to have a 10.5 kW electric range installed in each unit. Determine the demand load, in kW, on the grounded (neutral) service-entrance conductor for the ranges.

    A. 11.9 kW
    B. 13.6 kW
    C. 17.0 kW
    D. 10.4 kW

    ANSWER -   (A)   11.9 kW

Column C shows a demand of 17 kW for the demand on the ungrounded conductors for the four (4) electric ranges.

17 kW x **70%** = 11.9 kW neutral demand

> In a residential occupancy, a **75%** demand factor is permitted to be applied when **four(4) or more** fastened in place appliances such as water heaters, trash compactors, garage door openers, dishwashers, garbage disposers, sump pumps, attic fans, etc., are supplied from the same feeder or service. **[220.53]** **Note** this section does not apply to ranges, clothes dryers, space-heating and air-conditioning equipment.

> EXAMPLE - A one-family dwelling unit is to have the following fastened in place appliances installed:
>
> one – 1,200 VA dishwasher
> one – 4,000 VA water heater
> one – 1,150 VA garbage disposer
> one -   700 VA attic fan
> one – 1,920 VA garage door opener
>
> The demand load, in VA, on the ungrounded service-entrance conductors for the listed appliances is _____.
>
> A. 7,728 VA
> B. 6,728 VA
> C. 6,276 VA
> D. 8,970 VA
>
> ANSWER -   (B)   6,728 VA
>
> 1,200 VA dishwasher
> 4,000 VA water heater
> 1,150 VA garbage disposer
>   700 VA attic fan
> 1,920 VA garage door opener
> 8,970 VA connected load x **75%** = 6,728 VA demand

> In residential occupancies, demand factors may also be applied to electric clothes dryers; the use of demand factors in **Table 220.54** shall be permitted when sizing feeders and service entrance conductors. Each dryer shall be calculated at a **minimum of 5,000 watts (volt-amperes)** or the nameplate rating, whichever is larger. **[220.54]**

EXAMPLE - An eight (8) unit multifamily dwelling is to have the following electric clothes dryers installed in the laundry rooms of the tenants:

two – 4.5 kW rated
two – 5.5 kW rated
two – 6.0 kW rated
two – 6.5 kW rated

The demand load, in kW, to be added to the ungrounded feeder conductors for the listed electric dryers is _____.

A. 27.0 kW
B. 27.6 kW
C. 34.5 kW
D. 33.8 kW

ANSWER -   (B)   27.6 kW

two dryers @ 5.0 kW (minimum) = 10 kW
two dryers @ 5.5 kW   = 11 kW
two dryers @ 6.0 kW   = 12 kW
two dryers @ 6.5 kW   = 13 kW
                connected load = 46 kW x **60%** = 27.6 kW

➢ An additional demand factor of **70 percent** is permitted for the **neutral** (grounded conductor) for a feeder or service supplying electric clothes dryers for dwelling units. **[220.61(B)(1)]**

EXAMPLE - Refer to the previous example. The demand, in kW, on the grounded (neutral) conductor of the feeder conductors is _____.

A. 32.20 kW
B. 27.60 kW
C. 19.32 kW
D. 18.90 kW

ANSWER -   (C)   19.32 kW

27.6 kW (demand) load x **70%** (neutral demand) = 19.32 kW

➢ For commercial cooking related equipment, branch-circuits and overcurrent protection are sized according to the nameplate rating on the appliance. When sizing feeder and service conductors we may apply demand factors in accordance with **Table 220.56**. These demand factors shall not apply to space heating, ventilating or air-conditioning equipment. However, the feeder or service demand load is **not** permitted to be less than the sum of the **largest two** kitchen equipment loads. **[220.56]**

EXAMPLE - A feeder is to supply the following cooking related equipment in the kitchen of a restaurant:

oven	- 10 kW
booster heater	- 15 kW
dishwasher	- 2 kW
garbage disposal	- 1 kW
water heater	- 6 kW
steamer	- 4 kW

What is the demand load on the ungrounded feeder conductors for the appliances?

A. 38.0 kW
B. 24.7 kW
C. 26.6 kW
D. 25.0 kW

ANSWER - (D)   25.0 kW

oven - 10 kW
booster heater   - 15 kW
dishwasher - 2 kW
garbage disposal   - 1 kW
water heater   - 6 kW
steamer   - 4 kW
   Total = 38 kW (connected load)
       X **65%** (demand)
       = 24.7 kW **demand load**

But, the **two largest** loads are rated 10 kW and 15 kW which totals **25 kW**.

UNIT 4

CONDUCTOR AMPACITY AND SIZING

Upon successfully completing this unit of study, the student will be familiar with the concept of determining the ampacity of conductors, application of correction factors, proper sizing, and insulation ratings of conductors.

$$\text{Required Ampacity} = \frac{\textbf{Load}}{\textbf{Correction Factors}}$$

UNIT 4

CONDUCTOR AMPACITY AND SIZING

RELATED INFORMATION:

- The definition of **ampacity** is the maximum current, in amperes, that a conductor can carry continuously under the conditions of use **without exceeding** its temperature rating. **[Article 100]** To get a better understanding of **ampacity**, perhaps we might consider it as **current-carrying capacity**, or the maximum amperage a conductor can carry without damaging the conductor and/or its insulation.

- When determining the ampacity of a conductor, or sizing a conductor, there are several factors needed to be taken into consideration; the ambient temperature, the type and temperature rating of the conductor insulation, the number of current-carrying conductors contained in the raceway or cable, the temperature rating of the terminations, characteristics of the load to be served, the environment the conductor will be subject to and voltage drop, which will be discussed later.

- **Table 310.104 (A)** lists the various types of insulated conductors, rated 600 volts, that includes maximum operating temperatures, application provisions and insulation characteristics. Some conductors are dual rated in regard to the location in which they are installed. For example, type **THHW** is rated **75 deg. C** for wet locations and **90 deg. C** for dry locations.

- **Table 310.15(B)(16)** lists the ampacity values for copper, aluminum or copper clad aluminum conductors, up to 2000 volts, with temperature ratings of 60 deg. C through 90 deg. C. This table is based on **not more than three** current-carrying conductors in a raceway, cable or directly buried in the earth at an ambient temperature (temperature surrounding the wire) of **30 deg. C or 86 deg. F**.

Table 310.15(B)(16) (formerly Table 310.16) Allowable Ampacities of Insulated Conductors Rated Up to and Including 2000 Volts, 60°C Through 90°C (140°F Through 194°F), Not More Than Three Current-Carrying Conductors in Raceway, Cable or Earth (Directly Buried), Based on Ambient Temperature of 30°C (86°F)*

Size AWG or kcmil	Temperature Rating of Conductor (See Table 310.104(A)						Size AWG or kcmil
	60°C (140°F)	75°C (167°F)	90°C (194°F)	60°C (140°F)	75°C (167°F)	90° (194°F)	
	Types TW, UF	Types RHW, THHW, THW, THWN, XHHW, USE, ZW	Types TBS, SA, SIS, FEP, FEPB, MI, RHH, RHW-2, THHN, THHW, THW-2, THWN-2, USE-2, XHH, XHHW, XHHW-2, ZW-2	Types TW, UF	Types RHW, THHW, THW, THWN, XHHW, USE	Types TBS, SA, SIS, THHN, THHW, THW-2, THWN-2, RHH, RHW-2, USE-2, XHH, XHHW, XHHW-2, ZW-2	
	COPPER			ALUMINUM OR COPPER-CLAD ALUMINUM			
18	-	-	14	-	-	-	-
16	-	-	18	-	-	-	-
14**	15	20	25	-	-	-	-
12**	20	25	30	15	20	25	12**
10**	30	35	40	25	30	35	10**
8	40	50	55	35	40	45	8
6	55	65	75	40	50	55	6
4	70	85	95	55	65	75	4
3	85	100	115	65	75	85	3
2	95	115	130	75	90	100	2
1	110	130	145	85	100	115	1
1/0	125	150	170	100	120	135	1/0
2/0	145	175	195	115	135	150	2/0
3/0	165	200	225	130	155	175	3/0
4/0	195	230	260	150	180	205	4/0
250	215	255	290	170	205	230	250
300	240	285	320	195	230	260	300
350	260	310	350	210	250	280	350
400	280	335	380	225	270	305	400
500	320	380	430	260	310	350	500
600	350	420	475	285	340	385	600
700	385	460	520	315	375	425	700
750	400	475	535	320	385	435	750
800	410	490	555	330	395	445	800
900	435	520	585	355	425	480	900
1000	455	545	615	375	445	500	1000
1250	495	590	665	405	485	545	1250
1500	525	625	705	435	520	585	1500
1750	545	650	735	455	545	615	1750
2000	555	665	750	470	560	630	2000

* Refer to 310.15(B)(2) for the ampacity correction factors where the ambient temperature is other than 30°C (86°F).
*Refer to 240.4(D) for conductor overcurrent protection limitations.

➢ The body of **Table 310.15(B)(16)** lists ampacities of conductors used in areas where the ambient temperature is 30 deg. C or 86 deg. F, this is called **normal operating temperature**. The left half of the table is for **copper** conductors and the right half of the table is for **aluminum or copper clad aluminum** conductors.

➢ The temperature rating of a conductor is the maximum temperature, at any location along its length, that the conductor can withstand over a prolonged period of time without serious damage occurring. **[310.15(A)(3), INF. Note #1]**

➢ When conductors are subject to ambient temperatures above 86 deg. F, the resistance of the conductors are also increased proportionately. The greater the elevated ambient temperature, the greater the resistance. When the **resistance** of a conductor **increases** the **ampacity** of the conductor **decreases**. When this condition occurs, you must apply the appropriate temperature correction factors given in **Table 310.15(B)(2)(a).**

Table 310.15(B)(2)(a) Ambient Temperature Correction Factors Based on 30°C (86°F)					
For ambient temperatures other than 30°C (86°F), multiply the allowable ampacities specified in the ampacity table by the appropriate correction factor shown below.					
Ambient Temp. (°C)	Temperature Rating of Conductor			Ambient Temp. (°F)	
	60° C	75°C	90° C		
10 or less	1.29	1.20	1.15	50 or less	
11-15	1.22	1.15	1.12	51-59	
16-20	1.15	1.11	1.08	60-68	
21-25	1.08	1.05	1.04	69-77	
26-30	1.00	1.00	1.00	78-86	
31-35	0.91	0.94	0.96	87-95	
36-40	0.82	0.88	0.91	96-104	
41-45	0.71	0.82	0.87	105-113	
46-50	0.58	0.75	0.82	114-122	
51-55	0.41	0.67	0.76	123-131	
56-60	-	0.58	0.71	132-140	
61-65	-	0.47	0.65	141-149	
66-70	-	0.33	0.58	150-158	
71-75	-	-	0.50	159-167	
76-80	-	-	0.41	168-176	
81-85	-	-	0.29	177-185	

EXAMPLE - When a size 3 AWG copper conductor, with THW insulation, is installed in an area where the ambient temperature is 114 deg. F, the wire has an allowable ampacity of _____.

A. 100 amperes
B. 75 amperes
C. 82 amperes
D. 58 amperes

ANSWER -   (B)   75 amperes

100 amperes x .75 = 75 amperes

To solve this problem, first we locate the wire size on the left side of **Table 310.15(B)(16)** and look to the right under the copper THW column, with a temperature rating of 75°C, and note the ampacity of the wire is 100 amperes at normal operating temperature. Then, we apply the values as shown in **Table 310.15(B)(2)(a).** Look to the right side of the table where the ambient temperature is shown as **°F** and find the ambient temperature. Next, we follow that line to the left where the line intersects with the **75° C column** (temperature rating of conductor) to find our correction factor of **.75**, or 75%. Finally, to find the allowable ampacity of the conductor, multiply the two values together.

EXAMPLE - When a size 1/0 AWG THWN aluminum conductor is installed in an ambient temperature of 45 deg. C, the conductor has an allowable ampacity of _____.

A. 100 amperes
B. 90 amperes
C. 98 amperes
D. 104 amperes

ANSWER -   (C)   98 amperes

1/0 THWN aluminum ampacity before derating = 120 amperes
120 amps x .82 (correction factor) = 98.4 amperes

We use the same steps as before. First, we find the wire size which has an ampacity of 120 amperes. **[Tbl. 310.15(B)(16)]** Then, we find the ambient temperature, this time on the left portion of **Table 310.15(B)(2)(a)**, and go to the right under the THWN aluminum column (temperature rating of conductor) to find the correction factor of **.82**. Next, multiply the two values together.

➢ The temperature correction factors on **Table 310.15(B)(2)(a)** are to be applied when sizing conductors for a given load located in an area with an elevated ambient temperature. The following formula should be used:

Required ampacity = $\dfrac{\text{load}}{\text{correction factor}}$

EXAMPLE - Where a 100 ampere load is to be supplied with THWN copper conductors in an area where the ambient temperature will reach 110 deg. F, size _____ THWN conductors are required to serve the load.

    A. 1 AWG
    B. 2 AWG
    C. 3 AWG
    D. 1/0 AWG

    ANSWER -   (A)   1 AWG

required ampacity = $\dfrac{100 \text{ amps}}{.82}$ = 122 amperes

Table 310.15(B)(16) indicates size 1 AWG copper conductors with an ampacity of 130 amperes, should be selected. To cross reference:

130 amperes x .82 (correction factor) = 107 amperes

➢ Conductors are to be sized in accordance with the lowest temperature rating of the terminal, device or conductor of the circuit. **[110.14(C)]** In other words, conductors must be sized to the **lowest temperature rating** of the wire, circuit breaker, terminal or device.

➢ Conductors with temperature ratings higher than that of the terminations are permitted to be used for ampacity adjustment and/or correction. **[110.14(C)]** Today, most terminations are rated at **60 deg. C or 75 deg. C**. This permits us to use THHN conductors for derating purposes, but the conductor size is based on the lower terminal rating of the circuit breaker, equipment or device, not the 90 deg. C rating of the conductor insulation.

EXAMPLE - The load on a size 6 AWG THHN copper conductor is limited to _____ where connected to a circuit breaker with a termination rated at 60° C.

A. 75 amperes
B. 65 amperes
C. 60 amperes
D. 55 amperes

ANSWER -   (D)   55 amperes

Table 310.15(B)(16) lists the ampacity of size 6 AWG, copper, 60° C rated conductors to be 55 amperes.

EXAMPLE - The load, in amperes, on a size 6 AWG THHN copper conductor is permitted to be no more than _____ where connected to a fusible disconnect switch with terminals rated at 75 deg. C.

A. 75 amperes
B. 65 amperes
C. 60 amperes
D. 55 amperes

ANSWER -   (B)   65 amperes

Table 310.15(B)(16) lists the ampacity of size 6 AWG copper 75 deg. C rated conductors to be 65 amperes.

- Many circuit breakers and disconnect switches now have dual ratings marked **60/75 deg. C**. Under this condition, for 60 deg. C conductors, derating and ampacity values are to be based on the 60 deg. C terminal ratings; 75 deg. C and 90 deg. C conductors derating and ampacity values may be based on either the 60 deg. C or 75 deg. C terminal ratings.

- Many conductors now are dual rated such as **THWN/THHN**. The ampacity rating is based on the THWN, 75 deg. C values, but the derating factor(s) may be based on the THHN 90 deg. C values.

- The allowable **ampacity** of Types **NM**, **NMC** and **NMS** cable shall be in accordance with the **60 deg. C** conductor temperature rating. The **90 deg. C** rating shall be permitted to be used for **ampacity derating** purposes, provided the final ampacity does not exceed that for a 60 deg. C rated conductor. **[334.80]**

EXAMPLE - A size 12/2 AWG w/ground copper NM cable is to be installed in an attic of a dwelling where the ambient temperature is 125 deg. F. Determine the ampacity of the cable.

A. 22.8 amperes
B. 14.5 amperes
C. 24.6 amperes
D. 17.4 amperes

ANSWER -   (A)   22.8 amperes

Ampacity of 12 AWG at 90 deg. C before derating = 30 amperes
30 amperes x .76 (temperature correction) = 22.8 amperes

Under this condition, the ampacity of 22.8 amperes is NOT permitted, because this value is more than the 20 ampere rating of the 12 AWG conductors at the 60 deg. C temperature rating.

EXAMPLE - A size 10/3 AWG w/ground copper NM cable is to be installed in the crawl space of a dwelling where the ambient temperature is 100 deg. F. Determine the ampacity of the cable.

A. 24.6 amperes
B. 36.4 amperes
C. 32.3 amperes
D. 30.0 amperes

ANSWER -   (D)   30.0 amperes

Ampacity of 10 AWG at 90 deg. C before derating = 40 amperes
40 amperes x .91 (temp. correction) = 36.4 amperes

Under this condition the ampacity of 36.4 amperes is also NOT permitted, because this value is more than the 30 ampere rating of 10 AWG conductors at the 60 deg. C rating.

➢ When there are more than three (3) current-carrying conductors in a raceway or cable, the ability of the conductors to dissipate heat is reduced. Therefore, when this condition exists in a raceway or cable longer than 24 inches the allowable ampacity of each conductor shall be reduced as shown in **Table 310.15(B)(3)(a)**.

EXAMPLE - What is the allowable ampacity of a size 1/0 AWG THW copper conductor installed in a conduit longer than 24 inches, when there are three (3) other current-carrying conductors contained in the same pipe?

A. 150 amperes
B. 120 amperes
C. 105 amperes
D. 140 amperes

ANSWER -   (B)   120 amperes

150 amperes x .8 (adjustment factor) = 120 amperes

First, find the ampacity of the conductor, before derating, as shown in **Table 310.15(B)(16).** Then, apply the appropriate adjustment factor as shown in **Table 310.15(B)(3)(a).**

➤ When there are four (4) or more current-carrying conductors in a raceway or cable, longer than 24 inches, installed in an area with an elevated temperature, **both** the temperature correction and the adjustment factor for the number of current-carrying conductors must be applied.

EXAMPLE - Determine the allowable ampacity of a size 2 AWG THWN aluminum conductor installed in a 20 foot long conduit with seven (7) other current-carrying conductors of the same size and insulation, where the ambient temperature is 99 deg. F.

A. 59 amperes
B. 71 amperes
C. 55 amperes
D. 63 amperes

ANSWER -   (C)   55 amperes

Size 2 AWG THWN AL ampacity before derating = 90 amperes
90 amperes x .88 (temp. correction) x .7 (adj. factor) = 55 amps

First, find the ampacity of the conductor as shown in **Table 310.15(B)(16)** before derating. Then, apply the temperature correction factor. **[Table 310.15(B)(2)(a)]** Next, apply the adjustment factor for the multiple current-carrying conductors as shown in **Table 310.15(B)(3)(a),** and multiply the three values together.

➤ When sizing conductors for a given load in an area with an elevated ambient temperature, installed in a raceway or cable more than 24 inches in length, the following formula may be used when there are more than three current-carrying conductors in the raceway or cable.

$$\text{Required ampacity} = \frac{\text{Load}}{\text{temp. correction} \times \text{adj. factor}}$$

EXAMPLE - A 100 ampere load is located in an environment where the temperature reaches 115 deg. F, and is to be supplied with four (4) 75 deg. C rated copper current-carrying conductors. Determine the proper size wire to serve the load. All terminations are rated at 75 deg. C.

    A. 1/0 AWG
    B. 2/0 AWG
    C. 1 AWG
    D. 3 AWG

ANSWER - (B) 2/0 AWG

$$\text{ampacity} = \frac{100 \text{ amperes (load)}}{.76 \text{ (temp.)} \times .8 \text{ (adj.)}} = \frac{100}{0.6} = 167 \text{ amperes}$$

*NOTE – Size 2/0 AWG copper conductors rated at 75 deg. C with an ampacity of 175 amperes are required.

➤ Generally, where conductors or cables are installed in raceways exposed to direct sunlight on or above rooftops, the temperature values shown in **Table 310.15(B)(3)(c)** shall be added to the outdoor temperature and applied to the temperature correction factors in **Tables 310.15(B)(2)(a) and 310.15(B)(2)(b)**. **[310.15(B)(3)(c)]** The temperature adders must be applied up to a height of 36 inches above a rooftop. For example, when a conduit containing conductors rated at 75 deg. C is installed 3 inches above a rooftop and exposed to direct sunlight in an ambient temperature of 100 deg. F then, **40 degrees F** is to be added to the maximum ambient temperature. In this case, the value of **140 degrees F** must be used for the temperature correction factor adjustments from **Table 310.15(B)(2)(a)**.

Example - Determine the allowable ampacity of a size 10 AWG THWN copper conductor, installed in a conduit three (3) inches above a rooftop where the outdoor ambient temperature reaches 110 degrees F.

A. 33.60 amperes
B. 30.80 amperes
C. 20. 30 amperes
D. 11.55 amperes

Answer – (D) 11.5 amperes

outside ambient temperature =   110 ° F
adder (3 in. above roof)   = + 40 ° F
                Total   =   150 ° F

35 amperes x .33 (temperature correction) = 11.55 amperes

First, find the ampacity of the conductor as indicated in **Table 310.15(B)(16)** before derating. Then, locate the appropriate adder as shown in **Table 310.15(B)(3)(C)** and add this value to the ambient temperature. Next, find the correct temperature correction factor in **Table 310.15(B)(2)(a)** and multiple this value by the conductor ampacity value as given before derating.

➢ When considering current-carrying conductors, the neutral conductor is **not counted** when the neutral carries only the **unbalanced current** of the circuit; for example, 120/240 volt single-phase systems. **[310.15(B)(5)(a)]** The neutral does carry current, but is not required to be counted.

➢ The neutral **is considered** a current-carrying conductor on a 4-wire, 3-phase wye circuit where the major portion of the load consists of **nonlinear loads**. **[310.15(B)(5)(c)]** Examples of nonlinear loads are high intensity discharge (HID) lighting and fluorescent lighting, information technology equipment, computers, and data processing equipment.

➢ As per Section **310.15(B)(7)** for sizing **120/240-volt**, **3-wire**, **single-phase** service and feeder conductors rated 100 through 400 amperes, for one-family dwelling units and individual units of a multi-family dwelling, they are permitted to have an ampacity not less than 83 percent of the service or feeder rating.

EXAMPLE - A one-family dwelling is supplied with a 120/240-volt, single-phase electrical system from the local utility company and has a demand load of 200 amperes. What is the MINIMUM size THWN/THHN aluminum service-entrance conductors required?

A. 250 kcmil
B. 4/0 AWG
C. 3/0 AWG
D. 2/0 AWG

ANSWER -   (B)   4/0 AWG

200 amperes x .83 = 166 amperes

Size 4/0 AWG THWN/THHN aluminum service-entrance conductors with an ampacity of 180 amperes should be selected from **Table 310.15(B)(16).**

➤ When single-insulated conductors are installed in free air, they can dissipate the heat caused by the current flowing in the conductors more readily than when installed in raceways. The conductors have a greater allowable ampacity therefore, **Table 310.15(B)(17)** may be applied in the same manner as previously referenced in this unit.

EXAMPLE - When ambient temperature is not a consideration, when installed in free air, a size 6 AWG THWN copper conductor has a MAXIMUM allowable ampacity of _____.

A. 65 amperes
B. 75 amperes
C. 105 amperes
D. 95 amperes

ANSWER -   (D)   95 amperes

Table 310.15(B)(17) shows size 6 AWG THWN copper conductors to have an allowable ampacity of 95 amperes.

UNIT 5

BOX AND RACEWAY SIZING

Upon successfully completing this unit of study the student will be familiar with the concept of properly sizing electrical boxes and raceways.

$$\text{Number of Wires Permitted} = \frac{\text{Allowable Fill}}{\text{Wire Size}}$$

UNIT 5

BOX AND RACEWAY SIZING

Outlet and Device Box Sizing

RELATED INFORMATION:

- Device and junction boxes are required to be of a sufficient size to house conductors and/or devices, clamps and support fittings without damaging the conductor's insulation. Therefore, when sizing boxes, conductors, clamps and support fittings are required to be counted in order to select the proper size box. **[314.16]**

- To properly size outlet boxes you must count the conductors within the box correctly. **Section 314.16(B)(1)** is to be used as a guideline to count the conductors as follows:

    1) Conductors that originate outside the box or that are spliced within the box are counted **one** for each conductor.

    2) Conductors unbroken within the box, less than 12 inches in length, that pass through the box without splicing or terminating are counted **one** for each conductor.

    3) Conductors 12 inches or longer that are looped and unbroken are counted as **two** for a single conductor.

    4) Conductors that originate within the box and do not leave the box such as, bonding jumpers and pigtails are **not counted**.

    5) Conductors from a domed luminaire (fixture) that terminate within the box are **not counted**.

- When sizing device and junction boxes, the insulation of the conductors are not required to be taken into consideration. The volume required for the individual conductors is expressed in **cubic inches** and/or **cubic centimeters**, no matter what the insulation characteristics of the conductor(s) is/are.

- To determine the volume, in cubic inches, of a box simply multiply the length times the width times the depth of the box.

EXAMPLE - A box that measures 6 inches x 6 inches and is 4 inches deep has a volume of _____.

A. 96 cubic inches
B. 144 cubic inches
C. 24 cubic inches
D. 36 cubic inches

ANSWER -   (B)   144 cubic inches

6 in. x 6 in. x 4 in. = 144 cubic inches

➢ **Table 314.16(A)** may be used to determine the **MINIMUM** size outlet box required for a given number of conductors, or when determining the **MAXIMUM** number of conductors permitted in an outlet box when all of the conductors in the box are of the **same size**.

EXAMPLE - Determine the MAXIMUM number of size 12 AWG THWN conductors permitted in a 4 x 1½ in. square box.

A. seven
B. eight
C. nine
D. ten

ANSWER -   (C)   nine

The right hand side of **Table 314.16(B)** under the **12** column shows nine conductors permitted in the box.

EXAMPLE - Of the following listed, which one of the boxes is the MINIMUM required to house three (3) size 12 AWG THWN/THHN conductors and three (3) size 12 AWG THW conductors?

A. 4 x 1½ in. octagon
B. 4 x 2¼ in. octagon
C. 4 x 1½ in. square
D. 4 x 2¼ in. square

ANSWER -   (A)   4 x 1½ in. octagon

Table 314.16(B) permits six (6) size 12 AWG conductors in a 4 x 1½ in. octagon box.

➢ **Table 314.16(A)** shall apply where no fittings or devices, such as cable clamps, luminaire studs, hickeys, receptacles, switches or dimmers, are enclosed in the box. **Table 314.16(A)** does not take into consideration the fill requirements for these fittings or devices; where one or more of these items are contained in the box, the number of conductors permitted as shown in the table shall be reduced as follows:

   1) **cable clamps** – One or more internal cable clamps present in the box are counted as **one** conductor, based on the **largest** conductor in the box. **[314.16(B)(2)]**

   2) **support fittings** – One or more luminaire (fixture) studs and/or hickeys in the box are counted as **one** conductor for each type of fitting, based on the **largest** conductor in the box. **[314.16(B)(3)]**

   3) **devices** – For each yoke or strap containing one or more device present in the box, they are to be counted as **two wires**, based on the **largest** conductor connected to the device. **[314.16(B)(4)]**

   4) **equipment grounding conductors** – One or more equipment grounding conductors or bonding jumpers contained in a box are to be counted as **one** conductor, based on the **largest** equipment grounding conductor or bonding jumper in the box. **[314.16(B)(5)]** Where an **additional set** of isolated equipment grounding conductors are in the box, they are to be counted as **one** conductor, based on the **largest** equipment grounding conductor in the additional set.

➢ When doing box fill calculations we must take into consideration the volume taken up by all conductors, fittings and devices contained in the box to properly size the box.

   EXAMPLE - A device box contains two (2) internal clamps, two (2) equipment grounding conductors, one (1) bonding jumper and one (1) duplex receptacle. The number of conductors permitted in the box is to be reduced by _____ conductors.

   A. three
   B. four
   C. five
   D. six

   ANSWER -   (B)   four

   clamps   = 1 wire
   receptacle   = 2 wires
   equip. grounding & bonding wires   = <u>1 wire</u>
                              TOTAL   = 4 wires

➢ When calculating the proper size outlet box to be used when the conductors are of different sizes, you are to determine the volume of the conductors, in cubic inches, by applying **Table 314.16(B)**, and then size the box by using **Table 314.16(A)**.

EXAMPLE - Determine which one of the following listed outlet boxes is the MINIMUM size required to enclose the following conductors:

- six (6) size 12 AWG conductors
- two (2) size 14 AWG conductors
- one (1) size 14 AWG equipment grounding conductors

A. 4 x 1½ in. octagon
B. 4 x 1½ in. square
C. 4 x 2¼ in. square
D. 4¼ x 1½ in. square

ANSWER -   (B)   4 x 1½ in. square

Size 12 AWG = 2.25 cu. in. x 6   =   13.5 cubic inches
Size 14 AWG = 2.00 cu. in. x 2   =   4.0 cubic inches
Size 14 AWG Equip. grounding x 1 =   2.0 cubic inches
                                     19.5 cubic inches

Table 314.16(A) requires a 4 x 1½ inch square box having a volume of 21 cubic inches.

Junction and Pull Box Sizing

RELATED INFORMATION:

> **Section 314.16** states when boxes enclosing conductors of size **4 AWG or larger** are used as pull or junction boxes, they are to comply with the provisions of **314.28**. Under this condition, pull and junction boxes are to be sized by the raceways entering the box(es) and not by the size of the conductors contained in the box.

> In straight pulls, the length of the box shall not be less than **eight times** the trade diameter of the largest raceway entering the box. **[314.28(A)(1)]**

EXAMPLE - Determine the MINIMUM length of a pull box that has a trade size 3½ inch conduit entering at each end, and containing conductors of size 250 kcmil, when a straight pull of the conductors is to be made.

A. 21 inches
B. 24 inches
C. 28 inches
D. 32 inches

ANSWER -   (C)   28 inches

3.5 in. (conduit) x 8 = 28 inches

> Where splices, angle or U-pulls are made, the distance between each raceway entry inside the box and opposite wall of the box shall not be less than **six (6) times** the trade size of the raceway in a row. **[314.28(A)(2)]** Then, you are to add the sum of the trade size diameter of any additional raceways entering the box. In other words, for angle or U-pulls, the proper size junction box can be determined by multiplying the largest raceway by six (6) and add any additional conduits.

EXAMPLE - A junction box is to be installed where the conductors are larger than size 4 AWG and an angle (90 deg.) pull of the conductors is to be made. Two (2) trade size 3 inch conduits are to enter the box from the top and two (2) trade size 3 inch conduits are to enter the box from the side. Determine the MINIMUM size pull box required.

A. 36 in. x 36 in.
B. 27 in. x 27 in.
C. 24 in. x 24 in.
D. 21 in. x 21 in.

ANSWER -   (D)   21 in. x 21 in.

Top to bottom – 3 in. (largest conduit) x 6 = 18 in. + 3 in. = 21 in.
Side to side – 3 in. (largest conduit) x 6 = 18 in. + 3 in. = 21 in.

EXAMPLE - A pull box has one (1) trade size 2 inch conduit and one (1) trade size 1½ inch conduit entering the top and two (2) trade size 2 inch conduits on the left side. Where conductors are larger than 4 AWG and an angle (90 deg.) pull of the conductors is to be made, determine the MINIMUM distance required from the top wall to the bottom wall.

A. 13½ inches
B. 11 inches
C. 12 inches
D. 16 inches

ANSWER -   (A)   13½ inches

2 in. (largest conduit) x 6 = 12 + 1½ in. = 13½ inches

Conduit and Tubing Sizing

RELATED INFORMATION:

> When electrical conduit or tubing enclose conductors of the same size, with the same type of insulation, when the conduit or tubing is more than 24 inches in length, application of **Annex C, Tables C.1 through C.12(A)** is permitted to be used when determining the MAXIMUM number of conductors permitted. **[Chapter 9, Table 1]** This is the fastest and easiest method of determining the MAXIMUM number of conductors allowed in a standard trade size conduit or tubing.

> Located at the first part of **Annex C** there is a listing of the various types of standard electrical conduits. Use this table to find the particular type of conduit you are going to use when determining conduit fill.

EXAMPLE -   Determine the MINIMUM trade size electrical metallic tubing (EMT), more than 24 inches in length, permitted to enclose twelve (12) size 10 AWG THWN conductors.

A. 3/4 in.
B. 1 in.
C. 1¼ in.
D. 1½ in.

ANSWER -   (B)   1 inch

First locate **Table C.1** of **Annex C**. Next, refer to the type of insulation **(THWN)** of the conductors. Then, locate the wire size **(10 AWG)**, and you will find for twelve (12) size 10 AWG THWN conductors a trade size 1 inch EMT is required.

EXAMPLE - A trade size 1½ inch Schedule 40 PVC conduit, 25 feet in length, is permitted to enclose no more than _____ size 2 AWG XHHW compact aluminum conductors.

A. six
B. seven
C. eight
D. ten

ANSWER - (C) eight

First, locate **Table C.10(A)** of **Annex C**. Next, find the insulation type **(XHHW)** of the conductors. Then, locate the conduit size **(1½ in.)** and conductor size **(2 AWG)**, and you will find a trade size 1½ inch Schedule 40 PVC is permitted to enclose eight (8) size 2 AWG XHHW compact aluminum conductors.

➢ When conduit or tubing enclose conductors of different sizes and/or insulations, **Chapter 9**, **Tables 4, 5 and 5A**, with their related notes, are to be applied to determine the proper fill.

➢ **Table 1** of **Chapter 9** shows the permitted fill, in percent of conduit and tubing, when one, two or over two conductors are installed; for example, when more than two (2) conductors are installed in a conduit or tubing they shall be permitted to be filled to **40 percent** of their cross-sectional area.

➢ Where conduit or tubing nipples have a MAXIMUM length not to exceed 24 inches between boxes and enclosures, the nipples shall be permitted to be filled to **60 percent** of their total cross-sectional area.
   [Chapter 9, Note 4]

➢ **Table 4, Chapter 9** list the various types of conduit and tubing. Each type of conduit or tubing is shown as a separate table. At the top of each table is shown the internal diameter and the percent of fill. Under the percent of fill heading you will find the allowable fill of each size conduit or tubing expressed in square inches and millimeters. On the left side of the table the trade size and metric designator of the conduit or tubing are listed. To find the allowable fill of a specific conduit or tubing simply locate the conduit or tubing size and extend to the right under the proper **percent** of fill heading.

EXAMPLE -   When more than two (2) conductors are installed in a trade size 2 inch electrical metallic tubing (EMT) longer than 24 inches, the EMT has an allowable fill of _____.

   A. 2.013 square inches
   B. 1.778 square inches
   C. 1.040 square inches
   D. 1.342 square inches

ANSWER -   (D)   1.342 square inches

Under this condition the 2 in. EMT is permitted to have an allowable fill of 40 percent. **[Table 4, Chapter 9]**

EXAMPLE -   When four (4) current-carrying conductors are installed in a trade size 2 inch electrical metallic tubing (EMT) nipple 18 inches long, the EMT has a MAXIMUM allowable fill of _____.

   A. 2.013 square inches
   B. 1.778 square inches
   C. 1.040 square inches
   D. 1.342 square inches

ANSWER -   (A)   2.013 square inches

Under this condition the 2 in. EMT is permitted to have an allowable fill of 60 percent. **[Table 4, Chapter 9]**

➢ **Table 5**, **Chapter 9** shows the various sizes and insulations of conductors expressed in millimeters and square inches in accordance with appropriate diameter and area. In most cases we relate to the **approximate area** in **square inches** on the right side of the table.

EXAMPLE -   A size 8 AWG THWN copper conductor has an approximate area of _____.

   A. 0.0437 square inches
   B. 0.0366 square inches
   C. 0.0835 square inches
   D. 0.2160 square inches

ANSWER -   (B)   0.0366 square inches

First, we locate the insulation **(THWN)** of the conductor.
Then, the size **(8 AWG)**, and look to the extreme right side of the table to find the approximate area in square inches.
[Table 5, Chapter 9]

➢ **Table 5A, Chapter 9** shows the various sizes and insulations of **compact aluminum conductors** expressed in millimeters and square inches with approximate diameter and area, much like **Table 5 of Chapter 9**. This table is structured different than **Table 5** but, is easier to use because there is only four (4) types of conductor insulations listed. Again refer to the approximate area in square inches of the conductor when calculating raceway fill.

EXAMPLE - What is the area, in square inches, of a size 3/0 AWG XHHW compact aluminum conductor.

A. 0.590 square inches
B. 0.2733 square inches
C. 0.2290 square inches
D. 0.1885 square inches

ANSWER - (C) 0.2290 square inches

First, from **Table 5A of Chapter 9**, locate the insulation **(XHHW)** of the conductor.
Then, locate the wire size, **(3/0 AWG)**, and look under the **in.²** heading to find the area.

➢ Where equipment grounding or bonding conductors are installed in conduit or tubing, they shall be included when calculating the permitted fill. **[Chapter 9, Note 3]** If insulated, use the **Table 5** to find the approximate area; if bare find the area in square inches from **Table 8 of Chapter 9**, look under the heading of **in²**.

EXAMPLE - A size 8 AWG solid bare equipment grounding conductor has an area of _____.

A. 0.128 square inches
B. 0.146 square inches
C. 0.017 square inches
D. 0.013 square inches

ANSWER - (D) 0.013 square inches

First, locate the wire size and stranding properties from **Table 8 of Chapter 9**. Next, extend to the right under the **in.²** heading to find the area.

➢ Conduits or tubing enclosing different size conductors and/or conductors having different insulations are sized by locating the area, in square inches, of each conductor per **Table 5**, **Table 5A** or **Table 8** and multiplying by the number of conductors. This total is used to select the proper size raceway using **Table 4** in **Chapter 9**.

EXAMPLE - Determine the MINIMUM trade size intermediate metal conduit (IMC) permitted to enclose three (3) size 8 AWG XHHW copper branch-circuit conductors and six (6) size 12 AWG THWN copper control-circuit conductors. The IMC is to be fifty (50) feet in length.

    A. 1/2 in.
    B. 3/4 in.
    C. 1 in.
    D. 1¼ in.

    ANSWER - (B) 3/4 in.

8 XHHW = .0437 sq. in. x 3 conductors = .1311 square inches
12 THWN = .0133 sq. in. x 6 conductors = .0798 square inches
                                            TOTAL = .2109 square inches

A trade size 3/4 in. IMC having an allowable fill @ 40% of 0.235 square inches is the MINIMUM required.

EXAMPLE - Determine the MINIMUM trade size, one (1) foot long, rigid metal conduit (RMC) to enclose the following listed copper conductors.

- four (4) – 3/0 AWG THWN
- four (4) – 4/0 AWG THHN

    A. 3 in.
    B. 2 in.
    C. 3½ in.
    D. 2½ in.

    ANSWER - (D) 2½ inches

3/0 THWN = .2679 x 4 conductors = 1.0716 square inches
4/0 THHN = .3237 x 4 conductors = 1.2948 square inches
                                      TOTAL = 2.3664 square inches

A trade size 2½ in. RMC nipple having an allowable fill @ 60% of 2.919 square inches is the MINIMUM required.

➤ When determining the number of conductors, all of the same size, permitted in a conduit or tubing 24 inches or less in length, simply divide the allowable fill area of the conduit or tubing by the area of one (1) conductor.

EXAMPLE - Determine the MAXIMUM number of size 2/0 AWG THHN copper conductors permitted to be installed in a trade size 2 in. electrical metallic tubing (EMT) 18 inches long.

A. seven
B. eight
C. nine
D. ten

ANSWER -   (C)   nine

$\dfrac{2.013 \text{ sq. in. (allowable fill)}}{.2223 \text{ sq. in. (area of wire)}}$ = 9.05 or 9 wires

➢ When calculating the MAXIMUM number of conductors, all of the same size, permitted in a conduit or tubing, when the calculation results in a decimal of **0.8** or larger, an additional wire of the same size may be installed.   **[Chapter 9, Note 7]**

EXAMPLE - Determine the MAXIMUM number of size 1/0 AWG THWN copper conductors permitted to be installed in a trade size 1¼ in. rigid metal conduit (RMC) nipple.

A. four
B. five
C. six
D. seven

ANSWER -   (B)   five

$\dfrac{0.916 \text{ sq. in. (allowable fill)}}{.1855 \text{ sq. in. (area of wire)}}$ = 4.9 or 5 wires

Wireway and Gutter Sizing

RELATED INFORMATION:

➢ When calculating the number of conductors, all of the same size, permitted in a metal or nonmetallic wireway, or an auxiliary gutter, the fill shall not exceed **20 percent** of the interior cross-sectional area of the wireway or gutter where splices or taps are not made. **[366.22(A)&(B)]**, **[376.22(A)]** and **[378.22]** Use the same steps as before; first, find the allowable fill and divide by the area of one (1) conductor. Disregard the length of the wireway or gutter.

EXAMPLE - Determine the MAXIMUM number of size 4/0 AWG XHHW copper conductors permitted to be installed in a 4 in. x 4 in. metal wireway.

A. ten
B. eleven
C. twenty
D. sixteen

ANSWER - (A) ten

4 in. x 4 in. = 16 sq. in. x 20% = 3.2 sq. in. permitted fill

$$\frac{3.2 \text{ sq. in. (permitted fill)}}{.3197 \text{ sq. in. (area of wire)}} = 10 \text{ wires}$$

➢ When conductors are of different sizes and/or insulations, **wireways** and **gutters** can be properly sized by dividing the total area, in square inches, of the conductors by the **20 percent** permitted fill area, where splices or taps are not made. Or find the area, in square inches, of a specific wireway or gutter and multiply by **20 percent** to find the allowable fill. Using this method you may have to try more than one size gutter or wireway to find the proper size.

EXAMPLE - A wireway is to contain the following listed conductors.

- three – size 250 kcmil THHN compact aluminum
- three – size 4/0 AWG THHN compact aluminum
- three – size 1/0 AWG THHN compact aluminum

Which one of the following listed wireways is the MINIMUM size required to house the conductors?

A. 4 in. x 4 in.
B. 6 in. x 6 in.
C. 8 in. x 8 in.
D. 12 in. x 12 in.

ANSWER - (A) 4 in. x 4 in.

First, go to **Table 5A of Chapter 9** to determine the area of the conductors.

250 kcmil THHN compact AL = .3525 sq. in. x 3 = 1.0575 sq. in.
4/0 AWG THHN compact AL = .2780 sq. in. x 3 = 0.8340 sq. in.
1/0 AWG THHN compact AL = .1590 sq. in. x 3 = 0.4770 sq. in.
                                           TOTAL = 2.3685 sq. in.

2.3685 (area of wires) = 11.8425 sq. in. required area
  20% (permitted fill)

A 4 in. x 4 in. wireway with an area of 16 square inches is required.

To cross-check:
4 in. x 4 in. = 16 sq. in. x 20% = 3.2 square inches allowable fill
This wireway having an allowable fill of 3.2 square inches may contain the conductors having an area of 2.3685 square inches.

UNIT 6

VOLTAGE DROP CALCULATIONS

Upon successfully completing this unit of study the student will be familiar with the concept and causes of voltage drop, as well as the means to prevent excessive voltage drop in three-phase and single-phase circuits.

$$VD = \frac{2 \times K \times I \times D}{CM}$$

UNIT 6

VOLTAGE DROP CALCULATIONS

RELATED INFORMATION:

- The conductors of an electrical system should be of sufficient size so that the voltage drop is not excessive. Typical results of excessive voltage drop are as follows:

    1) luminaires (lighting fixtures) dimming when appliances or motors are turned on,
    2) overheating of motors and appliances,
    3) shortened life span of appliances such as computers, TVs, refrigerators and freezers,
    4) nuisance tripping of circuit breakers,
    5) delayed starting of high-intensity discharge lighting.

- The loss of voltage, known as voltage drop, is apparent in all electrical circuits due to the resistance of the circuit conductors. This loss of voltage varies with conductor material, conductor size, conductor length, ambient temperature and intensity of the current.

- The NEC® recommends the MAXIMUM voltage drop to be limited to 3 percent at the farthest outlet for branch circuits and 5 percent on both feeder and branch circuits to the farthest outlet. **[210.19(A)(1) IN#4]** and **[215.2(A)(3) IN#2]** In practical work, many engineers try to limit the voltage drop for lighting and power branch circuits to 2 percent and 4 percent for feeders.

- **The smaller the wire size, the greater the resistance** because, the small cross-sectional area of the conductor restricts the flow of electrons; thus, the greater the voltage drop. **The larger the wire size, the less the resistance** because, the larger cross-sectional area of the conductor permits the electrons to flow more freely; thus, the less voltage drop. So, the most practical way to limit voltage drop is increase the wire size. Although not always practical, voltage drop may be decreased by:

1) increasing the voltage, which reduces the intensity of the current,
2) change the conductor material say, from aluminum to copper which reduces the resistance,
3) move the load closer to its source voltage, which reduces the conductor resistance.

➢ A useful and common formula that may be used to determine the voltage drop in a single-phase circuit is:

$$VD = \frac{2 \times K \times I \times D}{CM}$$

Formula Definitions:

VD – Volts dropped from a circuit.

2 – Multiplying factor for single-phase circuits. The **2** represents the conductor length in a single-phase circuit.

K - Approximate resistivity of the conductor per mil foot at an operating temperature of 75°C/167°F. A mil foot is a wire one (1) foot long and one (1) mil in diameter. The approximate **K** value (constant) for copper wire is **12.9 ohms** and for aluminum wire is **21.2 ohms**.

I - Current or amperage draw of the load at 100 percent.

D - The distance, in feet, from the source voltage to the load.

CM - The area of the conductor expressed in **circular mils**, which can be found in **Chapter 9, Table 8**, which lists wire sizes from 18 AWG through 2,000 kcmil. For example, a size 10 AWG conductor has a cross-sectional area of 10,380 circular mils. For conductors of size 250 kcmil through size 2,000 kcmil, the cross-sectional area in circular mils can be determined by adding three (3) zeros to the kcmil size. For example, a size 300 kcmil conductor has a cross-sectional area of 300,000 circular mils.

EXAMPLE - A 120-volt, single-phase branch circuit, using size 12 AWG copper conductors, is supplying a 15 ampere load located sixty (60) feet from the panelboard. Determine the approximate voltage drop. (K = 12.9)

A. 2 volts
B. 4 volts
C. 6 volts
D. 8 volts

ANSWER -   (B)   4 volts

CM = 6,530 (12 AWG)
K = 12.9 ohms (copper)
I = 15 amperes
D = 60 feet

$$VD = \frac{2 \times 12.9 \times 15 \times 60}{6,530} = \frac{23,220}{6,530} = 3.55 \text{ volts}$$

➢ A useful and common formula that may be used to determine the voltage drop in a **three-phase** circuit is:

$$VD = \frac{1.732 \times K \times I \times D}{CM}$$

➢ The multiplying factor for **three-phase** circuits is **1.732**. The square root of 3 represents the conductor length in a three-phase circuit. The only difference between the single-phase and the three-phase formulas is that "**1.732**" has replaced "2".

EXAMPLE - A 208Y/120-volt, three-phase feeder, using size 4 AWG aluminum conductors is to supply an 80 ampere load located one hundred (100) feet from the switchboard. Determine the approximate voltage drop.
(K = 21.2)

A. 9.3 volts
B. 5.0 volts
C. 7.0 volts
D. 9.0 volts

ANSWER -   (C)   7.0 volts

CM = 41,740 (4 AWG)
K = 21.2 ohms (aluminum)
I = 80 amperes
D = 100 feet

$$VD = \frac{1.732 \times 21.2 \times 80 \times 100}{41,740} = \frac{293,747}{41,740} = 7.0 \text{ volts}$$

> As stated before, the size of the conductor affects voltage drop because of the resistance variables. Conductors are to be sized to prevent excessive voltage drop. A useful formula that may be used to size the conductors and prevent excessive voltage drop in a single-phase circuit is:

$$CM = \frac{2 \times K \times I \times D}{VD}$$

> When determining wire size, VD is the actual volts allowed to be dropped from the circuit. For example, the recommended voltage drop in a 240 volt, single-phase branch circuit is 3 percent; 3 percent of 240 volts is 7.2 volts. DO NOT enter 3 percent in the VD position in the formula, enter the value of the actual voltage permitted to be lost or dropped.

EXAMPLE - A 240-volt, single-phase, 52 ampere load is located two-hundred (200) feet from the panelboard. What MINIMUM size copper branch circuit conductors should be used to supply this load when voltage drop is to be limited to 3 percent? (K = 12.9)

A. 8 AWG
B. 6 AWG
C. 4 AWG
D. 2 AWG

ANSWER - (C) 4 AWG

VD = 240 x 0.03 = 7.2 volts
K = 12.9 ohms (copper)
I = 52 amperes
D = 200 feet

$$CM = \frac{2 \times 12.9 \times 52 \times 200}{7.2} = \frac{268,320}{7.2} = 37,267 \text{ CM}$$

In this situation, a size 4 AWG conductor with a circular mil area (CMA) of 41,740 CM is required because, a size 6 AWG conductor with a CMA of 26,240 CM would not limit the voltage drop to 3 percent.

> A useful formula that may be used to size conductors in a three-phase circuit to prevent excessive voltage drop is:

$$CM = \frac{1.732 \times K \times I \times D}{VD}$$

EXAMPLE - A 208Y/120-volt, 3-phase, 150 ampere load is located two hundred and fifty (250) feet from the main distribution switchboard. What MINIMUM size copper feeder conductors are required to supply the load when voltage drop is to be limited to 3 percent? (K = 12.9)

A. 4/0 AWG
B. 1/0 AWG
C. 2/0 AWG
D. 3/0 AWG

ANSWER - (D) 3/0 AWG

VD = 208 x 0.03 = 6.24 volts
K = 12.9 ohms (copper)
I = 150 amperes
D = 250 feet

$$CM = \frac{1.732 \times 12.9 \times 150 \times 250}{6.24} = \frac{83,786}{6.24} = 134,272 \text{ CM}$$

A size 3/0 AWG conductor with a CMA of 167,800 CM is required to limit the voltage drop to 6.24 volts.

➢ Voltage drop can be limited in a circuit by limiting the length of the circuit conductors. The following formula can be used to determine the approximate distance circuit conductors may be installed to prevent excessive voltage drop in a single-phase circuit.

$$D = \frac{CM \times VD}{2 \times K \times I}$$

EXAMPLE - What is the approximate MAXIMUM distance a 120-volt, single-phase, 1,800 VA load, supplied with size 12 AWG copper branch circuit conductors can be located from the panelboard, when the permitted voltage drop is to be not more than three percent?

A. 60 feet
B. 75 feet
C. 90 feet
D. 120 feet

ANSWER -   (A) 60 feet

CM = 6,530 (12 AWG)
VD = 120 volts x .03 = 3.6 volts
K = 12.9 ohms
$$I = \frac{VA}{volts} = \frac{1,800 \text{ VA}}{120 \text{ volts}} = 15 \text{ amperes}$$

$$D = \frac{6,530 \times 3.6}{2 \times 12.9 \times 15} = \frac{23,508}{387} = 60.7 \text{ feet}$$

➤ When determining the approximate distance circuit conductors may be installed in three-phase circuits to prevent excessive voltage drop, the following formula can be used:

$$D = \frac{CM \times VD}{1.732 \times K \times I}$$

EXAMPLE - A transformer having a 208Y/120-volt, 3-phase secondary is to supply a panelboard with a 130 ampere demand load. The feeder conductors are size 1/0 AWG THWN copper. What is the MAXIMUM approximate distance the panelboard can be located from the transformer so that the voltage drop does not exceed three percent?

A. 125 feet
B. 65 feet
C. 225 feet
D. 200 feet

ANSWER - (C) 225 feet

CM = 105,600 (1/0 AWG)
VD = 208 volts x .03 = 6.24 volts
K = 12.9 ohms
I = 130 amperes

$$D = \frac{105,600 \times 6.24}{1.732 \times 12.9 \times 130} = \frac{658,944}{2,905} = 227 \text{ feet}$$

➤ Another way of limiting voltage drop is to limit the intensity of the current on the conductors. Perhaps, you may have an existing installation and if additional loads are added, this may cause excessive voltage drop on the feeder conductors. The following formula can be used to determine the MAXIMUM load permitted when limiting voltage drop on single-phase circuits:

$$I = \frac{CM \times VD}{2 \times K \times D}$$

EXAMPLE - A 240-volt, single-phase feeder with size 2/0 AWG THWN aluminum conductors is supplying an existing panelboard located 260 feet from the main switchboard. What is the MAXIMUM load that can be placed on the panelboard so that the voltage drop is limited to three percent?

A. 143 amperes
B. 175 amperes
C. 122 amperes
D. 87 amperes

ANSWER - (D) 87 amperes

CM = 133,100 CM (2/0 AWG)
VD = 240 volts x .03 = 7.2 volts
K = 21.2 ohms (aluminum)
D = 260 feet

$$I = \frac{133,100 \times 7.2}{2 \times 21.2 \times 260} = \frac{958,320}{11,024} = 86.9 \text{ amperes}$$

➢ The following formula can be used to determine the MAXIMUM load permitted when limiting the voltage drop on three-phase circuits:

$$I = \frac{CM \times VD}{1.732 \times K \times D}$$

EXAMPLE - An existing 208Y/120-volt, three-phase, 4-wire, panelboard is supplied with size 2 AWG THW copper feeder conductors from the main switchboard. The panelboard is located three-hundred (300) feet from the main switchboard. What is the MAXIMUM load, in amperes, the conductors can carry without exceeding a three percent voltage drop?

A. 62 amperes
B. 54 amperes
C. 38 amperes
D. 79 amperes

ANSWER - (A) 62 amperes

CM = 66,360 (2 AWG)
VD = 208 x .03 = 6.24 volts
K = 12.9 ohms (copper)
D = 300 feet

$$I = \frac{66,360 \times 6.24}{1.732 \times 12.9 \times 300} = \frac{414,086}{6,703} = 61.77 \text{ amperes}$$

➤ Another method of determining the voltage drop of the conductors for **single-phase circuits only** is to apply the Ohm's Law Method, using the following formula:

VD = I x R

FORMULA DEFINITIONS:

VD = Volts dropped from a circuit
I = Intensity of the current, or the load, in amperes, at 100 percent.
R = Total conductor resistance, which can be found in **Chapter 9, Table 8** of the NEC®, under the ohm/KFT column. Using this method, you must take into consideration the **total length** of both the conductors to find total resistance.

EXAMPLE - Two (2) size 12 AWG THWN/THHN 120-volt, single-phase, copper branch circuit conductors are to supply a 15 ampere load located one-hundred (100) feet from the panelboard. Determine the approximate voltage drop.

A. 3 volts
B. 6 volts
C. 9 volts
D. 12 volts

ANSWER -   (B)   6 volts

R = 1.98 ohms per 1,000 feet **(Chapter 9, Table 8)**

R = 1.98 / 1,000 = 0.00198 ohms per ft. x 200 ft = .396 ohms total

I = 15 amperes

VD = 15 amps x .396 ohms = 5.94 volts

EXAMPLE - A 240-volt, single-phase branch circuit is to supply a 32 ampere load with size 8 AWG THWN copper conductors. The load is one-hundred and fifty (150) feet from the panelboard; determine the voltage drop.

A. 4 volts
B. 15 volts
C. 7.5 volts
D. 6 volts

ANSWER - (C) 7.5 volts

R = .778 ohms per 1,000 feet **(Chapter 9, Table 8)**

R = $\frac{.788}{1,000}$ = 0.000788 ohms per ft. x 300 ft. = .2334 ohms total

VD = 32 amps x .2334 ohms = 7.46 volts

UNIT 7

AC MOTOR CALCULATIONS

Upon successfully completing this unit of study the student will be familiar with the concept of properly sizing conductors, overcurrent protection, overload protection, and disconnects for AC electric motors.

UNIT 7

AC MOTOR CALCULATIONS

RELATED INFORMATION:

- In general, when sizing the conductors, disconnecting means and overcurrent protection for **continuous-duty** ac motors, the full-load current values of the motor(s) given in **Tables 430.247** through **430.250** shall be used, instead of the actual current rating marked on the motor nameplate. **[430.6(A)(1)]** Note this rule does not apply for motors built for low speeds (less than 1,200 RPM) or high torque which may have higher full-load currents and multispeed motors which will have full-load current varying with the speed. For these motors the current values given on the motor(s) nameplate shall be used instead of the NEC® tables.

- **All** motors shall be considered to be for **continuous-duty** unless the nature of the apparatus it drives is such that the motor cannot operate continuously with load under any condition of use. **[430.33]** Examples of motors **not** considered as continuous duty are motors operating elevators, cranes and assembly line machines.

- In general, in order to properly size branch circuit conductors supplying a single continuous duty motor you are to comply with **430.22** which requires the conductors to have an ampacity of at least **125 percent** of the motor's full-load current (FLC) rating as determined in the related tables in the NEC®. The actual conductor sizes are to be selected from **Tables 310.15(B)(16)** or from **Table 400.5(A)**. The conductors are to be sized according to the temperature ratings (60°C or 75°C) of the equipment terminations.

    EXAMPLE - Determine the MINIMUM size THHN copper conductors required to supply a 3 hp, 240-volt, single-phase continuous-duty motor when all terminations have a rating of 75°C.

    A. 14 AWG
    B. 12 AWG
    C. 10 AWG
    D. 8 AWG

    ANSWER - (B) 12 AWG

    motor FLC = 17 amperes **[Table 430.248]**
    17 amperes x 125% **[430.22]** = 21.25 amperes
    Size 12 AWG THHN is rated at 25 amperes at 75°C
    [Table 310.15(B)(16)]

➤ Conductors that supply a motor used in a short-time, intermittent, or varying duty application are permitted to have an ampacity of not less than the percentage values shown on **Table 430.22(E)**, based the full-load current rating indicated on the **motor's nameplate**.

EXAMPLE - Conductors supplying a 40 hp, 480-volt, three-phase, 5 minute rated elevator motor with an ampere rating of 50 amperes marked on the nameplate, shall have an ampacity of at least _____.

A. 42.5 amperes
B. 45.9 amperes
C. 62.5 amperes
D. 67.5 amperes

ANSWER -   (A)   42.5 amperes

motor FLA = 50 amperes x 85% **[Table 430.22(E)]** = 42.5 amps

➤ In general, conductors that supply more than one continuous-duty motor on a single circuit and/or motor(s) and other load(s), are required to have an ampacity of not less than **125 percent** of the full-load current rating of the **highest** rated motor in the group plus **100 percent** of the full-load current ratings of all the **remaining motors** in the group, also the ampacity required for the other load(s).**[430.24]**

EXAMPLE - Determine the MINIMUM size THWN/THHN copper feeder conductors required to supply two (2) induction type, 208-volt, three-phase, continuous-duty motors; one (1) 10 hp and one (1) 15 hp. Consider all terminations are rated 75°C.

A. 6 AWG
B. 4 AWG
C. 3 AWG
D. 2 AWG

ANSWER -   (C)   3 AWG

10 hp FLC = 30.8 amps **[Tbl. 430.250]** x 100% = 30.80 amperes
15 HP FLC = 46.2 amps **[Tbl. 430.250]** x 125% = <u>57.75 amperes</u>
                                                                           88.55 amperes

Size 3 AWG THWN is rated at 100 amperes. **[Table 310.15(B)(16)]**

➤ Each motor and its accessories is required to have branch circuit, short-circuit and ground fault protection by the use of overcurrent protective devices such as fuses or circuit breakers. The overcurrent protective devices are to be sized no larger than the percentage values given in **Table 430.52**. **[430.52(C)(1)]** Where the values for overcurrent protection determined from **Table 430.52** does not correspond with the standard sizes or ratings as listed per **240.6(A)** the next higher standard overcurrent protection device is permitted to be used.
[430.52(C)(1), Ex 1] This is known as **initial sizing**.

EXAMPLE - Determine the MAXIMUM initial rating of nontime delay fuses to be used for branch-circuit, short-circuit and ground-fault protection for a 5 hp, 230-volt, three-phase, squirrel cage, continuous-duty motor.

A. 40 amperes
B. 45 amperes
C. 50 amperes
D. 60 amperes

ANSWER - (C) 50 amperes

5 hp FLC = 15.2 amperes **[Table 430.250]**
15.2 amperes x 300% = 45.6 amperes **[Table 430.52]**

Since 45.6 amperes is not a standard rating for nontime delay fuses, as per **430.52(C)(1) Ex. 1**, you are permitted to go up to the next standard size fuse which is rated at 50 amperes.

➤ When sizing overcurrent protection for motors, the selected rating or setting, if adjustable, should be as low as possible for MAXIMUM protection. However, if the motor is under severe starting conditions, the rating or setting designated in **Table 450.52** or as permitted by **430.52(C)(1) Ex. 1** is not large enough for the starting current of the motor, you are permitted to go up to a higher value as allowed by **430.52(C)(1) Ex. 2**. This is known as **MAXIMUM** or **absolute MAXIMUM** sizing.

EXAMPLE - Determine the absolute MAXIMUM standard size time-delay fuses permitted for short-circuit, branch-circuit and ground-fault protection for a 40 hp, 480-volt, three-phase, induction type, continuous-duty motor.

A. 100 amperes
B. 110 amperes
C. 115 amperes
D. 125 amperes

ANSWER -   (B)   110 amperes

40 hp FLC = 52 amperes **[Table 430.250]**
52 amperes x 225% = 117 amperes **[430.52(C)(1)Ex.2(b)]**

Since you are NOT permitted to exceed 225% of the FLC of the motor, you must go down to the next smaller standard size fuse as listed in **240.6(A).**

> In general, to properly size the overcurrent protection device for **feeder** conductors supplying two or more motors, the rules as specified in **430.62(A)** are to be applied which states, the protective device is to be sized by:

(1) not greater than the largest overcurrent protection device provided for any motor in the group,

(2) plus the sum of the full-load currents of the other motors of the group.

When sizing **feeder** overcurrent protection for motors, when the value you select does not correspond with a standard rating as listed per **240.6(A)** you are NOT permitted to go up to the next standard size, you must go **down**.

EXAMPLE - What standard size time-delay fuses are required for the feeder overcurrent protection of a feeder supplying four (4), 15 hp, 480-volt, three-phase, continuous-duty induction-type motors, each protected with 40 ampere rated time-delay fuses?

A. 100 amperes
B. 110 amperes
C. 125 amperes
D. 150 amperes

ANSWER -   (A)   100 amperes

15 hp FLC = 21 amperes **[Table 430.250]**

40 A (largest OCP in group) + 21 A + 21 A + 21 A = 103 amps

You are required to go down to 100 ampere rated fuses.
[240.6(A)]

➤ In addition to overcurrent protection, most continuous-duty electric motors rated more than 1 hp and motors automatically started having a rating of 1 hp or less, are required to be protected from harmful **overloads**. **[430.32(A)]** To properly size the overload protective devices, they shall be selected to trip at no more than the percentage values of the motors nameplate rating given in **430.32(A)(1)**, **(MINIMUM)** or **430.32(C)**, **(MAXIMUM)** instead of the full-load current values from Tables 430.248, 430.249 and 430.250. Today, many manufacturers have adjustable overloads installed in motor controllers or starters for protecting the motor against overloads, which are harmful to it.

➤ The ampere trip setting value of the separate overloads is based upon **service factor** and **temperature rise** of the motor, as indicated on the motor **nameplate**. The running overload protection may range from **115%** to **125% (MINIMUM)** **[430.32(A)(1)]** to no more than **140% (MAXIMUM) [430.32(C)]** of the motor's ampere **nameplate** rating. The service factor indicated on the nameplate usually ranges from **1.00** to **1.30**. For example, if a motor has a service factor rating of 1.15 this means that the motor can operate up to **115%** of its rating without undue harm where the ambient temperature is not more than 104°F or 40°C. The temperature rise indicated on the motors nameplate relates to the heating effect of the motor when it is running properly in relation to the ambient temperature. The higher the temperature rise indicated on the nameplate the hotter the motor runs. For example, a motor with a 40°C temperature rise means, under normal operating conditions the motor should not get warmer than 40°C or 104°F. If too great a load is put on the motor or the ambient temperature is elevated, the motor will become excessively hot, causing probable injury to the insulation of the windings.

EXAMPLE - What is the MINIMUM size running overload protection, in amperes, required for a 2 hp, 208-volt, single-phase, squirrel cage motor with a temperature rise of 42°C and a FLA of 12 amperes indicated on the nameplate?

A. 13.20 amperes
B. 15.18 amperes
C. 15.00 amperes
D. 13.80 amperes

ANSWER - (D) 13.80 amperes

2 hp FLA (nameplate) = 12 amperes

12 amps x 115% (all other motors) = 13.8 amps **[430.32(A)(1)]**

EXAMPLE - Refer to the previous example. Assume the ampere rating you have selected is not sufficient to start the motor and trips. Determine the MAXIMUM size overload protection permitted.

A. 15.00 amperes
B. 15.60 amperes
C. 16.80 amperes
D. 17.16 amperes

ANSWER - (B) 15.60 amperes

2 hp FLA (nameplate) = 12 amperes

12 amps x 130% (all other motors) = 15.60 amps **[430.32(C)]**

> Some motors are provided with a **thermal protector integral** with the motor, located inside the motor housing, for overload protection. **[430.32(A)(2)]** Under this condition, the ultimate trip setting, in amperes, shall not exceed the percentage values as expressed in **430.32(A)(2)**, multiplied by the motor's full-load current as given in **Table 430.248**, **Table 430.249** or **Table 430.250**.

EXAMPLE - Determine the MAXIMUM current setting permitted for overload protection for a motor that has a thermal protector integral with the motor, given the following:

- 1 hp – squirrel cage
- single-phase, 120-volts

A. 24.96 amperes
B. 20.80 amperes
C. 22.40 amperes
D. 27.20 amperes

ANSWER - (A) 24.96 amperes

1 hp FLC = 16 amperes **[Table 430.248]**

16 amperes x 156% **[430.32(A)(2)]** = 24.96 amperes

> In general, each motor must be provided with some form of approved manual **disconnecting means**. The disconnecting means is required to have an ampere rating of not less than **115 percent** of the full-load current rating of the motor as determined in **Table 430.248** through **430.250**.**[430.110(A)]** For motors rated 2 hp through 100 hp the disconnecting means may be a general-use switch, rated in horsepower, a circuit breaker, or a manual motor controller when marked **"Suitable as Motor Disconnect"**. **[430.109(A)(6)]**

EXAMPLE - When an inverse time circuit breaker is used as a disconnecting means only for a 7½ hp, single-phase, 240-volt, ac motor, the circuit breaker must have a standard ampacity rating of at LEAST _____.

A. 40 amperes
B. 50 amperes
C. 100 amperes
D. 46 amperes

ANSWER - (B) 50 amperes

7½ hp FLA = 40 amperes **[Table 430.248]**

40 amperes x 115% = 46 amperes **[430.110A]**

As per **240.6(A),** the next standard size circuit breaker has a rating of 50 amperes.

➢ For stationary ac motors of 2 hp or less and 300 volts or less the disconnecting means is permitted to be an ac general-use snap switch where the motor full-load current rating is not more than **80 percent** of the ampere rating of the switch. **[430.109(C)(2)]**

EXAMPLE - A 20 ampere rated ac general-use snap switch is permitted for use as a disconnecting means for a 120-volt, single-phase, ac motor when the motor has a rating of 2 hp or less and a full-load current rating of _____ or less.

A. 20 amperes
B. 16 amperes
C. 12 amperes
D. 25 amperes

ANSWER - (B) 16 amperes

20 amperes (switch rating) x 80% = 16 amperes
[430.109(C)(2)]

UNIT 8

SINGLE-FAMILY DWELLING SERVICE CALCULATIONS

After completing this unit of study, the successful student will be familiar with the concept of properly sizing services for one-family dwellings.

UNIT 8

SINGLE-FAMILY DWELLING SERVICE CALCULATIONS

RELATED INFORMATION:

- A single-family dwelling is considered a building consisting solely of one dwelling unit with living and sleeping quarters and having permanent provisions for cooking, cleaning, and laundering.

- In order to properly size services for dwelling units you are to comply with the requirements as set forth in **Article 220** of the NEC® and additional Articles such as **210**, **230** and **240** that may also apply. As indicated in **Section 310.15(B)(7)**, for sizing residential **120/240-volt, 3-wire, single phase** ungrounded (line) service conductors rated **100 through 400 amperes,** they are permitted to have an ampacity not less than **83 percent** of the service rating. For example, if the dwelling unit has a service rating of 150 amperes, the service-entrance conductors are permitted to have a rating of 125 amperes. 150 amperes x .83 = 124.5 amperes

- The NEC® recognizes two (2) methods when calculating dwelling services, the **general method**, also known as the **standard method** and the **optional method**. The standard method starts at **220.12** and the optional method starts at **220.80**. Generally, the optional method is easier to use because you simply add the nameplate values of the utilization equipment together and apply only one demand factor. With the general method, there are several demand factors applied. With either method the most common service provided for a one-family dwelling unit is 120/240-volts, single-phase.

- When using either calculation method, the **MINIMUM** size service for a one-family dwelling is required to be rated **100 amperes** because the ampacity for the ungrounded conductors shall not be less than the rating of the service disconnecting means **[230.42(B)]** and the service disconnecting means shall have a rating of not less than **100 amperes. [230.79(C)]**

- **Annex D** of the NEC® shows examples of both calculation methods and the steps and procedures to be used. We will follow these examples and steps to learn how to properly size services for one-family dwellings. First, we will look at the general (standard) method of calculation. You will find a completed example of this form using the standard method of calculation on page 123 of this text.

General Calculation Method

Step 1 - Determine the total connected load, in VA, of the general lighting and general-purpose receptacles by applying **Table 220.12**. Use the outside dimension of the house but, do not include garages, open porches and enclosed areas not adaptable for future use. **[220.12]**

    EXAMPLE - What is the total connected load, in VA, for the general lighting and general-use receptacles of a one-family dwelling having 30 feet by 60 feet of livable space?

        A. 2,100 VA
        B. 3,600 VA
        C. 5,400 VA
        D. 6,300 VA

        ANSWER - (C) 5,400 VA

    First, find the area, in square feet, of the livable space, then multiply by the value given in **Table 220.12**.

    30 ft. x 60 ft. = 1,800 sq. ft. x 3 VA **[Table 220.12]** = 5,400 VA

Step 2 - Find the total connected load of the small appliance and laundry branch circuits. A MINIMUM of **two (2)** small appliance branch circuits are required **[210.11(C)(1)]** and they shall be calculated at **1,500 VA** per circuit. **[220.52(A)]** A MINIMUM of **one (1)** branch circuit is required to supply the laundry **[210.11(C)(2)]** and shall be calculated at **1,500 VA** per circuit. **[220.52(B)]**

    EXAMPLE - What is the MINIMUM total connected load, in VA, for the small appliance and laundry loads in a single-family dwelling?

        A. 4,500 VA
        B. 3,000 VA
        C. 6,000 VA
        D. 1,500 VA

        ANSWER - (A) 4,500 VA

    2 small appl. circuits @ 1,500 VA each = 3,000 VA
    1 laundry circuit @ 1,500 VA   = 1,500 VA
                              TOTAL = 4,500 VA

Step 3 - Apply the demand factors specified in **Table 220.42** for the general-purpose lighting and receptacle loads, plus the loads required for the small appliance and laundry branch circuits. **[220.42]**

EXAMPLE - What is the demand load, in VA, for a dwelling unit having a 5,400 VA total connected lighting load and a 4,500 VA connected load for small appliance and laundry branch-circuits?

A. 9,900 VA
B. 5,415 VA
C. 6,780 VA
D. 3,465 VA

ANSWER - (B) 5,415 VA

5,400 VA (ltg.) + 4,500 VA (laund. & sm. appl.) = 9,900 VA total

1st 3,000 VA @ 100% **[Table 220.42]** = 3,000 VA
9,900 VA − 3,000 VA = 6,900 VA (remainder) x 35% = 2,415 VA
DEMAND LOAD = 5,415 VA

Step 4 - Apply a demand factor of **75 percent** of the nameplate rating of **four (4)** or more fastened in place appliances.

*NOTE – This rule does **not apply** for electric ranges, clothes dryers, space heating or air-conditioning equipment. **[220.53]**

EXAMPLE - A one-family dwelling is to have the following fastened in place appliances:

garbage disposal – 864 VA
dishwasher – 1,100 VA
trash compactor – 1,188 VA
water heater – 4,500 VA
attic fan – 750 VA
swimming pool pump – 1,250 VA

Where using the standard method of calculation for dwelling units, determine the demand load.

A. 7,652 VA
B. 9,652 VA
C. 6,757 VA
D. 7,239 VA

ANSWER - (D) 7,239 VA

garbage disposal -   864 VA
dishwasher   - 1,100 VA
trash compactor - 1,188 VA
water heater   - 4,500 VA
attic fan   -   750 VA
pump   - 1,250 VA
        TOTAL = 9,652 VA (connected load)
           x   75%
                 7,239 VA (demand load)

Step 5 - Determine the electric clothes dryer demand load, using **5,000 watts (volt – amperes)** as a MINIMUM or the nameplate rating, **whichever is larger**, for each dryer served. **[220.54]** You are permitted to use the demand factors shown in **Table 220.54**. A demand of **70 percent** of this value may be applied to the **neutral** (grounded) conductor. **[220.61(B)(1)]**

EXAMPLE - When a one-family dwelling is to have only one (1) 4,500 VA electric clothes dryer installed, the demand load will be _____ on the ungrounded service-entrance conductors and _____ on the grounded (neutral) conductor.

A. 4,500 VA – 3,500 VA
B. 3,500 VA – 4,500 VA
C. 4,500 VA – 5,000 VA
D. 5,000 VA – 3,500 VA

ANSWER -   (D)   5,000 VA – 3,500 VA

5,000 VA MINIMUM ungrounded conductors **[220.54]**
5,000 VA x 70% = 3,500 VA neutral conductor **[220.61(B)(1)]**

Step 6 - Determine the demand load for the cooking appliances in accordance with **Table 220.55**. **[220.55]** This is explained in **Unit 3** of this book. A further demand of **70 percent** of the demand load on the ungrounded conductors may be applied to the **neutral** (grounded) conductor. **[220.61(B)(1)]**

EXAMPLE - A 12 kW electric range installed in a one-family dwelling will have a demand load of _____ on the ungrounded service-entrance conductors and a demand load of _____ on the grounded neutral conductor.

A. 8,000 VA – 5,600 VA
B. 12,000 VA – 8,400 VA
C. 12,000 VA – 8,000 VA
D. 8,000 VA – 3,920 VA

ANSWER -   (A)   8,000 VA – 5,600 VA

ungrounded conductors demand – 8 kW = 8,000 VA
          [Table 220.55, Col. C]
grounded conductor – 8,000 VA x 70% = 5,600 VA
          [220.61(B)(1)]

Step 7 - Determine the demand load for the fixed electric space heating or air-conditioning load; you are permitted to **omit the smaller** of the two because these loads are considered noncoincident loads, meaning, they are unlikely to be in use simultaneously. **[220.60]**

EXAMPLE - A one-family dwelling unit to be constructed will have a 10 kW (kVA), 240-volt, single-phase, fixed electric space heating unit and a 32 ampere, 240-volt, single-phase air-conditioning unit. When calculating the total load on the dwelling unit, what is the demand that should be applied to the service-entrance conductors?

  A. 10,000 VA
  B. 10,800 VA
  C. 9,600 VA
  D. 19,600 VA

ANSWER - (A) 10,000 VA

First, compare the two loads.

A/C unit - P = I x E P = 32 amperes x 240 volts = 7,680 VA
Heating unit - 10 kW = 10 kW x 1,000 = 10,000 VA

*NOTE – The heating unit is the larger of the loads, this value should be applied.

Step 8 - Add an additional **25 percent** of the full-load current of the **largest motor** in the dwelling. **[220.50]** Generally, the largest motor in the house is the air-conditioning unit.

EXAMPLE - A one-family dwelling will have the following motor loads installed:

garbage disposal – 864 VA
trash compactor – 1,188 VA
attic fan – 750 VA
pump motor – 1,250 VA

When applying the largest motor rule for residential service calculations, how many VA should be added?

  A. 1,013 VA
  B. 1,563 VA
  C. 1,266 VA
  D. 313 VA

ANSWER - (D) 313 VA

Largest motor (pump) 1,250 VA x 25% = 313 VA

Step 9 - Add together the values determined from steps 3-8 to find the required volt-amperes. Next, apply the current formula **(I=P/E)** to determine the demand load. Then, multiply the current value by **83%** and size the service-entrance conductors using **Table 310.15(B)(16)**. Use **Table 250.66** for sizing the grounding electrode conductor.

EXAMPLE - After all demand factors have been taken into consideration for a one-family dwelling unit, a demand load of 35,967 VA is determined. What MINIMUM size THWN aluminum ungrounded service-entrance conductors are required when the house is to have a 120/240-volt, single-phase, electrical system?

A. 1 AWG
B. 1/0 AWG
C. 2/0 AWG
D. 3/0 AWG

ANSWER -   (C)   2/0 AWG

First, find the load in amperes and multiply by 83%.

$I = \dfrac{P}{E} = \dfrac{35,967}{240 \text{ volts}} = 150 \text{ amperes} \times 83\% = 124.5 \text{ amperes}$

Table 310.15(B)(16) indicates size 2/0 AWG aluminum conductors having an ampacity of 135 amperes should be selected.

STANDARD CALCULATION: ONE-FAMILY DWELLING

1. GENERAL LIGHTING & RECEPTACLES: *Table 220.12*
   _____ sq. ft. x 3 VA =   _____ VA

2. SMALL APPLIANCES 220.52(A) & LAUNDRY 220.52(B)
   1,500 VA x _____ circuits =   _____ VA

3. APPLY DEMAND FACTORS: *Table 220.42*
   Total of gen. ltg. & small appl.   _____ VA
   First 3000 VA x 100%   =   3,000 VA
   Next _____ VA x 35%   =   _____ VA **LINE**   **NEUTRAL**
   Remaining _____ VA x 25% =   _____ VA
   Total   _____ VA   _____ VA   _____ VA

4. FIXED APPLIANCES: *220.53*
   Water Heater =   _____ VA
   Disposal   =   _____ VA
   Compactor   =   _____ VA
   Dishwasher   =   _____ VA
   _____   =   _____ VA
   _____   =   _____ VA
   _____   =   _____ VA

   Total   _____ VA (x 75% if 4 or more)=   _____ VA   _____ VA

5. DRYER: *220.54*; *Table 220.54*
   _____ VA   =   _____ VA x 70%= _____ VA

6. COOKING EQUIPMENT: *Table 220.55 & Notes*
   Col A _____ VA x _____% =   _____ VA
   Col B _____ VA x _____% =   _____ VA
   Col C _____ VA   =   _____ VA
   Total   _____ VA   _____ VA x 70%= _____ VA

7. HEATING or A/C (largest): *220.60*
   Heating unit = _____ VA x 100% = _____ VA
   A/C unit   = _____ VA x 100% = _____ VA
   Heat pump   = _____ VA x 100% = _____ VA
   Largest Load   _____ VA

8. LARGEST MOTOR: *220.14(C)*
   _____ VA x 25% =   _____ VA   _____ VA

9. TOTAL   _____ VA   _____ VA
   Line   I = _____ VA = _____ amperes
              240 volts
   Neutral I = _____ VA = _____ amperes
              240 volts

Conductors are permitted to be sized @ 83% of the demand load if 120/240-volts, single-phase and not greater than 400 amperes.

STANDARD CALCULATION: ONE-FAMILY DWELLING

1. GENERAL LIGHTING & RECEPTACLES: *Table 220.12*
 1,800 sq. ft. x 3 VA = 5,400 VA

2. SMALL APPLIANCES 220.52(A) & LAUNDRY 220.52(B)
 1,500 VA x __3__ circuits = 4,500 VA

3. APPLY DEMAND FACTORS: *Table 220.42*   LINE   NEUTRAL
 Total of gen. ltg. & small appl. 9,900 VA
 First 3000 VA x 100% = 3,000 VA
 Next 6,900 VA x 35% = 2,415 VA
 Remaining _-0-_ VA x 25% = _-0-_ VA
 Total 5,415 VA   5,415 VA   5,415 VA

4. FIXED APPLIANCES: 220.53
 Water Heater = 4,500 VA
 Disposal = 864 VA
 Compactor = 1,188 VA
 Dishwasher = 1,110 VA
 Attic fan = 750 VA
 Pump = 1,250 VA
 -0- = -0- VA

 Total 9,652 VA (x 75% if 4 or more)= 7,239 VA   7,239 VA

5. DRYER: 220.54; *Table 220.54*
 5,000 VA = 5,000 VA x 70%= 3,500 VA

6. COOKING EQUIPMENT: *Table 220.55 & Notes*
 Col A _-0-_ VA x _-0-_ % = -0- VA
 Col B _-0-_ VA x _-0-_ % = -0- VA
 Col C 8,000 VA = 8,000 VA
 Total 8,000 VA   8,000 VA x 70%= 5,600 VA

7. HEATING or A/C (largest): 220.60
 Heating unit = 10,000 VA x 100% = 10,000 VA
 A/C unit = 7,680 VA x 100% = 7,680 VA
 Heat pump = _-0-_ VA x 100% = _-0-_ VA
 Largest Load 10,000 VA

8. LARGEST MOTOR: 220.14(C)
 1,250 VA x 25% = 313 VA   313 VA

9. TOTAL 35,967 VA   22,067 VA
 Line   I = 35,967 VA = 150 amperes
            240 volts
 Neutral   I = 22,067 VA = 92 amperes
            240 volts

Conductors are permitted to be sized @ 83% of the demand load if 120/240-volts, single-phase and not greater than 400 amperes.

Optional Calculation Method

> In general, the **optional calculation method** for dwelling units provides an easier and less complex method than the standard (general) method for computing the total demand load for service-entrance conductors. The optional calculation method is reserved for dwelling units served by a single service with a connected load of **100 amperes or greater. [220.82(A)]** Therefore, since most one-family homes currently being constructed have a connected load of 100 amperes or more, this calculation method is frequently used. You will find a completed example of this form of calculation method on page 130 of this text.

> When using the **optional calculation method**, the calculated load shall not be less than **100 percent** of the **first 10 kW**, plus **40 percent** of the remainder of the **"general loads"**, including, general lighting and receptacles, laundry and small appliance branch circuits and nameplate VA rating of all fastened in place motors and appliances, plus the larger of the air-conditioner or heating load. **[220.82(A)]** The following steps may be applied when using the optional calculation method for dwellings.

Step 1 - Compare the heating and air-conditioning loads. As per **220.82(C)**, include the **largest** of the following:

1. 100 percent of the nameplate rating(s) of the air-conditioning equipment.
2. 100 percent of the nameplate rating(s) of the heat pump(s) only.
3. 100 percent of the nameplate ratings of electric thermal storage and other heating systems where the usual load is expected to be continuous.

4. 100 percent of the nameplate rating(s) of the heat pump compressor and 65 percent of the supplemental electric heating for central electric space heating systems. If the heat pumps compressor is interlocked with the supplementary heat in a manner that both cannot be operated at the same time, the heat pump does not need to be added.

5. 65 percent of the nameplate rating(s) of electric space heating, if there are less than four (4) units having separate controls.

6. 40 percent of the nameplate rating(s) of electric space heating, if there are four (4) or more units with separate controls.

EXAMPLE - A one-family dwelling is to have the following heating and air-conditioning equipment:

two (2) 10 kW (kVA) electric space heating systems
two (2) 240-volt, single-phase, 50 ampere rated air-conditioners

When using the optional method of calculation for one-family dwellings, what demand, in VA, should be applied to the ungrounded service-entrance conductors for the heating or air-conditioning loads?

A. 20,000 VA
B. 24,000 VA
C. 15,600 VA
D. 13,000 VA

ANSWER -   (B)   24,000 VA

Space heaters **[220.82(C)(5)]**
10 kVA + 10 kVA = 20 kVA x 1,000 = 20,000 VA
20,000 VA x 65% = 13,000 VA

A/C Equipment **[220.82(C)(1)]**
50 amps + 50 amps = 100 amperes x 240 volts = 24,000 VA

The A/C equipment with a computed load of 24,000 VA is to be used for this calculation.

Step 2 -   Determine the connected load, in VA, of the general lighting and general-use receptacles; calculated from the outside dimensions of the dwelling using 3 VA per square foot. Do not include open porches, garages or unused or unfinished spaces not adapted for future use.   **[220.82(B)(1)]**

EXAMPLE -   Before demand factors are taken into consideration, determine the connected load, in VA, for the general lighting and general-use receptacles for a one-family dwelling having 5,000 square feet of livable space, a 600 square foot garage and a 350 square foot open porch.

A. 15,000 VA
B. 17,500 VA
C. 17,850 VA
D. 5,000 VA

ANSWER -   (A)   15,000 VA

5,000 sq. ft. x 3 VA **[220.82(B)(1)]** = 15,000 VA

Step 3 - Find the total connected load of the small appliance and laundry branch circuits; each circuit is to be calculated at **1,500 VA each**. **[220.82(B)(2)]** A MINIMUM of two (2) small-appliance branch circuits are required **[210.11(C)(1)]** and a MINIMUM of one (1) laundry branch circuit is required. **[210.11(C)(2)]**

EXAMPLE - A one-family dwelling is to have three (3) small-appliance branch circuits and one (1) laundry branch circuit installed. Before demand factors are taken into consideration, what is the total connected load of these circuits?

A. 1,500 VA
B. 3,000 VA
C. 4,500 VA
D. 6,000 VA

ANSWER - (D) 6,000 VA

Small appliance circuits 3 x 1,500 VA = 4,500 VA **[220.52(A)]**
Laundry circuit   1 x 1,500 VA = 1,500 VA **[220.52(B)]**
            TOTAL Connected Load   = 6,000 VA

Step 4 - Find the total connected load of all fastened in place appliances, such as electric ranges, cooktops, ovens, clothes dryers and water heaters. This total is to be based on the nameplate rating of the appliances. **[220.82(B)(3)]** Also include the nameplate ratings of all motors, such as attic fans, sump pumps and water well and swimming pool pumps. **[220.82(B)(4)]**

EXAMPLE - A single family dwelling is to have the following fastened in place appliances and motors:

one – 12 kVA electric range
one – 6 kVA electric clothes dryer
one – 1,250 VA dishwasher
one – 1,176 VA trash compactor
one – 1,656 VA garbage disposer
one – 6,000 VA water heater
one – 1,176 VA attic fan
one – 1,250 VA microwave oven

What is the total connected load of this utilization equipment?

A. 26,508 VA
B. 30,508 VA
C. 25,508 VA
D. 26,805 VA

ANSWER - (B) 30,508 VA

range - 12 kVA x 1,000	= 12,000 VA
clothes dryer - 6 kVA x 1,000	= 6,000 VA
dishwasher	= 1,250 VA
trash compactor	= 1,176 VA
garbage disposer	= 1,656 VA
water heater	= 6,000 VA
attic fan	= 1,176 VA
microwave oven	= 1,250 VA
TOTAL Connected Load	= 30,508 VA

Step 5 - Total the **"general load"** as determined in steps 2, 3 and 4, then apply the demand factors as per **220.82(B)**, **100 percent** of the **first 10 kVA (10,000 VA)**, plus **40 percent** of the remainder.

EXAMPLE - Using the optional calculation method for one-family dwellings, determine the demand load on the ungrounded service-entrance conductors for a dwelling that has the following total connected general loads:

General lighting and receptacles	- 15,000 VA
Small appliance and laundry circuits	- 6,000 VA
Fastened in place appliances and motors	- 30,500 VA

A. 51,500 VA
B. 25,000 VA
C. 26,600 VA
D. 25,600 VA

ANSWER -   (C)   26,600 VA

General lighting and receptacles	- 15,000 VA
Small appliance and laundry circuits	- 6,000 VA
Fastened in place appliances and motors	- <u>30,500 VA</u>
TOTAL General Load	= 51,500 VA

1st 10,000 VA @ 100%	- 10,000 VA
Remainder (total – 10,000) = 41,500 VA @ 40%	- <u>16,600 VA</u>
DEMAND LOAD	= 26,600 VA

Step 6 - Add together the values determined from steps 1 and 5 to find the required volt-amperes. Next, apply the current formula **(I=P/E)** to determine the demand load. Then, multiply the current value by **83%** and size the service-entrance conductors using **Table 310.15(B)(16)**. Use **Table 250.66** for sizing the grounding electrode conductor.

EXAMPLE - When applying the optional method of calculation for a one-family dwelling, after all demand factors have been considered, a demand load of 50,600 VA is determined. Using standard overcurrent protective devices, determine the MAXIMUM ampere rating of the service overcurrent protective device and the MINIMUM size of 75°C aluminum ungrounded service-entrance conductors required. The electrical system is 120/240-volts, single-phase.

  A. 200 amperes OCP – 4/0 AWG aluminum conductors
  B. 250 amperes OCP – 4/0 AWG aluminum conductors
  C. 250 amperes OCP – 250 kcmil aluminum conductors
  D. 225 amperes OCP – 4/0 AWG aluminum conductors

ANSWER - (D) 225 amperes – 4/0 AWG aluminum conductors

First, find the load in amperes.

$I = \frac{P}{E} = \frac{50,600 \text{ VA}}{240 \text{ volts}} = 210.8$ amperes (demand load)

This value does not correspond with the standard ampere rating of an overcurrent protective device. Therefore, as per **240.4(B)**, the next higher standard overcurrent device is permitted to be used. **Section 240.6(A)** indicates a **225 ampere** rating is the next higher standard OCP rating.

To find the required ampacity of the conductors:

210.8 amperes **x 83% = 175 amperes**

Size 4/0 AWG 75°C aluminum conductors with an ampacity of 180 amperes should be selected from **[Table 310.15(B)(16)]**.

OPTIONAL CALCULATION: ONE-FAMILY DWELLING

1. HEATING or A/C: *220.82(C)(1-6)*
Heating units (3 or less) = _____ VA x 65% = _____ VA
Heating units (4 or more) = _____ VA x 40% = _____ VA
A/C unit = _____ VA x 100% = _____ VA
Heat pump = _____ VA x 100% = _____ VA **LINE**
Largest Load = _____ VA
Total = _____ VA _____ VA

2. GENERAL LIGHTING: *220.82(B)(1)* **NEUTRAL**
_____ sq. ft. x 3 VA per sq. ft. = _____ VA _____ VA

3. SMALL APPLIANCE & LAUNDRY LOADS: *220.82(B)(2)*
1,500 VA x _____ circuits _____ VA _____ VA

4. FIXED APPLIANCES & MOTORS: *220.82(B)(3)&(4)*
Dishwasher = _____ VA _____ VA
Disposal = _____ VA _____ VA
Compactor = _____ VA _____ VA
Water heater = _____ VA _____ VA
Range = _____ VA @ 70% _____ VA
Cooktop = _____ VA @ 70% _____ VA
Oven = _____ VA @ 70% _____ VA
Dryer = _____ VA @ 70% _____ VA
_____ = _____ VA _____ VA
_____ = _____ VA _____ VA
_____ = _____ VA _____ VA
Total = _____ VA _____ VA

5. APPLY DEMAND FACTORS: *220.82(B)*
First 10,000 VA x 100% = 10,000 VA
Remaining _____ VA x 40% = _____ VA
Total _____ VA _____ VA _____ VA

6. TOTAL _____ VA _____ VA

LINE   I = VA / 240 volts = _____ amperes
NEUTRAL   I = VA / 240 volts = _____ amperes

Conductors are permitted to be sized @ 83% of the demand load if 120/240-volts, single-phase, or 100% if 208Y/120-volts, three-phase, or the load is greater than 400 amperes.

OPTIONAL CALCULATION: ONE-FAMILY DWELLING

1. HEATING or A/C: *220.82(C)(1-6)*

Heating units (3 or less) = 20,000 VA x 65%	= 13,000 VA	
Heating units (4 or more) = ____ VA x 40%	= ____ VA	
A/C unit = 24,000 VA x 100%	= 24,000 VA	
Heat pump = ____ VA x 100%	= ____ VA	**LINE**
Largest Load	= 24,000 VA	
Total	= 24,000 VA	24,000 VA

2. GENERAL LIGHTING: *220.82(B)(1)*   **NEUTRAL**

5,000 sq. ft. x 3 VA per sq. ft.   = 15,000 VA   15,000 VA

3. SMALL APPLIANCE & LAUNDRY LOADS: *220.82(B)(2)*

1,500 VA x __4__ circuits   = 6,000 VA   6,000 VA

4. FIXED APPLIANCES & MOTORS: *220.82(B)(3)&(4)*

Dishwasher =	1,250 VA		1,250 VA
Disposal =	1,656 VA		1,656 VA
Compactor =	1,176 VA		1,176 VA
Water heater =	6,000 VA		6,000 VA
Range =	12,000 VA	@ 70%	8,400 VA
Cooktop =	-0- VA	@ 70%	-0- VA
Oven =	-0- VA	@ 70%	-0- VA
Dryer =	6,000 VA	@ 70%	4,200 VA
Attic fan =	1,176 VA		1,176 VA
Microwave =	1,250 VA		1,250 VA
_____ =	____ VA		____ VA
Total =	51,508 VA		____ VA

5. APPLY DEMAND FACTORS: *220.82(B)*

First 10,000 VA x 100% =	10,000 VA		
Remaining 41,508 VA x 40% =	16,603 VA		
Total	26,603 VA	26,603 VA	46,108 VA

6. TOTAL   50,603 VA   46,108 VA

LINE   I = 50,603 VA = 211 amperes
                240 volts

NEUTRAL   I = 46,108 VA = 192 amperes
                240 volts

Conductors are to be sized per Table 310.15(B)(7) if 120/240 volts, single-phase, or Table 310.15(B)(16) if 208Y/120 volts, three-phase, or the load is greater than 400 amperes.

UNIT 9

MULTI-FAMILY DWELLING SERVICE CALCULATIONS

After successfully completing this unit of study, the student will have the ability to properly size services for multiple-family dwelling units.

UNIT 9

MULTI-FAMILY DWELLING SERVICE CALCULATIONS

RELATED INFORMATION:

- A multi-family dwelling unit is considered a building containing three or more dwelling units; examples are apartments, condominiums, and town houses.

- Many similarities exist between multi-family dwelling service calculations and one-family dwelling service calculations. Both can be calculated using the **standard (general) method** as well as the **optional method**. I suggest you become familiar with one-family dwelling calculations before attempting multi-family dwelling calculations.

- For multi-family dwellings the service-entrance conductor sizes are to be selected from **Table 310.15(B)(16).** The neutral load is permitted to be determined per **Section 220.61**. The rule in **Section 310.15(B)(7)(a)** that permits a reduction in the ampacity of service conductors, is reserved for one-family dwellings and individual units in a two-family or multifamily dwelling.

- **Annex D** of the NEC® shows examples of both calculation methods and the steps and procedures to be used. We will follow these examples and steps to learn to properly size services for multi-family dwellings. First, we will look at the general (standard) method of calculation. You will find a completed example of the general (standard) method of calculation on page 145 of this text.

General Calculation Method

Step 1 - Determine the total connected load, in VA, of the general lighting and general-use receptacles. Simply multiply the number of units by the square footage of one unit, when they are all the same size, and multiply by **3 VA** per Table **220.12**. Do not include open porches, garages, and enclosed areas not adaptable for future use. **[220.12]**

EXAMPLE - What is the total connected load, in VA, for the general lighting and general-use receptacles for a six (6) unit multi-family dwelling, when each apartment is 750 square feet?

   A. 2,250 VA
   B. 4,500 VA
   C. 13,500 VA
   D. 15,300 VA

   ANSWER –   (C)   13,500 VA

   First, find the area, in square feet, of the habitable spaces.

   6 units X 750 sq.ft. = 4,500 sq.ft.

   Next, multiply by 3 VA **[Table 220.12]**

   4,500 sq.ft. X 3 VA = 13,500 VA

Step 2 - Find the total connected load of the small appliance and laundry branch circuits. A minimum of **two (2)** small appliance branch circuits are required per unit **[210.11(C)(1)]** and they shall be calculated at **1,500 VA** per circuit. **[220.52(A)]**. A minimum of **one (1)** branch circuit calculated at **1,500 VA** is required to supply the laundry of each unit having a laundry. **[210.11(C)(2)] & [220.52(B)]**. When the multi-family dwelling unit has a common laundry facility provided on the premises and available to all building occupants, this is considered a "house load" and the laundry load can be omitted in this step.

EXAMPLE - What is the minimum total connected load, in VA, for the small appliance and laundry loads for a six (6) unit multi-family dwelling, having laundry facilities in each unit?

A. 27,000 VA
B. 18,000 VA
C. 12,000 VA
D. 9,000 VA

ANSWER - (A) 27,000 VA

2 small appl. circuits @ 1,500 VA X 6 units = 18,000 VA
1 laundry circuit @ 1,500 VA X 6 units = 9,000 VA
Total = 27,000 VA

Step 3 - Apply the demand factors specified in **Table 220.42** for the general purpose lighting and receptacle loads, plus the loads required for the small appliance and laundry branch circuits. **[220.42]**

EXAMPLE - What is the demand load, in VA, for a multi-family dwelling unit having a total connected general-purpose receptacle and lighting load of 13,500 VA and a total connected small appliance and laundry branch circuit load of 27,000 VA? (Use general method of calculation.)

A. 13,125 VA
B. 16,125 VA
C. 37,500 VA
D. 40,500 VA

ANSWER -   (B)   16,125 VA

General purpose lighting & receptacles	= 13,500 VA
Laundry & small appliances	= 27,000 VA
Total Connected Load	= 40,500 VA

1st 3,000 VA @ 100% **[Table 220.42]** = 3,000 VA
40,500 VA – 3,000 VA = 37,500 VA
37,500 VA (Remainder) X 35%   = 13,125 VA
                    Demand Load = 16,125 VA

Step 4 - Apply a demand factor of **75%** of the nameplate rating of **four (4)** or more fastened in place appliances. Examples include, water heater, dishwasher, trash compactor, garbage disposal, etc. **[220.53]** Note that this rule **does not apply** for electric ranges, clothes dryers, space heating or air conditioning equipment.

EXAMPLE - Using the standard (general) method of calculation for dwellings, determine the demand load, in VA, of a six (6) unit multi-family dwelling unit having the following fixed appliances installed in each unit:

```
dishwasher         - 1,100 VA
water heater       - 3,500 VA
garbage disposal   - 850 VA
```

A. 32,700 VA
B. 23,700 VA
C. 22,890 VA
D. 24,525 VA

ANSWER -   (D)   24,525 VA

```
Dishwasher          - 1,100 VA X 6 =  6,600 VA
Water Heater        - 3,500 VA X 6 = 21,000 VA
Garbage Disposal    -   850 VA X 6 =  5,100 VA
                 Total Connected Load = 32,700 VA
                                       X 75% (demand)
                       Demand Load   = 24,525 VA
```

Step 5 - Determine the electric clothes dryer demand load, using **5,000 watts** (volt amperes) as the minimum or the nameplate rating, **whichever is larger**, for each dryer served. **[220.54]** Apply the demand factors listed in **Table 220.54**. A further demand of **70 percent** of this value may be applied to the **neutral** (grounded) conductor. **[220.61(B)(1)]**

EXAMPLE - When the standard (general) method of calculation for dwellings is applied, if a six (6) unit apartment building having a 3.5 kW electric clothes dryer in each unit, the demand load, in VA, on the ungrounded service-entrance conductors is _____.

A. 15,750 VA
B. 21,000 VA
C. 22,500 VA
D. 30,000 VA

ANSWER -   (C)   22,500 VA

```
5,000 VA (minimum) x 6 = 30,000 VA
Demand [Table 220.54]    x    75 %
                         22,500 VA
```

STEP 6 - Determine the demand load for the cooking appliances in accordance with **Table 220.55 [220.55]**. This is explained in **Unit 3** of this book. A further demand of **70 percent** of the demand load on the ungrounded conductors may be applied to the **neutral** (grounded) conductor. **[220.61(B)(1)]**

EXAMPLE - An 8 kW electric range installed in each unit of a six (6) unit apartment building will have a demand load of _____ on the ungrounded service-entrance conductors and demand load of _____ on the grounded (neutral) conductor, when the standard method of calculation for dwellings is applied.

A. 43,000 VA – 30,100 VA
B. 20,640 VA – 14,448 VA
C. 48,000 VA – 33,600 VA
D. 43,000 VA – 32,250 VA

ANSWER - (B) 20,640 VA – 14,448 VA

ungrounded conductor – **[Table 220.55, Column B.]**
8 kW x 6 units x 43% = 20.64 kW
20.64 kW x 1,000 = 20,640 VA

grounded conductor – **[220.61(B)(1)]**

20,640 VA x 70% = 14,448 VA

STEP 7 - Determine the demand load for the fixed electric space heating or air conditioning load; the smaller of the two is permitted to be omitted, because these loads are considered noncoincident loads, meaning they are unlikely to be used at the same time. **[220.60]**

EXAMPLE - A six (6) unit apartment building to be constructed will have a 3 kW (kVA), 240-volt, single-phase, fixed electric space heating unit and a 17 ampere, single-phase, 240-volt, air conditioning unit, installed in each dwelling unit. When using the standard (general) method of calculation for dwellings, what is the demand, in VA, that should be applied to the service-entrance conductors?

A. 24,480 VA
B. 18,000 VA
C. 7,080 VA
D. 42,840 VA

ANSWER - (A) 24,480 VA

First compare the two loads.
A/C unit – P = I x E   P= 17 amps x 240 volts = 4,080 VA
Heating unit – 3 kW x 1,000 = 3,000 VA

4,080 VA (larger) x 6 units = 24,480 VA

STEP 8 - Add the values determined from steps 3 – 7 together to find the required volt ampere rating of the service. Next, apply the current formula **(I = P ÷ E)**, and size the service-entrance conductors using **Table 310.15(B)(16)**.

EXAMPLE - After all demand factors have been taken into consideration for a multi-family dwelling unit, a demand load of 108,270 VA is determined for the ungrounded service-entrance conductors. What minimum size THWN copper ungrounded conductors are required for the dwelling service? (120/240-volt, 3-wire, single-phase electrical system.)

A. 400 kcmil
B. 500 kcmil
C. 600 kcmil
D. 700 kcmil

ANSWER -   (D)   700 kcmil

First, find the load in amperes.

I = P ÷ E

I = 108,270 VA / 240 volts = 451.125

Table 310.15(B)(16) is to be used for sizing the conductors. Size 700 kcmil conductors with an ampacity of 460 amperes should be selected.

STANDARD CALCULATION: MULTI-FAMILY DWELLING

1. GENERAL LIGHTING & RECEPTACLES: *Table 220.12*
_____ sq. ft. x 3 VA = _____ VA

2. SMALL APPLIANCES 220.52(A) & LAUNDRY 220.52(B)
1,500 VA x _____ circuits = _____ VA

3. APPLY DEMAND FACTORS: *Table 220.42*
Total of gen. ltg. & small appl. _____ VA
First 3000 VA x 100% = 3,000 VA
Next _____ VA x 35% = _____ VA   **LINE**   **NEUTRAL**
Remaining _____ VA x 25% = _____ VA
Total =   _____ VA   _____ VA   _____ VA

4. FIXED APPLIANCES: *220.53*
Water Heater   _____ VA x _____ units = _____ VA
Disposal   _____ VA x _____ units = _____ VA
Compactor   _____ VA x _____ units = _____ VA
Dishwasher   _____ VA x _____ units = _____ VA
_____   _____ VA x _____ units = _____ VA
_____   _____ VA x _____ units = _____ VA
_____   _____ VA x _____ units = _____ VA

Total =   (x 75% if 4 or more) _____ VA = _____ VA   _____ VA

5. CLOTHES DRYERS: *220.54; Table 220.54*
_____ VA x _____ units = _____ VA x _____%   _____ VA x 70% = _____ VA

6. COOKING EQUIPMENT: *Table 220.54 & Notes*
Col A _____ VA x _____ units x _____ % = _____ VA
Col B _____ VA x _____ units x _____ % = _____ VA
Col C _____ VA x _____ units   = _____ VA
Total =   _____ VA   _____ VA x 70% = _____ VA

7. HEATING or A/C at 100% (largest): *220.60*
Heating unit = _____ VA x _____ units = _____ VA
A/C unit   = _____ VA x _____ units = _____ VA
Heat pump   = _____ VA x _____ units = _____ VA
Largest Load   = _____ VA

8. TOTAL   ☐ VA   ☐ VA

Line   I = _____ VA = _____ amperes
            240 volts

Neutral I = _____ VA = _____ amperes
            240 volts

Conductors are to be sized per Table 310.15(B)(16).

STANDARD CALCULATION: MULTI-FAMILY DWELLING

1. GENERAL LIGHTING & RECEPTACLES: *Table 220.12*
  4,500 sq. ft. x 3 VA =   13,500 VA

2. SMALL APPLIANCES 220.52(A) & LAUNDRY 220.52(B)
  1,500 VA x 18 circuits =   27,000 VA

3. APPLY DEMAND FACTORS: *Table 220.42*
  Total of gen. ltg. & small appl. 40,500 VA
  First 3000 VA x 100% =   3,000 VA
  Next 37,500 VA x 35% =   13,125 VA   **LINE**   **NEUTRAL**
  Remaining ____ VA x 25% =   ____ VA
  Total   16,125 VA   16,125 VA   16,125 VA

4. FIXED APPLIANCES: 220.53
  Water Heater 3,500 VA x 6 units = 21,000 VA
  Disposal   850 VA x 6 units = 5,100 VA
  Compactor   ____ VA x ____ units = ____ VA
  Dishwasher   1,100 VA x 6 units = 6,600 VA
  _____   ____ VA x ____ units = ____ VA
  _____   ____ VA x ____ units = ____ VA
  _____   ____ VA x ____ units = ____ VA
  Total   (x 75% if 4 or more) 32,700 VA = 24,525 VA   24,525 VA

5. CLOTHES DRYERS: 220.54; *Table 220.54*
  5,000 VA x 6 units = 30,000 VA x 75 %   22,500 VA x 70% =   15,750 VA

6. COOKING EQUIPMENT: *Table 220.54 & Notes*
  Col A ____ VA x ____ units x ____ % = ____ VA
  Col B 8,000 VA x 6 units x 43 % = 20,640 VA
  Col C ____ VA x ____ units   = ____ VA
  Total   = 20,640 VA   20,640 VA x 70% = 14,448 VA

7. HEATING or A/C at 100% (largest): 220.60
  Heating unit = 3,000 VA x ____ units = ____ VA
  A/C unit   = 4,080 VA x 6 units = 24,480 VA
  Heat pump   = ____ VA x ____ units = ____ VA
  Largest Load   =   24,480 VA

8. TOTAL   108,270 VA   70,848 VA
  Line   I = 108,270 VA = 451 amperes
               240 volts   **220.61(B)(2)**
  Neutral I = 70,848 VA = 295 amperes – First 200 amps @ 100%   = 200 amperes
               240 volts   Next 95 amps @ 70%   = 67 amperes
                                        TOTAL NEUTRAL = 267 amperes

Conductors are to be sized per Table 310.15(B)(16).

OPTIONAL CALCULATION METHOD

- When calculating the service size for multi-family dwellings, the **optional calculation method** is commonly applied, because it is an easier and less complex calculation method than the general (standard) method; less steps are used and it results in a smaller service size. The optional method is specifically designed for dwelling units having an electrical load of greater than 100 amperes. **[220.82(A)]** You will find a completed example of this calculation method on page 152 of this text.

- In general, the optional calculation method for multi-family dwellings may be applied when all of the following conditions are met: **[220.84(A)]**

    1. No dwelling unit is supplied by more than one feeder.

    2. Each dwelling unit is equipped with electric cooking equipment.

    3. Each dwelling unit is equipped with either electric space heating or air conditioning, or both.

- The following steps may be applied when using the optional calculation method for multi-family dwellings. Notice the first two steps are the same for both calculation methods.

STEP 1 - Determine the total connected load, in VA, of the general lighting and general-use receptacle. Simply multiply the number of units by the square footage of all units of the same size and multiply by 3 VA per square foot. **[220.84(C)(1)]** Do not include open porches, balconies, and garages.

> EXAMPLE - What is the connected load, in VA, for the general lighting and general-use receptacles for an eight (8) unit multi-family dwelling, when each apartment has 840 square feet of livable space?
>
> A. 20,160 VA
> B. 10,080 VA
> C. 16,020 VA
> D. 6,720 VA
>
> ANSWER - (A)   20,160 VA
>
> First, find the total area in square feet.
>
> 8 units x 840 sq. ft. = 6,720 sq. ft.
>
> Next, multiply by 3 VA **[220.84(C)(1)]**
>
> 6,720 sq. ft. x 3 VA = 20,160 VA

STEP 2 - Find the connected load of the small appliances and laundry branch circuits. **[220.84(C)(2)]** Each unit is required to have at least **two (2)** small appliance branch circuits, **[210.11(C)(1)]** and **one (1)** laundry branch circuit, **[210.11(C)(2)]** and they shall be calculated at **1,500** VA per circuit. **[220.52(A)&(B)]**

> EXAMPLE - Determine the minimum connected load, in VA, for the small appliance and laundry loads for an eight (8) unit apartment building having a laundry facility in each unit.
>
> A. 24,000 VA
> B. 36,000 VA
> C. 42,000 VA
> D. 12,000 VA
>
> ANSWER- (B)   36,000 VA
>
> 2 small appl. circuits @ 1,500 VA x 8 units = 24,000 VA
> 1 laundry circuit @ 1,500 va x 8 units   = 12,000 VA
>   TOTAL   36,000 VA

STEP 3 - Calculate the connected load, at the nameplate rating, of all fastened in place appliances, such as electric ranges, cooktops, ovens, clothes, dryers, dishwashers, garbage disposers, and water heaters. **[220.84(C)(3)]**

EXAMPLE - An eight (8) unit apartment building is to have the following fastened in place appliances installed in each unit.

water heater	– 3.6 kW	– 240 volts
electric range	– 8 kW	– 240 volts
dishwasher	– 1.1 kW	– 120 volts
garbage disposal	– 850 VA	– 120 volts
clothes dryer	– 3.5 kW	– 240 volts

Determine the total connected load, in VA, for the appliances.

A. 17,050 VA
B. 102,300 VA
C. 136,400 VA
D. 51,150 VA

ANSWER - (C) 136,400 VA

water heater	- 3,600 VA x 8 units = 28,800 VA
electric range	- 8,000 VA x 8 units = 64,000 VA
dishwasher	- 1,100 VA x 8 units = 8,800 VA
garbage disposal	- 850 VA x 8 units = 6,800 VA
clothes dryer	- 3,500 VA x 8 units = <u>28,000 VA</u>
	TOTAL 136,400 VA

STEP 4 - Calculate the connected load of the larger of the air-conditioning or space heating equipment. Omit the smaller. **[220.84(C)(5)]**

EXAMPLE - An eight(8) unit apartment building to be constructed will have a 3.5 kW (kVA), 240 volt, single-phase, fixed electric space heating unit and a 17 ampere, single-phase, 240-volt air-conditioning unit installed in each dwelling unit. When applying the optional method of calculation for multi-family dwellings for services and feeders, what MINIMUM value, in VA, is permitted to be used?

A. 60,640 VA
B. 28,000 VA
C. 24,480 VA
D. 32,640 VA

ANSWER - (D) 32,640 VA

First, compare the two loads.
A/C unit – P = I x E   P= 17 amps x 240 volts = 4,080 VA
Heating unit – 3.5 kW x 1,000 = 3,500 VA

4,080 (larger) x 8 units = 32,640 VA

STEP 5 - Add steps 1 through 4 to determine the total connected VA load of the dwelling units and apply the demand factors as per **Table 220.84**.

EXAMPLE - An eight (8) unit apartment building has the following total connected loads:

general lighting & receptacles – 20,160 VA
small appliances & laundry circuits – 36,000 VA
Fixed appliances - 136,400 VA
A/C- heating equipment – 32,640 VA

Use the optional method of calculation for multi-family dwellings, and determine the demand load, in VA, on the ungrounded service-entrance conductors.

A. 96,836 VA
B. 222,500 VA
C. 225,500 VA
D. 99,088 VA

ANSWER -   (A)   93,836 VA

```
  20,160 VA
  36,000 VA
 136,400 VA
  32,640 VA
 225,200 VA    (connected load)
   x 43%       Table 220.84
  96,836 VA    (demand load)
```

STEP 6 - Add the "house loads" at the nameplate rating of the equipment. When the multi-family dwelling has a common laundry facility provided on the premises and available to all building occupants, this is considered a commercial occupancy and dwelling demand factors are **not** to be applied. If there are no "house loads," this step is omitted.

STEP 7 - Add the values determined from steps 5 and 6 (if any) together to find the required volt ampere rating of the service. Next, apply the current formula **(I = P ÷ E)** and size the service-entrance conductors using **Table 310.15(B)(16)**. The neutral load is determined per **220.61**.

EXAMPLE - After all demand factors have been taken into consideration for a multi-family dwelling, a demand load of 96,836 VA is determined for the ungrounded service-entrance conductors. What minimum size THWN/THHN copper ungrounded conductors are required for the service? (120/240-volts, single-phase electrical system)

A. 500 kcmil
B. 600 kcmil
C. 700 kcmil
D. 750 kcmil

ANSWER -   (B)   600 kcmil

First, find the load in amperes.

I = P ÷ E

I = $\dfrac{96,836 \text{ VA}}{240 \text{ volts}}$ = 403 amperes

Select 75°C rated conductors from **Table 310.15(B)(16)**.
Size 600 kcmil conductors with an ampacity of 420 amperes should be selected.

OPTIONAL CALCULATION: MULTI-FAMILY DWELLING

1. GENERAL LIGHTING & RECEPTACLES: *220.84(C)(1)*   **Line**   **Neutral**
   _____ sq. ft. x 3 VA =   (____) VA   (_____) VA

2. SMALL APPLIANCES & LAUNDRY *220.84(C)(2)*
   Small Appl. 1,500 VA x _____ circuits x _____ units=   _____ VA   _____ VA
   Laundry   1,500 VA x _____ circuits x _____ units=   _____ VA   _____ VA
   Total =   (_____) VA (_____) VA

3. FIXED APPLIANCES: *220.84(C)(3)*
   Water Heater   _____ VA x _____ units =   _____ VA   _____ VA
   Disposal   _____ VA x _____ units =   _____ VA   _____ VA
   Compactor   _____ VA x _____ units =   _____ VA   _____ VA
   Dishwasher   _____ VA x _____ units =   _____ VA   _____ VA
   Range   _____ VA x _____ units =   _____ VA x 70%   _____ VA
   Cooktop   _____ VA x _____ units =   _____ VA x 70%   _____ VA
   Oven   _____ VA x _____ units =   _____ VA x 70%   _____ VA
   Dryer   _____ VA x _____ units =   _____ VA x 70%   _____ VA
   _____   _____ VA x _____ units =   _____ VA   _____ VA
   _____   _____ VA x _____ units =   _____ VA   _____ VA
   Total =   (_____) VA   (_____) VA

4. HEATING or A/C at 100% (largest): *220.84(C)(5)*
   Heating unit = _____ VA x _____ units = _____ VA
   A/C unit   = _____ VA x _____ units = _____ VA
   Heat pump   = _____ VA x _____ units = _____ VA
   Largest Load = _____ VA x _____ units = _____ VA   (_____) VA   (_____) VA

5. APPLY DEMAND FACTORS: *Table 220.84 Total of steps 1 -4*
   LINE   _____ VA x _____ % =   [_____] VA
   NEUTRAL   _____ VA x _____ % =   [_____] VA

6. HOUSE LOADS: *220.84(B)*
   Lighting   _____ VA   _____ VA   _____ VA
   Receptacles _____ VA   _____ VA   _____ VA
   Motors   _____ VA   _____ VA   _____ VA
   _____   _____ VA   _____ VA   _____ VA
   _____   _____ VA   _____ VA   _____ VA
   Total =   [_____] VA [_____] VA

7. TOTAL of STEPS 5 & 6   [_____] VA [_____] VA

   Line   I = _____ VA = _____ amperes
                 240 volts
   Neutral   I = _____ VA = _____ amperes
                 240 volts

   Conductors are to be sized per Table 310.15(B)(16).

OPTIONAL CALCULATION: MULTI-FAMILY DWELLING

1. GENERAL LIGHTING & RECEPTACLES: 220.84(C)(1) Line   Neutral
   6,720 sq. ft. × 3 VA =   (20,160) VA   (20,160) VA

2. SMALL APPLIANCES & LAUNDRY 220.84(C)(2)
   Small Appl. 1,500 VA × __2__ circuits × __8__ units =   24,000 VA   24,000 VA
   Laundry   1,500 VA × __1__ circuits × __8__ units =   12,000 VA   12,000 VA
   Total =   (36,000) VA (36,000) VA

3. FIXED APPLIANCES: 220.84(C)(3)
   Water Heater 3,600 VA × __8__ units =   28,800 VA   28,800 VA
   Disposal   850 VA × __8__ units =   6,800 VA   6,800 VA
   Compactor   ____ VA × ____ units =   _____ VA   _____ VA
   Dishwasher   1,100 VA × __8__ units =   8,800 VA   8,800 VA
   Range   8,000 VA × __8__ units =   64,000 VA × 70%   44,800 VA
   Cooktop   ____ VA × ____ units =   _____ VA × 70%   _____ VA
   Oven   ____ VA × ____ units =   _____ VA × 70%   _____ VA
   Dryer   3,500 VA × __8__ units =   28,000 VA × 70%   19,600 VA
   _____   ____ VA × ____ units =   _____ VA   _____ VA
   _____   ____ VA × ____ units =   _____ VA   _____ VA
   Total =   (136,400) VA   (108,800) VA

4. HEATING or A/C at 100% (largest): 220.84(C)(5)
   Heating unit = 3,500 VA × ____ units = _____ VA
   A/C unit   = 4,080 VA × __8__ units = 32,640 VA
   Heat pump   = ____ VA × ____ units = _____ VA
   Largest Load = 4,080 VA × __8__ units = 32,640 VA   (32,640) VA   (0) VA

5. APPLY DEMAND FACTORS: Table 220.84 Total of steps 1-4
   LINE   225,200 VA × 43 % =   [96,836] VA
   NEUTRAL 164,960 VA × 43 % =   [70,933] VA

6. HOUSE LOADS: 220.84(B)
   Lighting   _____ VA   _____ VA   _____ VA
   Receptacles _____ VA   _____ VA   _____ VA
   Motors   _____ VA   _____ VA   _____ VA
   _____   _____ VA   _____ VA   _____ VA
   _____   _____ VA   _____ VA   _____ VA
   Total =   [_____] VA   [_____] VA

7. TOTAL of STEPS 5 & 6   _____ VA   70,933 VA
   Line   I = 96,836 VA = 403 amperes
              240 volts   **220.61(B)(2)**
   Neutral I = 70,933 VA = 296 amperes — First 200 amps @100% = 200 amperes
              240 volts   Next 96 amps @ 70%   = 67 amperes
                                     TOTAL NEUTRAL = 267 amperes

Conductors are to be sized per Table 310.15(B)(16).

UNIT 10

COMMERCIAL LOAD CALCULATIONS

Upon successfully completing this unit of study, the student will be familiar with the concept of properly sizing overcurrent protection, branch circuit, feeder, and service conductors for commercial occupancies.

UNIT 10

COMMERCIAL LOAD CALCULATIONS

RELATED INFORMATION:

> ➤ Examples of commercial occupancies are office buildings, banks, retail stores, restaurants, warehouses, laundries, mobile home and recreational vehicle (RV) parks, automobile dealerships, sporting facilities, motels, etc.

> ➤ The loads in commercial locations are diversified and are to be calculated based upon the type of occupancy, how the loads are to be used in the electrical system, and the requirements of the equipment to be supplied. A good example of a commercial occupancy with diverse loads would be a motel or hotel. The sleeping rooms are calculated much like residential occupancies but the lobby, hallways, meeting rooms, restaurant, and area lighting are considered commercial locations. Let's look at some of the requirements that apply to commercial occupancies.

> ➤ Most of the lighting for commercial locations is to be considered a **continuous load**. Examples of exceptions to this statement would be the sleeping rooms of hotels and motels, which will be addressed later in this unit, and temporary commercial storage facilities and warehouses. The definition of a **continuous load** is a load where the maximum current is expected to continue for **3 hours** or more. **[Article 100]**

> ➤ In general, branch circuit conductors shall have an allowable ampacity (current carrying capacity) of NOT less than **125%** of the **continuous load**, plus **100%** of the **non-continuous** load to be served. **[210.19(A)(1)(a)]**

EXAMPLE -   A branch circuit conductor supplying a continuous load of 24 amperes, must have an ampacity of at least _____.

   A. 24 amperes
   B. 30 amperes
   C. 19 amperes
   D. 36 amperes

   ANSWER -   (B)   30 amperes

   24 amperes x 125% = 30 amperes

➢ In general, overcurrent devices (fuses and circuit breakers) protecting branch circuits, shall have a rating of not less that **125%** of the **continuous load** to be served plus **100%** of the **non-continuous** load to be served. **[210.20(A)]** Another way to look at it is, fuses and circuit breakers protecting branch circuits are not permitted to be loaded more than **80%** of their rated value when protecting **continuous loads**.

EXAMPLE -   When a 30 ampere rated circuit breaker is used to protect a branch circuit supplying a continuous load, the load shall not exceed_____.

   A. 30 amperes
   B. 38 amperes
   C. 24 amperes
   D. 36 amperes

   ANSWER -   (C)   24 amperes

   30 amperes x 80% = 24 amperes

➢ If the overcurrent device is listed for **continuous operation**, it shall be permitted to have a rating of **100%** of the **continuous load(s)** to be supplied. **[210.20(A)EX.]** But, circuit breakers are **NOT** listed for continuous operation, unless they have a rating of at least **400 amperes** or more. The NEC® does not address this issue.

➢ This continuous load requirement also applies to feeders **[215.2(A)(1)]** & **[215.3]** and services. **[230.42(A)(1)&(2)]**

Lighting Loads

➢ In general, 15- or 20-ampere rated branch circuits are used to supply lighting loads. **[210.23(A)]**

➢ General lighting loads for specific occupancies shall be based on the unit load per square feet depending on the type of occupancy as shown on Table **220.12**, and calculated from the outside dimensions of the building. **[220.12]** This is a **MINIMUM** requirement.

➤ Most commercial occupancies now contain fluorescent and/or HID lighting systems. When the occupancies contain lighting systems of this category, the **larger** of either the area load of the VA per square foot of the facility, or the total connected load of the ampere ratings of the ballast or transformers of the luminaries (lighting fixtures) shall be used to size branch circuit, feeder, and service-entrance conductors. **[220.18(B)]**

EXAMPLE - A retail department store having dimensions of 100 feet by 150 feet is to be constructed. The store will have three-hundred (300) fluorescent luminaires (lighting fixtures) installed for general lighting. Each luminaire will contain two (2), 120-volt ballasts that draw 0.75 amperes each. Determine the demand load, in VA, that must be applied to the service-entrance conductors for the general lighting.

A. 45,000 VA
B. 54,000 VA
C. 56,250 VA
D. 67,500 VA

ANSWER - (D) 67,500 VA

Compare the two methods and use the larger value.

Table 220.12
150 ft. x 100 ft. = 15,000 sq. ft.

15,000 sq. ft. x 3 VA = 45,000 VA
   (continuous load)   x 125%
                           56,250 VA

220.18(B)
300 (fixt.) x 2 (ballast) x 120 volts x .75 amps = 54,000 VA
                          (continuous load)   x 125%
                                                 67,500 VA

➤ Show window lighting for retail stores is commonly calculated at 200 volt-amperes per linear foot of show window. **[220.43(A)]** Such lighting is usually considered a **continuous load** because it is normally operated continuously for three (3) hours or more. Multiply **200 VA** per linear foot times **125%** to determine the load in VA.

EXAMPLE - A retail store is to have 125 feet of show window lighting, which will be operated continuously during the business day. Determine the demand load in VA.

A. 31,250 VA
B. 25,000 VA
C. 28,125 VA
D. 12,500 VA

ANSWER - (A)   31,250 VA

200 VA x 125 ft. x 125% = 31,250 VA

➢ When calculating the number of branch circuits required for lighting systems or receptacles, you can use the following formula:

$$\text{Number of circuits} = \frac{\text{Load VA}}{\text{circuit VA}}$$

EXAMPLE - The total demand load for the show window lighting of a retail store is determined to be 31,250 VA. Determine the MINIMUM number of 120 volt, 20 ampere branch circuits required to supply the show window lighting.

A. ten
B. twelve
C. thirteen
D. none of these

ANSWER - (C)   thirteen

$$\text{\# of circuits} = \frac{31,250 \text{ VA}}{120 \text{ volts} \times 20 \text{ amps}} = \frac{31,250 \text{ VA}}{2,400 \text{ VA}} = 13 \text{ circuits}$$

➢ In addition to the general lighting, many commercial occupancies, particularly retail stores, have track lighting mounted for display or accent lighting. Again, commercial lighting systems are usually considered as continuous use. For track lighting in non-dwelling occupancies a load of **150 volt-amperes** shall be included for every **two (2) feet** of track. **[220.43(B)]** Multiply **150 VA** per linear foot times **125%** and divide by **two (2)** to determine the load in VA.

EXAMPLE - A retail store is to have eighty (80) feet of accent track lighting installed and will be in use continuously during business hours. For the purpose of sizing branch-circuits, feeders and service-entrance conductors, determine the load in VA.

A. 15,000 VA
B. 10,000 VA
C. 12,500 VA
D. 7,500 VA

ANSWER - (D) 7,500 VA

$$\frac{150 \text{ VA} \times 80 \text{ ft.} \times 125\%}{2} = \frac{15,000}{2} = 7,500 \text{ VA}$$

- The general lighting and general-use receptacles for the guest rooms and suites of hotels and motels are permitted to be calculated by applying a demand load of **2 VA** per square foot **[Table 220.12]** and is permitted to be reduced by applying the demand factors as shown in **Table 220.42**. Even though this is a commercial occupancy, loads of this category are not considered as continuous use.

EXAMPLE - Determine the general lighting and general-use receptacle demand load, in VA, for the guest rooms of a twenty-four (24) unit motel. Each guest room has 600 square feet of living area.

A. 14,400 VA
B. 13,520 VA
C. 21,600 VA
D. 28,800 VA

ANSWER - (B) 13,520 VA

24 units x 600 x 2 VA **[Table 220.12]** = 28,800 VA

First 20,000 VA at 50% = 10,000 VA **[Table 220.42]**
8,800 VA   at 40% =   3,520 VA
        Demand Load = 13,520 VA

Electric Sign Loads

- The NEC® requires each commercial occupancy with grade level access to pedestrians to be provided with at least one (1) outlet for an exterior electric sign or outline lighting system. The outlet(s) is/are to be supplied by a branch-circuit rated at least 20 amperes. **[600.5(A)]**

- The branch-circuits that supply electric signs with incandescent and fluorescent lighting are not to exceed 20 amperes. **[600.5(B)(1)]**

> When calculating feeder and service-entrance conductors, each electric sign branch-circuit is to be calculated at a MINIMUM of **1,200 VA**. **[220.14(F)]** This VA rating is to be multiplied by **125%**; for the purpose of calculations electric signs are to be considered continuous loads. **[600.5(B)]**

EXAMPLE -   A motel to be constructed will have two (2) 20 ampere, 120-volt branch-circuits provided for the exterior electric signs. Determine the minimum demand load, in VA, on the feeder and service-entrance conductors.

A. 2,400 VA
B. 3,000 VA
C. 4,800 VA
D. 6,000 VA

ANSWER -   (B)   3,000 VA

1,200 VA x 2 (signs) x 125% = 3,000 VA

Receptacle Loads

> For non-dwelling occupancies each general-use receptacle outlet is to be calculated at **180 VA** for each single or duplex receptacle on one yoke or strap **[220.14(I)]**; receptacle loads are permitted to be made subject to the demand factors given in **Table 220.44** when calculating the demand loads on feeders and services. **[220.44]** General-use receptacle loads are generally not considered to be a continuous load.

Table 220.44 Demand Factors for Non-dwelling Receptacle Loads

Portion of Receptacle Load to Which Demand Factor Applies (Volt-Ampere)	Demand Factor (Percent)
First 10 kVA or less	100
Remainder over 10 kVA at	50

EXAMPLE –   What is the service demand load, in VA, for one-hundred and fifty (150), 20 ampere, 120-volt general-use duplex receptacles installed in an office building?

A. 27,000 VA
B. 23,125 VA
C. 24,250 VA
D. 18,500 VA

ANSWER -   (D)   18,500 VA

150 receptacles x 180 VA = 27,000 VA (connected load)

First 10 kVA at 100%   = 10,000 VA
remainder (17,000 VA) at 50% = 8,500 VA
                       Total = 18,500 VA

➤ When the exact number of general-use receptacle outlets to be installed in a bank or an office building has not yet been determined, **one (1) VA** per square foot of interior space is to be applied when calculating feeders or services. **[Table 220.12, Note B]** and **[220.14(K)]** When this condition occurs, the receptacle loads are **not** permitted to be made subject to the demand factors given in **Table 220.44. [220.44]**

EXAMPLE -   A 20,000 square foot bank building is to be constructed and the exact number of general-use receptacles to be installed in unknown. Determine the demand load, in VA, on the service-entrance conductors for the unknown receptacles.

A. 20,000 VA
B. 18,000 VA
C. 36,000 VA
D. 60,000 VA

ANSWER -   (A)   20,000 VA

20,000 sq. ft. x 1 VA = 20,000 VA

➤ When calculating the service and/or feeder demand load for multioutlet assemblies installed in commercial, industrial and educational facilities, the calculation is to be based on the use of the supplied cord-connected equipment that is expected to be used at the same time. **[220.14(H)]** (1) Where the cord-connected equipment are **unlikely** to be used simultaneously, each **five (5) feet** or fraction thereof shall be considered as one (1) outlet of not less than **180 VA**. (2) Where the cord-connected equipment are **likely** to be used simultaneously each **one (1) foot** or fraction thereof shall be considered as one outlet of not less than **180 VA**.

➤ The demand factors shown on **Table 220.44** may also be applied to fixed multioutlet assemblies when located in non-dwelling occupancies. Multioutlet assembly receptacles are generally not to be considered a continuous load; if they are **continuous, multiply by 125%.**

EXAMPLE - What is the service demand load, in VA, for one-hundred (100), 20 ampere, 120-volt, general-use receptacles and one-hundred (100) feet of multioutlet assembly, installed in an office building, where the cord connected appliances are unlikely to be used simultaneously?

A. 21,600 VA
B. 15,800 VA
C. 10,800 VA
D. 8,100 VA

ANSWER -   (B)   15,800 VA

Receptacles – 180 VA x 100   = 18,000 VA
Multioutlet assembly – 100 ft. / 5 = 20 x 180 VA = 3,600 VA
                                  connected load = 21,600 VA

Apply demand factors **[Table 220.44]**

First 10 kVA at 100%   = 10,000 VA
Remainder (11,600 VA) at 50%   = 5,800 VA
                                  demand load   = 15,800 VA

EXAMPLE - Refer to the previous example and consider the cord-connected appliances are to be used simultaneously and determine the demand load.

A. 15,800 VA
B. 36,000 VA
C. 23,000 VA
D. 18,000 VA

ANSWER -   (C)   23,000 VA

Receptacles – 180 VA x 100   = 18,000 VA
Multioutlet assembly – 100 ft. x 180 VA   = 18,000 VA
                                  Connected load   = 36,000 VA

First 10 kVA at 100%   = 10,000 VA
Remainder (26,000 VA) at 50%   = 13,000 VA
                                  Demand Load   = 23,000 VA

Air Conditioning Loads

- When sizing overcurrent protection, branch-circuit, feeder and service conductors for air-conditioning equipment, you will find many air-conditioning condensing units are sized according to **TONS** and not horsepower. The NEC® does not address this issue. A useful and practical method to convert **tons** to **VA** is to consider **one (1) ton** of air-conditioning condensing load equals **2,400 VA**. To find the load, in amperes, simply apply the current formula I = P ÷ E. Multiply 2,400 VA times the tonage of the A/C unit and divide by the voltage. For the purpose of calculating loads in this text this is the method that will be used.

EXAMPLE -   A 240-volt, single-phase, 3½ ton A/C condensing unit will draw_____ of current.

A. 30 amperes
B. 35 amperes
C. 40 amperes
D. 45 amperes

ANSWER -   (B)   35 amperes

$$I = \frac{3.5 \times 2,400 \text{ VA}}{240 \text{ volts}} = \frac{8,400}{240} = 35 \text{ amperes}$$

- Branch-circuit conductors supplying a single air-conditioning condensing unit are required to have a current-carrying capacity (ampacity) of not less than **125 percent** of the rated-current of the air-conditioning unit supplied. **[440.32]**

EXAMPLE -   Branch-circuit conductors supplying an air-conditioning condensing unit having a rated-current of 35 amperes, are required to have an ampacity of at LEAST _____.

A. 28 amperes
B. 35 amperes
C. 44 amperes
D. 53 amperes

ANSWER -   (C)   44 amperes

35 amperes x 125% = 43.75 amperes

- A value of not less than **100%** of the rated-current of the air-conditioning equipment is to be applied to feeder and service equipment and conductors.

- Fuses and circuit breakers provided for the protection of air-conditioning equipment shall be capable of carrying the starting current of the motor. **[440.22(A)]** The overcurrent protection device is mandated to be sized between **175 percent** and no more than **225 percent** of the rated-current of the air-conditioning equipment.

EXAMPLE - A circuit breaker provided to protect an air-conditioning condensing unit with a rated current of 35 amperes is required to have a MAXIMUM ampere rating of no more than _____.

A. 60 amperes
B. 80 amperes
C. 75 amperes
D. 70 amperes

ANSWER -   (D)   70 amperes

35 amperes x 225% = 78.75 amperes

*NOTE: Under this condition, you must go down to the next standard size circuit breaker, because you may not exceed **225%** of the rated-current of the A/C unit.

Electric Space-Heating Loads

- All fixed space heating equipment, including blower motors, shall be considered as **continuous load(s)**, when sizing branch-circuit conductors and overcurrent protection for the heating units. **[424.3(B)]** The branch-circuit conductors supplying electric space-heating equipment are required to have an ampacity of not less than **125 percent** of the current rating of the heating unit(s) to be served.**[210.19(A)(1)]** This rule does not apply when sizing feeders and/or services. The feeder and/or service demand load is calculated at **100 percent** of the total heating load. **[220.51]**

EXAMPLE - The branch-circuit conductors supplying a 240-volt, single-phase, 15 kW rated fixed electric space heater provided with a 10 ampere blower motor are required to have an ampacity of at LEAST _____.

A. 63 amperes
B. 78 amperes
C. 91 amperes
D. 109 amperes

ANSWER -   (C)   91 amperes

First find the current rating of the heater.

$I = P \div E$ $I = \dfrac{15 \text{ kW} \times 1{,}000}{240 \text{ volts}} = 62.5$ amperes

```
  62.5 amperes (heater)
+ 10.0 amperes (blower)
  72.5 amperes x 125% = 91 amperes
```

EXAMPLE -   The overcurrent protection device for the above referenced heating unit is required to have a standard rating of not less than _____.

A. 75 amperes
B. 80 amperes
C. 90 amperes
D. 100 amperes

ANSWER -   (D)   100 amperes

The next standard size overcurrent device has a rating of 100 amperes. **[240.6(A)]**

EXAMPLE -   Determine the service demand load, in VA, for an office building that has three (3), 208-volt, three-phase, 10 kW fixed electric space heaters, provided with a 1,945 VA blower motor in each heating unit.

A. 35,835 VA
B. 44,794 VA
C. 53,585 VA
D. 55,583 VA

ANSWER -   (A)   35,835 VA

10,000 VA + 1,945 VA = 11,945 x 3 units = 35,835 VA

> When determining the demand load on the service-entrance conductors for the fixed electric space heating or air-conditioning load, the smaller of the two loads is permitted to be omitted; because both loads are unlikely to be used at the same time. **[220.60]** Apply only the largest load(s) that will be used at one time for calculating the total load on feeder or service conductors.

EXAMPLE - A retail store is to have a ten (10) ton A/C unit and a thirty-five (35) kW electric heating unit installed. Both units are 240-volts, single-phase. Determine the demand load, in amperes on the service-entrance conductors for the A/C and heating equipment.

A. 100 amperes
B. 125 amperes
C. 146 amperes
D. 183 amperes

ANSWER -   (C)   146 amperes

First compare the two loads.

A/C Unit
10 tons x 2,400 VA = 24,000 VA
$I = \dfrac{24,000 \text{ VA}}{240 \text{ volts}} = 100$ amperes

Heating Unit
$I = \dfrac{35 \text{ kW} \times 1,000}{240 \text{ volts}} = \dfrac{35,000}{240} = 146$ amperes

*NOTE: The heating unit is the larger load therefore, the A/C unit is permitted to be omitted.

➢ Today, many buildings are provided with roof-mounted heating and cooling systems that are in one complete unit in order to save space. The cooling capacity usually range from 5 tons up to 200 tons. Examples of good applications for roof-mounted heating and cooling systems are schools, office buildings, retail stores, super markets and manufacturing facilities.

Kitchen Equipment

> For electric kitchen equipment in commercial occupancies the branch circuits and overcurrent protection are sized according to the nameplate rating on the appliance. When sizing feeder and service conductors the demand factors shown on **Table 220.56** may be applied. However, the feeder or service demand load is **not** permitted to be **less** than the sum of the **two (2) largest** kitchen equipment loads. **[220.56]**

EXAMPLE - A catering service is to have the following cooking related equipment in the kitchen:

- water heater – 5.5 kW
- booster heater – 7.0 kW
- dishwasher – 2.0 kW
- sterilizer - 2.5 kW
- oven - 6.0 kW
- grill - 5.0 kW
- mixer - 3.0 kW
- freezer - 3.5 kW
- refrigerator - 2.5 kW

What is the demand load, in kW, on the service-entrance conductors for the appliances?

A. 37.00 kW
B. 25.90 kW
C. 13.00 kW
D. 24.05 kW

ANSWER - (D) 24.05 kW

water heater	- 5.5 kW
booster heater	- 7.0 kW
dishwasher	- 2.0 kW
sterilizer	- 2.5 kW
oven	- 6.0 kW
grill	- 5.0 kW
mixer	- 3.0 kW
freezer	- 3.5 kW
refrigerator	- 2.5 kW
(connected load)	37 kW
(demand)	x 65 % **[Table 220.56]**
Demand Load	= 24.05 kW

Laundry Equipment

> The branch-circuit conductors and overcurrent protection for laundry equipment in commercial occupancies are to be sized in accordance to the appliance **nameplate rating**. The NEC® does not permit a demand factor to be applied to service, feeder or branch-circuit conductors for commercial laundry equipment therefore, the laundry equipment demand load is to be calculated at **100%**.

EXAMPLE -   The laundry room of a multi-family dwelling will have the following laundry equipment installed:

- two – clothes dryers   -   7,000 VA each
- three – washing machines -   1,920 VA each
- three – washing machines -   1,500 VA each

What is the demand load, in VA, on the service and feeder conductors for the listed appliances?

A. 24,260 VA
B. 18,500 VA
C. 16,982 VA
D. 14,000 VA

ANSWER -   (A)   24,260 VA

clothes dryers	– 2 x 7,000 VA =	14,000 VA
washing machine	– 3 x 1,920 VA =	5,760 VA
washing machine	– 3 x 1,500 VA =	4,500 VA
	TOTAL =	24,260 VA

Mobile Home and Manufactured Home Parks

> ➤ The distribution system to mobile home lots is required to be 120/240 volts, single-phase. **[550.30]** Because appliances, luminaries, and other equipment are installed in a mobile home when manufactured and are rated 120/240-volts single-phase; three-phase systems and systems of a different voltage would not be compatible to the loads to be supplied.

> ➤ Each mobile home lot is required to be calculated on the basis of the larger of (1) a minimum of not less than **16,000 VA** for each mobile home lot or (2) the calculated load of the largest typical mobile home the lot will accommodate. **[550.31]** However, for each mobile home to be served the service equipment is to be rated at least 100 amperes, **[550.32(C)]** and the mobile home lot feeder conductors shall have a current carrying capacity (ampacity) of not less than 100 amperes. **[550.33(B)]**

> ➤ When sizing service-entrance conductors for a mobile home park the demand factors, based on the number of mobile homes in the park, displayed in **Table 550.31** are permitted to be applied.

EXAMPLE - What is the MINIMUM demand load, in amperes, on the service conductors of a mobile home park consisting of fifteen (15) lots?

A. 250 amperes
B. 260 amperes
C. 400 amperes
D. 1,000 amperes

ANSWER - (B) 260 amperes

15 lots x 16,000 VA (MINIMUM) = 240,000 VA
                   demand   = x   .26 **[Tbl. 550.31]**
                   demand load   = 62,400 VA

I = P ÷ E
I = 62,400 VA = 260 amperes
     240 volts

EXAMPLE - A twenty-five (25) lot mobile home park is to be constructed. Each lot in the park is capable of accommodating a mobile home with a rating of 24,000 VA. Determine the demand load, in amperes, on the park service conductors.

A. 1,000 amperes
B. 650 amperes
C. 400 amperes
D. 600 amperes

ANSWER -   (D)   600 amperes

25 lots x 24,000 VA = 600,000 VA
                       x   .24 [Tbl.550.31]
Demand load   = 144,000 VA

I = P ÷ E
I = 144,000 VA = 600 amperes
     240 volts

Recreational Vehicle Parks

> For recreational vehicle parks the NEC® requires electrical equipment connected line-to-line shall have a voltage rating of 208-230 volts. **[551.40(A)]** Therefore, recreational vehicle parks are permitted to be provided with 120-volt, 120/240-volt, single-phase or 208Y/120-volt, three-phase electrical systems. Typically, most older recreational vehicle parks have 120/240-volt, single-phase distribution systems.

> When sizing service-entrance or feeder conductors for a recreational vehicle park, the demand factors, reflected in **Table 551.73(A)**, based on the number of sites in the park, are permitted to be applied.

> **Each RV site** supplied with electrical power is required to be provided with at least **one (1) 20 ampere**, 125-volt receptacle outlet. **[551.71]** For the basis of calculation, 20 ampere, 125-volt sites are considered as **2,400 VA per site**. **[551.73(A)]**

> At least **20 percent** of all RV sites in the park supplied with electrical power are required to be provided with a **50 ampere**, 125/250-volt receptacle outlet. **[551.71]** The 50 ampere sites are considered as **9,600 VA** per site, for the basis of calculation. **[551.73(A)]** Where the RV site has more than one (1) receptacle outlet, the calculated load shall only be calculated for the highest rated receptacle.

EXAMPLE - When a forty (40) site RV park supplies all campsites with electrical power, the NEC® requires at LEAST _____ of the sites to be provided with a 50 ampere, 125/250-volt receptacle.

A. eight
B. two
C. twelve
D. forty

ANSWER- (A) eight

40 sites x 20% = 8 sites

> At least **70 percent** of all RV sites in the park supplied with electrical power are required to be provided with a **30-ampere**, 125-volt receptacle. **[551.71]** For the basis of calculation 30-ampere, 125-volt, RV sites are considered as **3,600 VA** per site. **[551.73(A)]**

EXAMPLE - Refer to the previous example. How many sites in the RV park are required to be provided with a 30-ampere, 125-volt receptacle outlet?

A. eight
B. twelve
C. twenty-eight
D. forty

ANSWER - (C) twenty-eight

40 sites x 70% = 28 sites

> Dedicated **tent sites** in a RV park that are provided with only 20 ampere, 125-volt receptacles are considered as **600 VA** per site, for the basis of calculation. Because these sites are not intended to accommodate recreational vehicles, the calculated load is permitted to be smaller. **[551.73(A)]**

> When determining the total load for a recreational vehicle park, you must take into consideration the loads required for the recreational buildings, swimming pools, stores, service buildings, etc. These amenities are to be considered commercial loads and are to be sized separately and then added to the value calculated for the RV sites, where they are all supplied by one service. **[551.73(D)]**

> Typically, recreational vehicle parks are provided with one service and the RV sites are supplied from a common feeder through one or more sub-panel(s). The demand factors shown on **Table 551.73(A)** are to be applied when sizing RV site feeders and service-entrance conductors.

EXAMPLE -   What is the feeder/service demand load, in amperes, for the RV sites of a recreational vehicle park that has twenty (20) sites provided with 50 ampere 125/250-volt receptacles, fifteen (15) sites provided with both 30 ampere and 20 ampere receptacles and five (5) RV sites provided with 20 ampere, 125-volt receptacles? The electrical system is 120/240-volts, single-phase.

A. 392 amperes
B. 441 amperes
C. 213 amperes
D. 1,075 amperes

ANSWER -   (B)   441 amperes

```
50 ampere sites      – 9,600 VA x 20 sites = 192,000 VA
30/20 ampere sites   – 3,600 VA x 15 sites =  54,000 VA
20 ampere sites      – 2,400 VA x 5 sites  =  12,000 VA
                                             258,000 VA
           Table 551.73(A) (demand)    x        .41
                       Demand Load           105,780 VA
```

I = P ÷ E
I = 105,780 VA = 441 amperes
      240 volts

Electric Welders

> The NEC® provides rules governing two general types of electric welding machines.
>   1. Arc welders
>   **Non-motor generator** – a transformer supplies current for an AC arc welder.
>   **Motor generator** – A generator or rectifier supplies current for DC arc welder.
>   2. Resistance welders, which are commonly referred to as "spot" welders which derive their power from an AC power source.

> The ampacity of the supply conductors to individual arc welders is determined by selecting the appropriate factor shown in **Table 630.11(A)** based on the type of welding machine and the duty cycle of the welder. **[630.11(A)]** An arc welder with a 60% duty cycle means the welding machine will be used approximately for 6 minutes out of every 10 minutes. The selected factor is then multiplied by the primary current rating displayed on the welder nameplate to determine the minimum current-carrying capacity (ampacity) of the circuit conductors. The actual size of the conductors are selected from **Table 310.15(B)(16).**

EXAMPLE - The minimum ampacity of the branch-circuit conductors supplying a transformer arc welder with a 60 percent duty cycle and a primary current of 50 amperes indicated on the nameplate is _____.

A. 40 amperes
B. 44 amperes
C. 39 amperes
D. 50 amperes

ANSWER - (C) 39 amperes

50 amperes x .78 (multiplier) = 39 amperes

➢ When a feeder supplies more than one arc welding machine the conductor ampacity rating is based on the sum of the current ratings of the individual arc welders determined by applying **Table 630.11(A)** and multiplying by **100 percent** of the **two** largest welders, plus **85 percent** of the **third** largest welder, plus **70 percent** of the **fourth** largest welder, plus **60 percent** of **all remaining** welders in the group. **[630.11(B)]**

EXAMPLE - A feeder at a school welding shop is to supply the following listed transformer arc welders all with a 50 percent duty cycle.

- two (2) 60 ampere primary current
- two (2) 50 ampere primary current
- two (2) 40 ampere primary current

The feeder is required to have an ampacity of at LEAST _____.

A. 213 amperes
B. 196 amperes
C. 182 amperes
D. 176 amperes

ANSWER - (D) 176 amperes

60 amperes x .71 = 43 x 100% = 43 amperes
60 amperes x .71 = 43 x 100% = 43 amperes
50 amperes x .71 = 36 x 85% = 31 amperes
50 amperes x .71 = 36 x 70% = 25 amperes
40 amperes x .71 = 28 x 60% = 17 amperes
40 amperes x .71 = 28 x 60% = 17 amperes
                               176 amperes

➢ The ampacity of the supply conductors for a resistance type welder, when the primary current and duty cycle are known, shall not be less than the product of the actual primary current when welding and the multiplication factors shown in **Table 630.31(A)(2)**.

EXAMPLE -   A resistance type (spot) welder with a duty cycle of 25 percent and with an actual primary current of 30 amperes is to be served. The conductors supplying the welder are required to have an ampacity of at LEAST _____.

A. 15 amperes
B. 20 amperes
C. 25 amperes
D. 30 amperes

ANSWER -   (A)   15 amperes

30 amperes x .50 = 15 amperes

➢ When conductors supply two or more resistance type welding machines, the conductors ampacity rating is based on the sum of the primary current of the individual welders determined by applying **Table 630.31(A)(2)** and multiplying by 100% of the largest welder, plus 60 percent of the values obtained for all remaining welders in the group. **[630.31(B)]**

EXAMPLE -   Three (3) spot welders, each having a primary current of 30 amperes and a duty cycle of 10 percent are to be supplied by a common branch circuit. The branch-circuit conductors are required to have an ampacity of at LEAST_____.

A. 15 amperes
B. 22 amperes
C. 66 amperes
D. 99 amperes

ANSWER -   (B)   22 amperes

30 amperes x .32 = 10 amperes x 100% = 10 amperes
30 amperes x .32 = 10 amperes x 60% = 6 amperes
30 amperes x .32 = 10 amperes x 60% = 6 amperes
                                        22 amperes

Commercial Service and Feeder Sizing

> For the purpose of sizing the service for a commercial building, the following steps may be used to determine the demand load.

Step 1   Determine the lighting load. Include:
(1) the **larger** of the area load of the VA per square foot of the facility **[Table 220.12]** or the connected loads of the lighting fixtures **[220.18(B)]** and apply **Table 220.42 if applicable**,
(2) sign lighting, **[220.14(F)]**
(3) show windows, **[220.43(A)]**
(4) track lighting **[220.43(B)]**

Step 2   Calculate the receptacle load. Include:
(1) 180 VA per receptacle outlet **[220.14(I)]**
(2) fixed multi-outlet assemblies **[220.14(H)]** apply demand factors per **Table 220.44**

Step 3   Compare the air-conditioning loads or the space heating loads. Use the **larger** of the two loads at **100%**.

Step 4   Determine the kitchen equipment load. Apply **Table 220.56** for 3 or more units of kitchen equipment.

Step 5   Calculate the laundry equipment at **100%**

Step 6   Add any other miscellaneous loads not covered in the above steps. Examples: walk-in coolers, water heaters, frozen food display cases, welders, exhaust fans, motors, etc.

Step 7   Add the value determined from the above listed steps together to find the volt ampere rating of the service. Next, apply the current formula (I = P ÷ E) and size the service-entrance conductors using 75°C conductors selected from **Table 310.15(B)(16)**.

EXAMPLE -   A hair salon is 4,000 square feet; the service is 208Y/120-volts, three-phase. Determine the service demand load and the service conductor size for the hair salon which has the following equipment.

- 20 feet of show window lighting
- 150 feet of track lighting
- 120 feet of fixed multi-outlet assembly (appliances will be used simultaneously)
- 50 – 120-volt, 20 ampere duplex receptacles
- one – 12 ton A/C unit, 3-phase (gas heating)
- one – 5 kW cooktop, 208-volt, single-phase
- one – 4 kW oven, 208-volt, single-phase
- one – 1,200 VA, microwave oven
- one – 1,200 VA, refrigerator/freezer
- two – 1,800 VA, washing machines
- one – 5 kW, clothes dryer, 208-volt, single-phase
- one – electric sign circuit

SOLUTION -

LIGHTING
General lighting	– 4,000 sq. ft. x 3 VA x 125%	= 15,000 VA
Show Window	- 20 ft. x 200 VA x 125%	= 5,000 VA
Track Lighting	- 150 ft./2 x 150 VA x 125%	= 14,063 VA
Sign Circuits	- 1 x 1,200 VA x 125%	= 1,500 VA

RECEPTACLES
Multi-outlet Assembly	– 120 ft. x 180 VA	= 21,600 VA
Receptacles	- 50 x 180 VA	= 9,000 VA
		30,600 VA

Table 220.44
1st 10 kVA @ 100%		= 10,000 VA
20,600 VA @50%		= 10,300 VA
	20,300 VA	= 20,300 VA

COMPARE A/C VERSUS HEATING
A/C – 12 ton x 2,400 VA per ton	= 28,800 VA	= 28,800 VA
HTG. – N/A	= N/A	

KITCHEN EQUIPMENT
Cooktop	- 5 kW	= 5,000 VA
Oven	- 4 kW	= 4,000 VA
Microwave	- 1,200 VA	= 1,200 VA
Refrigerator	- 1,200 VA	= 1,200 VA
		11,400 VA
Table 220.56		x .8
		9,120 VA = 9,120 VA

LAUNDRY EQUIPMENT
Washing Machine – 2 x 1,800 VA	= 3,600 VA	
Clothes Dryer - 1 x 5,000 VA	= 5,000 VA	
	8,600 VA	= 8,600 VA

DEMAND LOAD = 102,383 VA

$$I = \frac{102,383 \text{ VA}}{208 \times 1.732} = \frac{102,383 \text{ VA}}{368.25} = 284 \text{ amperes}$$

Size 300 kcmil copper 75°C rated service-entrance conductors or size 500 kcmil aluminum 75°C rated service-entrance conductors should be selected from **Table 310.15(B)(16).**

*NOTE – See page 182 of this text for an example of this calculation method using the following completed form.

COMMERCIAL CALCULATION

1. LIGHTING: *Table 220.12 or 220.18(B)*
   General Lighting: _____ sq. ft. x _____ VA x 125% =   _____ VA
   220.18(B): _____ fixtures x _____ VA x 125% =   _____ VA
   Show Window: _____ ft. x 200 VA x 125% =   _____ VA
   Track Lighting: _____ ft. / 2 x 150 VA x 125% =   _____ VA
   Sign Ckts. _____ x 1,200 VA x 125% =   _____ VA
   Misc. Lighting: _____ VA
                                           Total Lighting = (_____) VA   [_____] VA

2. RECEPTACLES: 220.14(I) and/or 220.14(H)
   Receptacles: 180 VA x _____ receptacles =   _____ VA
   Multi-outlet Assembly: 180 VA x _____ ft. =   _____ VA
   Total =   (_____) VA
   Table 220.44
   First 10,000 VA x 100% =   _____ VA
   Remainder: _____ VA x 50% =   _____ VA
                                            Demand = (_____) VA   [_____] VA

3. HEATING or A/C at 100% (largest):
   Heating unit = _____ VA x _____ units = _____ VA
   A/C unit = _____ VA x _____ units = _____ VA
   Heat pump = _____ VA x _____ units = _____ VA
   Largest Load = _____ VA x _____ units = _____ VA   (_____) VA   [_____] VA

4. KITCHEN EQUIPMENT: 220.56
   Range _____ VA x _____ units =   _____ VA
   Cooktop _____ VA x _____ units =   _____ VA
   Oven _____ VA x _____ units =   _____ VA
   Dishwasher _____ VA x _____ units =   _____ VA
   Water Heater _____ VA x _____ units =   _____ VA
   _____ _____ VA x _____ units =   _____ VA
   _____ _____ VA x _____ units =   _____ VA
                                         Total = (_____) VA
                                         Table 220.56 x _____ %
                                         Demand = (_____) VA   [_____] VA

5. LAUNDRY EQUIPMENT:
   Washing Machine _____ VA x _____ units   _____ VA
   Clothes Dryer _____ VA x _____ units   _____ VA
   Water Heater _____ VA x _____ units   _____ VA
   _____ _____ VA x _____ units   _____ VA
                                         Total = (_____) VA   [_____] VA

6. MISCELLANEOUS LOADS: _____ VA
                                                       _____ VA
                                         Total = (_____) VA   [_____] VA

7. TOTAL   [_____] VA
   Line   I = _____ VA = _____ amperes
                  volts
   Conductors are to be sized per Table 310.15(B)(16)

COMMERCIAL CALCULATION

1. LIGHTING: *Table 220.12 or 220.18(B)*

General Lighting: **4,000** sq. ft. x **3** VA x 125% = **15,000** VA
220.18(B): _____ fixtures x _____ VA x 125% = _____ VA
Show Window: **20** ft. x 200 VA x 125% = **5,000** VA
Track Lighting: **150** ft. / 2 x 150 VA x 125% = **14,063** VA
Sign Ckts. **1** x 1,200 VA x 125% = **1,500** VA

Total Lighting = (**35,563**) VA [**35,563**] VA

2. RECEPTACLES: 220.14(I) and/or 220.14(H)

Receptacles: 180 VA x **50** receptacles = **9,000** VA
Multi-outlet Assembly: 180 VA x **120** ft. = **21,600** VA
Total = (**30,600**) VA

Table 220.44
First 10,000 VA x 100% = **10,000** VA
Remainder: **20,600** VA x 50% = **10,300** VA

Demand = (**20,300**) VA [**20,300**] VA

3. HEATING or A/C at 100% (largest):

Heating unit = **20,000** VA x **1** units = **20,000** VA
A/C unit = **28,800** VA x **1** units = **28,800** VA
Heat pump = _____ VA x _____ units = _____ VA
Largest Load = **28,800** VA x **1** units = **28,800** VA (**28,800**) VA [**28,800**] VA

4. KITCHEN EQUIPMENT: 220.56

Range _____ VA x _____ units = _____ VA
Cooktop **5,000** VA x **1** units = **5,000** VA
Oven **4,000** VA x **1** units = **4,000** VA
Dishwasher _____ VA x _____ units = _____ VA
_____ _____ VA x _____ units = _____ VA
Microwave **1,200** VA x **1** units = **1,200** VA
Refrigerator **1,200** VA x **1** units = **1,200** VA

Total = (**11,400**) VA
Table 220.56 x **80** %
Demand = (**9,120**) VA [**9,120**] VA

5. LAUNDRY EQUIPMENT:

Washing Machine **1,800** VA x **2** units **3,600** VA
Clothes Dryer **5,000** VA x **1** units **5,000** VA
Water Heater _____ VA x _____ units _____ VA
_____ _____ VA x _____ units _____ VA

Total = (**8,600**) VA [**8,600**] VA

6. MISCELLANEOUS LOADS: _____ VA
_____ VA

Total = (_____) VA [_____] VA

7. TOTAL **102,383** VA

Line I = **102,383** VA = **284** amperes
208 x 1.732

Conductors are to be sized per Table 310.15(B)(16).

MASTER ELECTRICIAN'S EXAM PREP GUIDE
EXAM #1

The following questions are based on the 2014 edition of the National Electrical Code® and are typical of questions encountered on most Master Electricians' Licensing Exams. On each question select the best answer from the choices given and review your answers with the answer key included in this book. Typically, the only material permitted for use on this type of exam is a calculator, scratch paper and a current edition of the NEC® book. Each question on this test has a value of 4 points; passing score is 70% therefore, in order to pass you need to get 18 of the 25 questions correct.

ALLOTTED TIME: 75 minutes

1. For solar photovoltaic systems, locating the system grounding connection point as close as practicable to the photovoltaic source better protects the system from _____.

A. voltage surges due to ground-faults
B. excessive voltage-drop
C. voltage surges due to lightning
D. excessive resistance in the grounding system

2. What is the MINIMUM height allowed for a fence enclosing an outdoor installation of 2,400 volt electrical equipment?

A. 6 feet
B. 7 feet
C. 8 feet
D. 9 feet

3. Where power for equipment is directly associated with the radio frequency distribution system is carried by the coaxial cable, and the power source is a power limiting transformer, what is the MAXIMUM voltage this coaxial cable may carry?

A. 50 volts
B. 60 volts
C. 120 volts
D. 150 volts

4. Where a 15-ampere rated general-use ac snap switch is used as a disconnecting means for an ac motor, the NEC® requires the MAXIMUM full-load current rating of the motor to be NO more than _____ .

A. 7.5 amperes
B. 10 amperes
C. 12 amperes
D. 15 amperes

5. Determine the MAXIMUM number of 125-volt, general-purpose receptacles the NEC® permits to be protected by a 20-ampere, 120-volt, single-pole inverse time circuit breaker in a commercial occupancy.

A. 18
B. 15
C. 13
D. 10

6. Which of the following statements, if any, is/are true regarding illumination for service equipment installed in electrical equipment rooms?

  I. The illumination shall not be controlled by means of three way switches.
  II. The illumination shall not be controlled by automatic means only.

A. I only
B. II only
C. both I and II
D. neither I nor II

7. In regard to the tenant spaces in a retail shopping mall; each occupant shall have access to the main disconnecting means, EXCEPT:

A. where the service and maintenance are provided by the building management.
B. where there are more than six disconnecting means provided.
C. where the primary feeder transformer does not exceed 600 volts.
D. where the secondary of the service transformer does not exceed 240-volts to ground.

8. Determine the conductor allowable ampacity given the following conditions:

* ambient temperature of 44 deg. C
* 250 kcmil THWN copper conductors
* four (4) current-carrying conductors are in the raceway
* length of raceway is 25 feet

A. 160 amperes
B. 167 amperes
C. 200 amperes
D. 209 amperes

9. Determine the MAXIMUM overcurrent protection permitted for size 14 THWN copper motor control circuit conductors tapped from the load side of a motor overcurrent protection device. Given: the conductors require short-circuit protection and do not extend beyond the motor control equipment enclosure.

A. 20 amperes
B. 25 amperes
C. 30 amperes
D. 100 amperes

10. Circuit breakers rated _____ or less and 1000 volts or less shall have the ampere rating molded, stamped, etched or similarly marked into their handles or escutcheon areas.

A. 600 amperes
B. 200 amperes
C. 400 amperes
D. 100 amperes

11. In the kitchen of a dwelling unit where a single-phase, 125-volt, 15-or 20-ampere rated receptacle outlet is installed for a refrigerator and is located within 6 feet of the kitchen sink, the receptacle outlet shall be provided with _____.

A. GFCI protection only
B. AFCI protection only
C. both GFCI and AFCI protection
D. neither GFCI nor AFCI protection

12. Where a rooftop mounted air-conditioning unit is supplied with three (3) size 8 AWG THWN copper conductors, enclosed in an electrical metallic tubing (EMT) within three (3) inches of the rooftop, and exposed to direct sunlight and an ambient temperature of 100 degrees F, the allowable ampacity of the conductors is _____ .

A. 50 amperes
B. 44 amperes
C. 29 amperes
D. 25 amperes

13. Which of the following listed conductor insulations is oil resistant?

A. TW
B. TFE
C. THWN
D. MTW

14. All exposed non-current-carrying metal parts of an information technology system shall _____ or shall be double insulated.

A. be bonded to the equipment grounding conductor
B. not be bonded to the equipment grounding conductor
C. be bonded to the grounded conductor
D. be isolated

15. Determine the MINIMUM number of 15-ampere, 120-volt general lighting branch circuits required for a 12,000 square feet multifamily condo where each dwelling unit has cooking facilities provided.

A. 15
B. 20
C. 24
D. 30

16. Storage batteries used as a source of power for emergency systems shall be of a suitable rating and capacity to supply and maintain the total load for at LEAST _____ .

A. 1/2 hour
B. 1 hour
C. 1½ hours
D. 2 hours

17. When a conduit containing service-entrance conductors runs

beneath a building, what is the MINIMUM depth of concrete required to cover the conduit for it to be considered "outside" the building?

A. 2 inches
B. 6 inches
C. 12 inches
D. 18 inches

18. The entire area of an aircraft hangar, including any adjacent and communicating areas not suitably cut off from the hangar, shall be classified as a Class I, Division 2 or Zone 2 location up to a level _____ above the floor.

A. 12 inches
B. 18 inches
C. 24 inches
D. 30 inches

19. Where a 240-volt, single-phase 90 ampere load is located 225 feet from a panelboard and supplied with size 3 THWN copper conductors; what is the approximate voltage drop on this circuit? (K = 12.9)

A. 6 volts
B. 4 volts
C. 8 volts
D. 10 volts

20. The continuity of the equipment grounding conductor system for portable electrical carnival equipment shall be verified _____ .

A. and recorded on an annual basis
B. and recorded on a quarterly basis
C. and recorded on a monthly basis
D. each time the equipment is connected

21. Electrical services and feeders for recreational vehicle parks shall be calculated on the basis of NOT less than _____ per RV site equipped with both 20-ampere and 30-ampere supply facilities.

A. 2400 volt-amperes
B. 9600 volt-amperes
C. 4800 volt-amperes
D. 3600 volt-amperes

22. In a commercial garage work area, which of the following 125-volt, single-phase receptacles, if any, are required to have GFCI protection?

I. 15-ampere general-purpose receptacles for hand tools and portable lighting equipment.
II. 20-ampere receptacles serving electrical diagnostic equipment only.

A. I only
B. II only
C. both I and II
D. neither I nor II

23. When sizing time-delay Class CC fuses for motor branch-circuit, short-circuit and ground-fault protection, they are to be sized at the same value as _____ .

A. inverse-time circuit breakers
B. nontime-delay fuses
C. instantaneous trip circuit breakers
D. adjustable trip circuit breakers

24. The MINIMUM spacing required between the bottom of a 600 volt rated switchboard and the noninsulated busbars mounted in the switchboard cabinet is _____ .

A. 6 inches
B. 8 inches
C. 10 inches
D. 12 inches

25. Given: A rigid metal conduit (RMC) to be installed will contain only the following three (3) circuits on the load side of the service overcurrent protective devices:

* two - 150 ampere, 3-phase circuits
* one - 300 ampere, single-phase circuit

The load side equipment bonding jumper for this conduit must be a MINIMUM size of _____ copper.

A. 1 AWG
B. 2 AWG
C. 4 AWG
D. 6 AWG

END OF EXAM #1

MASTER ELECTRICIAN'S EXAM PREP GUIDE
EXAM #2

The following questions are based on the 2014 edition of the National Electrical Code® and are typical of questions encountered on most Master Electricians' Licensing Exams. On each question select the best answer from the choices given and review your answers with the answer key included in this book. Typically, the only material permitted for use on this type of exam is a calculator, scratch paper and a current edition of the NEC® book. Each question on this test has a value of 4 points; passing score is 70% therefore, in order to pass you need to get 18 of the 25 questions correct.

ALLOTTED TIME: 75 minutes

1. Where conduits enter a floor-standing switchboard, switchgear or, panelboard at the bottom, the conduits, including their end fittings, shall NOT rise more than _____ above the bottom of the enclosure.

A. 6 inches
B. 4 inches
C. 2 inches
D. 3 inches

2. For emergency systems where internal combustion engines are used as the prime mover, an on-site fuel supply shall be provided with an on-site fuel supply sufficient for NOT less than _____ full-demand operation of the system.

A. 2 hours
B. 3 hours
C. 4 hours
D. 6 hours

3. Conductors supplying outlets for arc and xenon motion picture projectors of the professional type shall be a MINIMUM size of _____.

A. 12 AWG
B. 10 AWG
C. 8 AWG
D. 6 AWG

4. Thermostatically controlled switching devices serving as both controllers and disconnecting means for fixed electric space heating equipment shall _____.

A. be prohibited
B. be located not more than 5 feet above the floor level
C. directly open all grounded conductors when manually placed in the OFF position
D. be designed so that the circuit cannot be energized automatically after the device has been manually placed in the OFF position

5. A bonding jumper connected between the communications grounding electrode and power grounding electrode system at the building or structure service where separate electrodes are used shall NOT be smaller than size _____ copper.

A. 8 AWG
B. 6 AWG
C. 12 AWG
D. 10 AWG

6. Given: A straight pull of size 4 AWG and larger conductors is to made in a junction box that will have a trade size 3 in. conduit and two (2) trade size 2 in. conduits entering on the same side and exiting on the opposite wall. No splices or terminations will be made in the box. Which of the following listed junction boxes is the MINIMUM required for this installation?

A. 18 in. x 12 in.
B. 20 in. x 18 in.
C. 20 in. x 12 in.
D. 24 in. x 24 in.

7. Given: A dairy farm with a 120/240-volt, single phase electrical system will have the following three loads supplied from a common service; one – 18,000 VA, one - 16,000 VA, and one – 10,000 VA. What is the demand load, in amperes, on the ungrounded service-entrance conductors?

A. 183 amperes
B. 152 amperes
C. 304 amperes
D. 114 amperes

8. All 15- or 20-ampere, single-phase, 125-volt receptacles located within at LEAST _____ of the edge of a decorative fountain shall be provided with GFCI protection for personnel.

A. 10 feet
B. 15 feet
C. 20 feet
D. 25 feet

9. The emergency controls for attended self-service gasoline stations or convenience stores with motor fuel dispensing facilities must be located NOT more than _____ from the motor fuel dispensers.

A. 20 feet
B. 50 feet
C. 75 feet
D. 100 feet

10. Given: A transformer is fed with four (4) parallel size 500 kcmil conductors per phase. The conductors enter the enclosure on the opposite wall of the terminals. What is the MINIMUM wire-bending space required for the conductors?

A. 16 inches
B. 14 inches
C. 12 inches
D. 10 inches

11. What MINIMUM size THWN copper conductors are required to supply a continuous-duty, 25 hp, 208-volt, 3-phase motor, where the motor is on the end of a short conduit run that contains only three (3) conductors, at an ambient temperature of 115 deg. F?

A. 6 AWG
B. 3 AWG
C. 2 AWG
D. 1 AWG

12. Where time-delay (dual-element) fuses are used for short-circuit and ground-fault protection for both windings of a part-winding synchronous motor, the fuses shall be permitted to have a rating NOT exceeding _____ of the full-load current of the motor.

A. 200 percent
B. 150 percent
C. 175 percent
D. 225 percent

13. Where a conductor is marked *RHW-2* on the insulation, what does the *-2* represent?

A. The cable has 2 conductors.
B. The conductor is double insulated.
C. The conductor has a nylon outer jacket.
D. The conductor has a maximum operating temperature of 90°C.

14. Apply the general method of calculation for dwellings and determine the demand load, in kW, on the ungrounded service-entrance conductors for four (4) household electric ranges rated 19 kW each.

A. 34 kW
B. 17 kW
C. 38 kW
D. 23 kW

15. In movie theaters, all switches for controlling the emergency lighting systems shall be located _____.

A. on the stage
B. in the lobby
C. in the manager's office
D. in the projection booth

16. Single-conductor cable Type _____ shall be permitted in exposed outdoor locations in photovoltaic source circuits for photovoltaic module interconnections within the photovoltaic array.

A. UF
B. THHN
C. USE-2
D. THWN

17. What percent of electrical supplied spaces in a recreational vehicle park must be equipped with at least one (1) 30-ampere 125-volt receptacle outlet?

A. 60 percent
B. 70 percent
C. 90 percent
D. 100 percent

18. Each operating room of a health care facility shall be provided with a MINIMUM of _____ listed hospital grade receptacles.

A. 12
B. 24
C. 30
D. 36

19. Where a 3-phase, 25 kVA rated transformer with a 480-volt primary and a 208Y/120-volt secondary is to be installed where both primary and secondary protection is required to be provided, determine the MAXIMUM standard ampere rating of the secondary overcurrent protection as permitted by the NEC®.

A. 80 amperes
B. 90 amperes
C. 100 amperes
D. 110 amperes

20. Where ungrounded conductors are run in parallel in multiple raceways, the equipment grounding conductor, where used, shall be _____.

A. omitted
B. run in parallel in each raceway
C. installed in one raceway only
D. bare

21. Where track lighting is installed in a continuous row, each individual section of NOT more than _____ in length shall be securely supported.

A. 2 feet
B. 4 feet
C. 6 feet
D. 8 feet

22. Determine the MINIMUM size THWN copper feeder conductors required by the NEC® to supply the following 480 volt, continuous duty, 3-phase, induction-type, Design C, motors.

* one - 40 hp
* one - 50 hp
* one - 60 hp

A. 2/0 AWG
B. 3/0 AWG
C. 4/0 AWG
D. 250 kcmil

23. In health care facilities, essential electrical systems shall have a MINIMUM _____ .

A. of one (1) hour back-up time
B. capacity of 200 gallons of fuel for the auxillary generator
C. of two (2) independent sources of power
D. capacity of 150 kVA

24. Where compressed natural gas vehicles are repaired in a major repair garage, the area within _____ of the ceiling shall be considered unclassified where adequate ventilation is provided.

A. 18 inches
B. 24 inches
C. 30 inches
D. 36 inches

25. Where a 3-phase, 480-volt, 100 ampere demand load is located 390 feet from a panelboard, what MINIMUM size THWN aluminum conductors are required to supply the load where the voltage drop is required to be limited to 3 percent? (K = 21.2)

A. 2 AWG
B. 1 AWG
C. 1/0 AWG
D. 2/0 AWG

END OF EXAM #2

ASTER ELECTRICIAN'S EXAM PREP GUIDE
EXAM #3

The following questions are based on the 2014 edition of the National Electrical Code® and are typical of questions encountered on most Master Electricians' Licensing Exams. On each question select the best answer from the choices given and review your answers with the answer key included in this book. Typically, the only material permitted for use on this type of exam is a calculator, scratch paper and a current edition of the NEC® book. Each question on this test has a value of 4 points; passing score is 70% therefore, in order to pass you need to get 18 of the 25 questions correct.

ALLOTTED TIME: 75 minutes

1. A listed _____ shall be installed in or on all emergency systems switchboards and panelboards.

A. ground-fault circuit interrupter (GFCI)
B. surge-protective device (SPD)
C. arc-fault circuit interrupter (AFCI)
D. leakage-current detector-interrupter (LCDI)

2. In general, where a cablebus system is rated 95 amperes, the MAXIMUM allowable rating of the overcurrent device that may be used to protect the cablebus is _____ .

A. 80 amperes
B. 90 amperes
C. 95 amperes
D. 100 amperes

3. A feeder tap less than 25 feet in length is not required to have overcurrent protection if the ampacity of the tap conductors is NOT less than _____ of the rating of the overcurrent device protecting the feeder conductors.

A. one-half
B. one-fourth
C. one-third
D. 75 percent

4. Given: A flexible metal conduit (FMC) to be installed will contain three (3) size 400 kcmil THWN copper conductors and one (1) size 250 kcmil copper conductor. Where the FMC is more than 24 inches long, what MINIMUM trade size FMC is permitted for this installation?

A. 3 in.
B. 3½ in.
C. 2½ in.
D. 4 in.

5. In general, which of the following MUST be provided at a patient bed location used for general care in a hospital?

A. One branch circuit from the normal system.
B. One branch circuit from the critical branch of the essential electrical system.
C. "Hospital-grade" receptacles.
D. All of these.

6. When an electrical service is required to have a grounded conductor present, what is the smallest grounded conductor permitted for an electric service using size 1000 kcmil copper ungrounded conductors installed in a single raceway?

A. 3/0 copper
B. 2/0 copper
C. 1/0 copper
D. 4/0 copper

7. Determine the MINIMUM number of 20-ampere, 277-volt, general-lighting branch circuits required for a 150,000 square foot retail department store where the actual connected load is 400 kVA; consider circuit breakers of this size are NOT rated for continuous use.

A. 72
B. 82
C. 91
D. 102

8. Where a 2-gang box contains two (2) single-pole switches, unless the box is equipped with permanently installed barriers, voltage between the switches shall NOT be in excess of _____.

A. 120 volts
B. 277 volts
C. 480 volts
D. 240 volts

9. Where electrical metallic tubing (EMT) is installed under metal-corrugated sheet roofing decking, a clearance of at LEAST _____ must be maintained between the top of the tubing and the surface of the roof decking.

A. 1 in.
B. 1¼ in.
C. 1½ in.
D. 1¾ in.

10. Fluorescent luminaires installed MORE than _____ above the floor in patient care areas in a hospital, shall NOT be required to be grounded by an insulated equipment grounding conductor.

A. 6 feet
B. 6½ feet
C. 7 feet
D. 7½ feet

11. Where nonmetallic conduit is used to enclose conductors supplying a wet-niche luminaire located in a permanently installed swimming pool, a size _____ insulated copper grounding conductor shall be installed in the conduit, unless a listed low-voltage lighting system not requiring grounding is used.

A. 12 AWG
B. 10 AWG
C. 8 AWG
D. 6 AWG

12. The ampacity of phase conductors from the generator terminals to the first overcurrent device shall NOT be less than _____ of the nameplate current rating of the generator where the design of the generator does not prevent overloading.

A. 100 percent
B. 115 percent
C. 125 percent
D. 150 percent

13. In Class II, Division 1 locations, an approved method of connection of conduit to boxes or cabinets is _____ .

A. compression fittings
B. threaded bosses
C. welding
D. all of these

14. The upward discharging vent of an underground fuel tank of motor fuel dispensing facilities is classified as a Class I, Division 1 location WITHIN _____ of the open vent, extending in all directions.
A. 3 feet
B. 5 feet
C. 6 feet
D. 8 feet

15. Conductors between the controller and the diesel engine of a fire pump are required to be _____ .

A. 90 deg. C rated
B. 104 deg. C rated
C. stranded
D. solid

16. The MAXIMUM allowable ampacity of a size 750 kcmil XHHW aluminum conductor when there are six (6) current-carrying conductors all of the same size and insulation in the raceway, installed in a dry location where the ambient temperature will reach 22 deg. C is _____.

A. 323.40 amperes
B. 365.40 amperes
C. 361.92 amperes
D. 348.00 amperes

17. Where resistance heating element type duct heating equipment is located above a lay-in type suspended ceiling in a commercial or retail occupancy, a clearance of not less than the width of the enclosure or NOT less than _____ whichever is greater must be maintained.

A. 24 inches
B. 30 inches
C. 36 inches
D. 48 inches

18. According to the NEC®, flat conductor cable (FCC) is permitted to be used for:

I. general-purpose circuit conductors.
II. appliance circuit conductors.

A. I only
B. II only
C. both I and II
D. neither I nor II

19. Determine the MINIMUM size USE aluminum cable permitted for use on an underground 120/240-volt, single-phase, service for a small office building that has a total load of 23,600 VA after all demand factors have been taken into consideration. Consider all conductor terminations are rated for 75 deg. C.

A. 1/0 AWG
B. 2/0 AWG
C. 1 AWG
D. 2 AWG

20. For track lighting installed in a retail store, a MAXIMUM of two (2) feet of lighting track or fraction thereof shall be considered _____ .

A. 150 VA
B. 180 VA
C. 200 VA
D. 100 VA

21. Where an apartment complex has a connected lighting load of 205.4 kVA, what is the demand load, in kVA, on the ungrounded service-entrance conductors? Consider each apartment unit has provisions for cooking by tenants and apply the general (standard) method of calculation for dwelling units.

A. 60.2 kVA
B. 16.5 kVA
C. 63.0 kVA
D. 65.3 kVA

22. All of the following copper conductors are to be installed in an electrical metallic tubing (EMT) ten (10) feet long:

* 24 - size 10 AWG THHW
* 10 - size 10 AWG THHN
* 14 - size 12 AWG THHN

Determine the MINIMUM trade size EMT required.

A. 2 in.
B. 2½ in.
C. 3 in.
D. 3½ in.

23. Given: A 40 unit apartment complex with a 120/240-volt, single-phase electrical system is to add a 6,000 watt, 240 volt, single-phase clothes dryer in each unit. How many amperes will the clothes dryers add to the ungrounded (line) service-entrance conductors when applying the general method of calculation?

A. 265 amperes
B. 270 amperes
C. 300 amperes
D. 350 amperes

24. When sizing fuses for a branch circuit serving a hermetic refrigerant motor-compressor, the device shall NOT exceed _____ of the rated load current marked on the nameplate of the equipment.

A. 115 percent
B. 125 percent
C. 175 percent
D. 225 percent

25. Given: You are to install 90 feet of multioutlet assembly in the computer lab of a school where the computers are likely to be used simultaneously. Determine the MINIMUM number of 20-ampere, 120-volt, single-phase branch circuits required to supply the multioutlet assembly.

A. six
B. seven
C. eight
D. nine

END OF EXAM #3

MASTER ELECTRICIAN'S EXAM PREP GUIDE
EXAM #4

The following questions are based on the 2014 edition of the National Electrical Code® and are typical of questions encountered on most Master Electricians' Licensing Exams. On each question select the best answer from the choices given and review your answers with the answer key included in this book. Typically, the only material permitted for use on this type of exam is a calculator, scratch paper and a current edition of the NEC® book. Each question on this test has a value of 4 points; passing score is 70% therefore, in order to pass you need to get 18 of the 25 questions correct.

ALLOTTED TIME: 75 minutes

1. Overcurrent protection for size 18 AWG non-power-limited fire alarm (NPLFA) circuit conductors shall NOT exceed _____ and the overcurrent protection for size 16 AWG NPLFA circuit conductors shall NOT exceed _____.

A. 8 amperes, 10 amperes
B. 7 amperes, 12 amperes
C. 8 amperes, 12 amperes
D. 7 amperes, 10 amperes

2. The general rule is where raceways and cables are exposed to direct sunlight on or above rooftops, the adjustments shown in Table 310.15(B)(3)(c) shall be added to the outdoor temperature to determine the applicable ambient temperature for application of the correction factors. An exception to this rule is _____.

A. prohibited
B. where the raceway or cables contain 3 or less current-carrying conductors
C. where the insulated conductors or cables have a temperature rating of 90ºC or more
D. where the insulated conductors or cables are Type XHHW-2

3. An emergency system is required to have NO more than, _____ to have power available in the event of failure of the normal supply system.

A. 10 seconds
B. 15 seconds
C. 60 seconds
D. 3 minutes

4. X-ray equipment installed in a hospital may be served by a hard-service cord with a suitable attachment plug, provided the branch circuit rating does NOT exceed _____.

A. 15 amperes
B. 20 amperes
C. 30 amperes
D. 50 amperes

5. Elevator driving motors used with a generator field control are rated as _____ duty motors.

A. intermittent
B. continuous
C. variable
D. controlled

6. Where a direct burial cable has a voltage of 45 kV, the NEC® mandates the MINIMUM burial depth of the cable to be at LEAST _____ .

A. 24 inches
B. 36 inches
C. 42 inches
D. 48 inches

7. Given: A recreational vehicle campground has a total of 150 campsites with electrical power. Twenty-five (25) of the campsites are reserved as tent sites. How many sites are required to have at LEAST one (1) 20 ampere, 125-volt, receptacle outlet?

A. 105
B. 125
C. 150
D. None

8. Determine the MINIMUM size type SO cord permitted to supply a 40 hp, 460-volt, 3-phase, continuous-duty, ac wound rotor, motor installed in an area with an ambient temperature of 86 degrees F.

A. 2 AWG
B. 4 AWG
C. 6 AWG
D. 8 AWG

9. Where a 30 hp, 240-volt, 3-phase synchronous motor has a power factor of 90 percent, as per the NEC® the full-load running current of the motor is _____ .

A. 63.0 amperes
B. 69.3 amperes
C. 76.23 amperes
D. 86.62 amperes

10. When water reaches the height of the established electrical datum plane for an irrigation pond, the electrical service equipment must _____ .

A. be installed in a NEMA 6 enclosure
B. float
C. be installed in a NEMA 6P enclosure
D. disconnect

11. Disregarding exceptions, when installing emergency battery pack lighting unit equipment, the branch-circuit feeding this equipment shall:

A. be connected to the nearest receptacle outlet.
B. come from the closest outlet of power that is compatible with the emergency lights rated voltage.
C. be fed only from an identified emergency lighting panel.
D. be on the same branch-circuit serving the normal lighting in the area.

12. In an industrial establishment, what is the MAXIMUM length of 200 ampere rated busway that may be tapped to a 600 ampere rated busway without providing additional overcurrent protection?

A. 10 feet
B. 25 feet
C. 50 feet
D. 75 feet

13. Size 4/0 AWG, 75 deg. C aluminum secondary conductors of a 3-phase delta-wye transformer, shall be protected at NOT more than _____ .

A. 175 amperes
B. 200 amperes
C. the calculated load connected to the transformer
D. none of these, because secondary protection is not required for multiphase, delta-wye transformer secondary conductors

14. For trade size 3/4 in. MI cable, the radius of the inner edge of the bend shall NOT be less than _____ times the external diameter of the cable.

A. three
B. four
C. five
D. seven

15. Where a flat cable assembly, Type FC, is installed LESS than _____ above the floor or fixed working platform, it shall be protected by a cover identified for the use.

A. 6 feet
B. 7 feet
C. 8 feet
D. 10 feet

16. The MINIMUM burial depth for conduit or cables installed under an airport runway, concourse or tarmac is _____.

A. 1½ feet
B. 2 feet
C. 3 feet
D. 4 feet

17. Determine the MINIMUM size overload protection required for a 480 volt, 3-phase, 15 hp, continuous-duty motor given the following related information:

* Design C
* temperature rise - 40 deg. C
* service factor - 1.12
* actual nameplate rating - 18 amperes

A. 20.7 amperes
B. 18.0 amperes
C. 22.5 amperes
D. 23.4 amperes

18. Assume where the overload protection you have selected on the above motor is not sufficient to start the motor and trips, therefore, modification of this value is necessary, determine the MAXIMUM size overload protection permitted.

A. 22.5 amperes
B. 20.7 amperes
C. 25.2 amperes
D. 23.4 amperes

19. Where a 50 kVA transformer with a 480-volt, 3 phase primary and a 208Y/120-volt, 3-phase secondary is to be installed and overcurrent protection is required on both the primary and secondary side of the transformer; determine the MAXIMUM size overcurrent protection device permitted for the primary side.

A. 125 amperes
B. 150 amperes
C. 175 amperes
D. 200 amperes

20. What is the demand load, in VA, for the general-use receptacles in an office building that has a total of 150 general-use, 125-volt, 20-ampere, single-phase receptacle outlets installed?

A. 18,500 VA
B. 10,000 VA
C. 27,000 VA
D. 13,500 VA

21. Determine the MAXIMUM number of size 12 AWG conductors permitted to be housed in a 3½ in. deep, 3-gang masonry box that contains three (3) switches.

A. 21
B. 23
C. 24
D. 27

22. A horizontal raceway entering a dust-ignition proof enclosure from one that is not, need not have a seal-off if it is at LEAST_____ in length.

A. 18 inches
B. 5 feet
C. 10 feet
D. 25 inches

23. Where abandoned communications cables are identified for future use with a tag, the tag shall be _____.

A. red in color
B. orange in color
C. located outside the junction box
D. of sufficient durability to withstand the environment

24. All 125-volt, 15- and 20-ampere receptacles located within _____ of the inside walls of a storable pool, storable spa, or storable hot tub shall be protected by a ground-fault circuit interrupter.

A. 6 feet
B. 8 feet
C. 10 feet
D. 20 feet

25. A dry type transformer of 1000 volts or less and NOT exceeding _____ is permitted to be installed in a hollow space of a building, such as above a lift-out ceiling, provided there is adequate ventilation.

A. 25 kVA
B. 37½ kVA
C. 50 kVA
D. 112½ kVA

END OF EXAM #4

MASTER ELECTRICIAN'S EXAM PREP GUIDE
EXAM #5

The following questions are based on the 2014 edition of the National Electrical Code® and are typical of questions encountered on most Master Electricians' Licensing Exams. On each question select the best answer from the choices given and review your answers with the answer key included in this book. Typically, the only material permitted for use on this type of exam is a calculator, scratch paper and a current edition of the NEC® book. Each question on this test has a value of 4 points; passing score is 70% therefore, in order to pass you need to get 18 of the 25 questions correct.

ALLOTTED TIME: 75 minutes

1. In Class II, Division 1 locations, where pendant mounted luminaires are suspended by rigid metal conduit (RMC) and a means for flexibility is not provided, the RMC shall have a length of NOT more than _____.

A. 12 inches
B. 18 inches
C. 24 inches
D. 30 inches

2. All hydromassage bathtub metal piping systems and all grounded metal parts in contact with the circulating water associated with the bathtub shall be bonded together using a solid copper bonding jumper NOT smaller than _____.

A. 10 AWG
B. 8 AWG
C. 6 AWG
D. 12 AWG

3. Where power-limited fire alarm (PLFA) circuit conductors pass through a wall, the conductors shall be protected by a metal raceway or nonmetallic conduit up to a of at LEAST _____ above the floor, unless other means of protection is provided.

A. 8 feet
B. 6 feet
C. 7 feet
D. 10 feet

4. Luminaires installed in exposed or concealed locations under metal-corrugated sheet roof decking shall be installed and supported so there is NOT less than _____ clearance from the lowest surface of the roof decking to the top of the luminaire.

A. 1 in.
B. 1¼ in.
C. 1½ in.
D. 1¾ in.

5. Transformers with ventilation openings shall be installed so the ventilating openings are not blocked by walls or other obstructions. The required clearances shall be _____.

A. of not less than 3 inches
B. of not less than 6 inches
C. clearly marked on the transformer
D. as specified on the approved plans

6. Where a dwelling unit has a three (3) car attached garage, the NEC® requires a MINIMUM of _____ 125-volt, single-phase, 15- or 20-ampere receptacles to be installed in the garage.

A. one
B. two
C. three
D. four

7. With respect to messenger-supported service-drop conductors and open overhead wiring operating at 0 to 750 volts to ground, the MINIMUM vertical clearance that must be maintained from the base of a swimming pool diving board and the conductors is _____ .

A. 22½ feet
B. 19½ feet
C. 14½ feet
D. 10 feet

8. Determine the MINIMUM required size 75 deg. C rated conductors permitted to be used to supply a demand load of 200 amperes where provided with a 208Y/120-volt, 3-phase 4-wire, electrical system. Consider all four (4) conductors to be current-carrying and the ambient temperature is 120 deg. F.

A. 250 kcmil
B. 300 kcmil
C. 400 kcmil
D. 500 kcmil

9. A metal junction box to be installed will contain the following conductors:

* three - size 6 AWG ungrounded conductors
* three - size 6 AWG grounded conductors
* one size 8 AWG grounding conductor
* three - size 12 AWG ungrounded conductors
* three - size 12 AWG grounded conductors
* one - size 12 AWG grounding conductor

The junction box is required to have a volume of at LEAST _____.

A. 51.50 cubic inches
B. 53.75 cubic inches
C. 46.50 cubic inches
D. 56.50 cubic inches

10. In regard to permanently installed swimming pools, where necessary to employ flexible connections to a pool pump motor, _____ shall be permitted as the wiring method(s).

   I. UF cable
   II. liquidtight flexible metal conduit (LFMC)

A. I only
B. II only
C. neither I nor II
D. both I and II

11. Which of the following listed wiring methods is NOT approved for use in assembly locations, UNLESS encased in concrete?

A. EMT
B. Schedule 80 PVC
C. Type MC cable
D. Type AC cable

12. In regard to commercial garages, lamps and lampholders for fixed lighting located over lanes through which vehicles are commonly driven, shall be located NOT less than _____ above the floor level, unless the luminaires are of the totally enclosed type.

A. 8 feet
B. 10 feet
C. 12 feet
D. 14½ feet

13. Determine the maximum permitted operational setting of an adjustable inverse time circuit breaker used for branch-circuit, short-circuit and ground-fault protection of a 10 hp, 208-volt, 3-phase, squirrel cage, Design B, continuous-duty motor. Assume the motor will start at this setting and exceptions are not applicable.

A. 30.8 amperes
B. 35.7 amperes
C. 77.0 amperes
D. 338.8 amperes

14. Where transformer vaults are not protected with an automatic fire-suppression system, they shall be constructed of approved materials that have a MINIMUM fire-resistance rating of _____.

A. 1 hour
B. 2 hours
C. 3 hours
D. 4 hours

15. At a truck plaza, every electrified truck parking space intended to provide an electrical supply for transport refrigerated units, shall be equipped with a _____ receptacle outlet.

   I. 30 ampere, 480-volt, 3-phase, 3-pole, 4-wire
   II. 60 ampere, 208-volt, 3-phase, 3-pole, 4-wire

A. I only
B. II only
C. either I or II
D. both I and II

16. What is the MAXIMUM distance allowed to support intermediate metal conduit (IMC) from a junction box, where structural members do not readily permit fastening?

A. 3 feet
B. 5 feet
C. 6 feet
D. 8 feet

17. Explosionproof apparatus is required for electrical equipment placed in _____ locations.

A. Class I, Division 1 and 2
B. Class I Division 3
C. Class II, Division 1 and 2
D. all of these

18. Multiconductor cable Type TC-ER or Type _____ shall be permitted in outdoor locations in photovoltaic inverter output circuits where used with utility-interactive inverters mounted in locations that are not readily accessible.

A. USE
B. MI
C. UF
D. USE-2

19. Determine the MAXIMUM standard size inverse time circuit breaker permitted for branch-circuit, short-circuit, and ground-fault protection for a 50 hp, ac motor, when given the following related information.

   * continuous-duty
   * induction type
   * 3-phase, 480 volt
   * Design L
   * nameplate rating 62 amperes

A. 175 amperes
B. 200 amperes
C. 250 amperes
D. 300 amperes

20. In general, on the load side of the point of grounding of a separately derived system such as a transformer, a grounded conductor is NOT permitted to be connected to _____ .

A. equipment grounding conductors
B. normally noncurrent-carrying metal parts of equipment
C. ground, the earth
D. any of these

21. The life safety branch of the essential electrical system of a health care facility shall provide power to _____ .

   I. automatic doors used for building egress
   II. illumination of electrical equipment rooms

A. I only
B. II only
C. both I and II
D. neither I nor II

22. Intrinsically safe apparatus, associated apparatus, and other equipment shall be installed _____.

A. in accordance with the control drawings
B. in the electrical equipment room
C. on a backboard of at least 3/4 in. thick plywood
D. in a dedicated enclosure

23. The grounded conductor of a 3-phase, 3-wire, delta service shall have an ampacity NOT less than _____ .

A. that of the grounding conductor
B. that of the ungrounded conductors
C. 80 percent of the ungrounded conductors
D. 125 percent of the grounding conductor

24. Where a 150 kVA service transformer has a 480Y/277-volt, 3-phase primary and a 208Y/120-volt, 3-phase secondary, the full-load ampere rating on the primary side of the transformer is _____ .

A. 180 amperes
B. 312 amperes
C. 542 amperes
D. 416 amperes

25. Direct-buried cables or conductors located in a trench below 2 inch thick concrete or equivalent shall have a MINIMUM cover requirement of _____ .

A. 6 inches
B. 12 inches
C. 18 inches
D. 24 inches

END OF EXAM #5

MASTER ELECTRICIAN'S EXAM PREP GUIDE
EXAM #6

The following questions are based on the 2014 edition of the National Electrical Code® and are typical of questions encountered on most Master Electricians' Licensing Exams. On each question select the best answer from the choices given and review your answers with the answer key included in this book. Typically, the only material permitted for use on this type of exam is a calculator, scratch paper and a current edition of the NEC® book. Each question on this test has a value of 4 points; passing score is 70% therefore, in order to pass you need to get 18 of the 25 questions correct.

ALLOTTED TIME: 75 minutes

1. The lightning protection system ground terminals shall be bonded to the building or structure grounding electrode system. The bonding shall be _____ and to all raceways, boxes, and enclosures between the cabinets or equipment and the grounding electrode.

A. insulated from one end
B. insulated at each end
C. bonded at both ends
D. bonded at one end only

2. Type AC cable shall provide an adequate path for:

A. grounding conductors.
B. fault current.
C. water drainage.
D. a grounding electrode.

3. A totally enclosed ac motor located in a Class I, Division 1 location shall _____.

A. be double insulated
B. be located no more than 5 ft. above the floor
C. have a temperature rise of not more than 40°C
D. be supplied with positive air ventilation

4. Color coding shall be permitted to identify intrinsically safe conductors where they are colored _____ and where no other conductors of the same color are used.

A. orange
B. light blue
C. yellow
D. green

5. Mandatory rules of the NEC® are those that identify actions that are specifically required or prohibited, are characterized by the use of the terms _____.

A. shall or shall not
B. may or may not
C. will or will not
D. can or cannot

6. A surge arrestor is required on each ungrounded conductor of an industrial facility that experiences severe thunderstorms. If the electrical system is a 4-wire, wye-connected grounded system, how many surge arrestors shall be required?

A. one
B. two
C. three
D. four

7. As per the NEC®, a _____ location may be temporarily subject to dampness and wetness.

A. dry
B. damp
C. moist
D. wet

8. High-impedance grounded neutral systems shall be permitted for 3-phase ac systems of 480-volts to 1,000 volts where _____.

A. the conditions of maintenance ensure that only qualified persons service the installation
B. ground detectors are installed on the electrical system
C. line-to-neutral loads are not served
D. all of these conditions are met

9. Where the overcurrent protection specified is not sufficient for the starting current of an air-conditioner motor-compressor, the rating or setting shall be permitted to be increased, but shall not exceed _____ of the motor-rated-load current or branch circuit selection.

A. 225%
B. 175%
C. 125%
D. 115%

10. Floor duct installed in the concrete floor of an aircraft hangar shall be classified as a _____ location.

A. Class II, Division2
B. Class II, Division 1
C. Class I, Division 2
D. Class I, Division 1

11. Generally, where installed on the outside of a raceway, the length of the equipment bonding jumper shall NOT exceed _____ and shall be routed with the raceway.

A. 4 feet
B. 6 feet
C. 5 feet
D. 8 feet

12. Unless otherwise permitted by the local authority having jurisdiction, Type AC cable shall be secured within _____ of every box, cabinet, or fitting and at intervals not exceeding 4½ ft. where installed on or across framing members.

A. 8 inches
B. 18 inches
C. 12 inches
D. 24 inches

13. Energized electrical equipment operating at 120-volts to ground with exposed live parts on one side and a concrete block tile wall on the other side of the working space, is Condition _____.

A. one
B. two
C. three
D. four

14. Where corrosion protection is necessary and rigid metal conduit (RMC) or intermediate metal conduit (IMC) is threaded in the field, the threads shall be coated with a/an _____ material compound.

A. grounding
B. moisture-resistant
C. non-conductive, corrosion-resistant
D. approved, electrically conductive, and corrosion-resistant

15. In general, flexible metal conduit (FMC) shall be supported by an approved means at intervals NOT exceeding _____.

A. 1 foot
B. 3 feet
C. 4½ feet
D. 6 feet

16. The accessible portions of abandoned supply circuits and interconnecting cables for information technology equipment, or any systems in an information technology equipment room, shall be _____.

A. removed unless contained in a metal raceway
B. required to be secured in place
C. protected by a nonmetal covering
D. tagged to avoid potential damage

17. Disregarding exceptions, the maximum distance permitted for seven (7) current-carrying Type NM cables to be bundled together without requiring the allowable ampacity of the conductors to be reduced is _____.

A. 12 inches
B. 24 inches
C. 30 inches
D. 36 inches

18. For other than dwelling units, all single-phase, 125-volt, 15- and 20-ampere receptacle outlets shall be calculated at NOT less than _____ for each single or for each multiple receptacle mounted on one yoke.

A. 100 VA
B. 150 VA
C. 180 VA
D. 200 VA

19. Where underground installed service conductors emerge from grade and are exposed to physical damage, which of the following listed raceways are NOT approved for such use?

A. rigid metal conduit
B. Schedule 80 PVC
C. Schedule 40 PVC
D. RTRC-XW

20. One who has skills and knowledge related to the construction and operation of the electrical equipment and installations and has received safety training to recognize and avoid the hazards involved, is defined in the NEC® as a/an _____ person.

A. exposed
B. knowledgeable
C. safety certified
D. qualified

21. Cable splices made and insulated by approved methods are permitted to be located within a cable tray, provided they are _____.

A. accessible
B. copper conductors only
C. conductors with a temperature rating of not less than 90°C
D. exposed to ambient temperatures of not more than 110°F

22. Transformers containing oil or a liquid that will burn where located in Class I, Division 1 locations shall be _____.

A. enclosed in a fence
B. installed in vaults only
C. identified for Class I locations
D. installed in a fire-proof room

23. Given: A 240-volt, single-phase, 5,000 VA non-motor operated appliance is supplied by a circuit with size 8 AWG Type NM cable. The MAXIMUM standard rating permitted for a circuit breaker providing overcurrent protection for this appliance is _____.

A. 30 amperes
B. 35 amperes
C. 40 amperes
D. 45 amperes

24. What is the general lighting demand load, in VA, on the ungrounded (line) service entrance conductors of an industrial commercial (loft) building having dimensions of 100 ft. by 300 ft.?

A. 60,000 VA
B. 75,000 VA
C. 90,000 VA
D. 105,000 VA

25. According to the NEC®, when an installation uses metal conduits entering service equipment or enclosures with concentric or eccentric knockouts, as a MINIMUM requirement, the raceway(s) shall be equipped with _____.

A. double locknuts
B. single locknuts
C. at least one locknut and one bushing
D. bonding jumpers, and locknuts or bushings

END OF EXAM #6

MASTER ELECTRICIAN'S EXAM PREP GUIDE
EXAM #7

The following questions are based on the 2014 edition of the National Electrical Code® and are typical of questions encountered on most Master Electricians' Licensing Exams. On each question select the best answer from the choices given and review your answers with the answer key included in this book. Typically, the only material permitted for use on this type of exam is a calculator, scratch paper and a current edition of the NEC® book. Each question on this test has a value of 4 points; passing score is 70% therefore, in order to pass you need to get 18 of the 25 questions correct.

ALLOTTED TIME: 75 minutes

1. As a general rule, for an ac electrical system operating at less than 1000 volts, a main bonding jumper shall connect the grounded conductor(s) to _____.

A. each service disconnecting means grounded conductor terminal
B. each meter base only
C. the grounding electrode
D. each sub-panel

2. Every circuit breaker having an interrupting rating other than _____ shall have its interrupting rating shown on the circuit breaker.

A. 20,000 amperes
B. 15,000 amperes
C. 10,000 amperes
D. 5,000 amperes

3. Electrically operated residential kitchen waste disposers shall be permitted to be cord-and-plug connected however, the flexible cord is to be not less than 18 inches in length and NOT over _____ in length.

A. 36 inches
B. 48 inches
C. 30 inches
D. 24 inches

4. Excluding neon signs, branch circuits that supply all other electric signs and outline lighting systems shall be rated NOT to exceed _____.

A. 40 amperes
B. 30 amperes
C. 20 amperes
D. 25 amperes

5. When considering the support distance for rigid metal conduit (RMC), in compliance with the rules established by the NEC®, what is the MAXIMUM horizontal unsupported length permitted of a trade size 2 in. raceway?

A. 16 feet
B. 10 feet
C. 12 feet
D. 14 feet

6. Generally, receptacle outlets provided for the small appliance countertop circuits in the kitchen of a dwelling shall be located above the countertop, but NOT more than_____ above the countertop.

A. 6 inches
B. 12 inches
C. 18 inches
D. 20 inches

7. What is the general lighting demand load, in VA, on the ungrounded (line) service entrance conductors, of a building consisting of four (4) offices each having a floor space of 20 feet by 30 feet?

A. 8,400 VA
B. 7,200 VA
C. 4,800 VA
D. 10,500 VA

8. For electrical systems of 1,000 volts or less, overhead spans of open individual conductors up to 50 feet in length and not supported by a messenger wire, shall be at LEAST size _____ copper.

A. 8 AWG
B. 10 AWG
C. 6 AWG
D. 12 AWG

9. An unbroken length of rigid metal conduit (RMC) or intermediate metal conduit (IMC) is permitted to support a luminaire in a billboard sign in lieu of a box where the _____.

A. luminaire is at least 8 feet above grade or standing area when accessible to unqualified persons
B. length of conduit exceeds 4 feet from the last point of conduit support
C. luminaire is 15 inches in any direction from a single conduit entry
D. total support weight on a single conduit exceed 20 pounds

10. Isolated ground receptacles that incorporate an isolating grounding conductor connection intended for the reduction of electrical noise or electromagnetic interference, shall be clearly identified by a/an _____ located on the front or face of the receptacle.

A. red circle
B. orange triangle
C. red triangle
D. yellow happy face

11. A mobile home that is factory-equipped with gas or oil-fired central heating equipment and cooking appliances may be provided with a listed mobile home power-supply cord NOT less than _____.

A. 50 amperes
B. 40 amperes
C. 60 amperes
D. 100 amperes

12. The sum of the cross-sectional areas of all contained conductors at any cross-section of a nonmetallic wireway shall NOT exceed _____ of the interior cross-sectional area of the wireway.

A. 40%
B. 30%
C. 60%
D. 20%

13. The disconnecting means for motors and their controllers shall open _____ conductors of the circuit.

A. the "A" phase
B. the grounded
C. the "B" phase
D. simultaneously all ungrounded phase

14. Where a feeder system includes a short run of trade size 1 in. listed liquidtight flexible metal conduit (LFMC), the circuit conductors contained in the LFMC must be protected by overcurrent devices rated NOT more than _____ in order for the LFMC to be an approved type of equipment grounding conductor.

A. 30 amperes
B. 20 amperes
C. 60 amperes
D. 80 amperes

15. A general-use, 125-volt, 15-ampere rated receptacle located in a hallway of a dwelling unit is required to be _____.

A. listed tamper-resistant
B. on a dedicated circuit
C. replaced with a 20-ampere rated receptacle
D. provided with GFCI protection

16. Type NM cable is permitted for use under all the following conditions or locations EXCEPT:

A. as a feeder.
B. in Type V construction.
C. in a wet or damp location.
D. in a multifamily dwelling unit.

17. According to the NEC®, which MINIMUM enclosure type letter would be required where the installation is a motor controller located outdoors, in an area that is subject to heavy rain and snow?

A. Type 1
B. Type 3
C. Type 4
D. Type 6

18. Given: A commercial building provided with a 208Y/120-volt, 3-phase, electrical system has a calculated demand load of 72,200 VA; the ungrounded service entrance conductors must have an ampacity of at LEAST _____.

A. 200 amperes
B. 350 amperes
C. 300 amperes
D. 250 amperes

19. As per the NEC, the definition of a motor controller is _____.

A. a device to open the circuit automatically on a predetermined overcurrent
B. an interconnected combination of equipment that provides a means of adjusting the motor speed
C. a device which allows circuit conductors to be disconnected from their source of supply
D. a device to stop or start a motor by making or breaking the current

20. What is the MINIMUM of 20-ampere, 120-volt, general lighting branch circuits required for a dwelling unit having a lighting load of 9,600 VA?

A. three
B. five
C. four
D. two

21. Where a sub-panel is fed with CU Type NM cable and the circuit is protected by a 60 ampere overcurrent protective device, in compliance with the NEC®, the equipment grounding conductor should be at LEAST size _____.

A. 12 AWG
B. 10 AWG
C. 8 AWG
D. 6 AWG

22. A service disconnect may be installed in all of the following locations, EXCEPT _____.

A. outdoors
B. an exit foyer
C. a bathroom
D. a transformer vault

23. Where a sign in a public parking lot is fed with 200 ampere, 120/240-volt, single phase, service conductors installed in a rigid metal conduit (RMC), what is the MINIMUM required burial depth of the conduit?

A. 24 inches
B. 12 inches
C. 18 inches
D. 30 inches

24. Where all of the multiconductor cables are smaller than 4/0 AWG, the sum of the cross-sectional areas of all cables shall NOT exceed _____ when installed in a 9 inch wide ladder-type cable tray.

A. 7.0 sq. in.
B. 10.5 sq. in.
C. 14.0 sq. in.
D. 21.0 sq. in.

25. Conduit bodies enclosing size 6 AWG or smaller conductors shall have a cross-sectional area NOT less than _____ than the cross-sectional area of the largest conduit or tubing to which they are attached.

A. 1.25 times larger
B. 1.50 times larger
C. 1.75 times larger
D. 2.00 times larger

END OF EXAM #7

MASTER ELECTRICIAN'S EXAM PREP GUIDE
EXAM #8

The following questions are based on the 2014 edition of the National Electrical Code® and are typical of questions encountered on most Master Electricians' Licensing Exams. On each question select the best answer from the choices given and review your answers with the answer key included in this book. Typically, the only material permitted for use on this type of exam is a calculator, scratch paper and a current edition of the NEC® book. Each question on this test has a value of 4 points; passing score is 70% therefore, in order to pass you need to get 18 of the 25 questions correct.

ALLOTTED TIME: 75 minutes

1. An acceptable color for conductors intended for use as ungrounded conductors is _____.

A. white
B. gray
C. green
D. orange

2. A metal underground water pipe is permitted for use as a grounding electrode where the water pipe is in direct contact with the earth for at LEAST _____ or more.

A. 3 feet
B. 6 feet
C. 8 feet
D. 10 feet

3. For lighting systems operating at 30 volts or less, the output circuits of the power supply are to be rated for NOT more than _____.

A. 20 amperes
B. 25 amperes
C. 30 amperes
D. 15 amperes

4. Where a 12-kW portable generator is used for temporary wiring on a construction site, which of the following listed single-phase, 125-volt receptacle outlets are mandated to provide ground-fault circuit-interrupter protection for personnel?

A. All 20- and 30-ampere rated receptacles.
B. Only one 20-ampere rated receptacle.
C. Two 20-ampere rated receptacles.
D. Only one 30-ampere rated receptacle.

5. An unintentional, electrically conducting connection between an ungrounded conductor of an electrical circuit and the normally non-current-carrying conductors, metallic enclosures, metallic raceways, metallic equipment or earth is referred to as a _____ in the NEC®.

A. grounded conductor
B. short
C. ground-fault
D. bonding jumper

6. Where GFCI protection is not provided, ceiling-suspended (paddle) fans are NOT permitted to be located _____.

A. in a kitchen
B. in a garage
C. under an open porch
D. over a spa or hot tub, less than 12 ft. above the maximum water level

7. Which of the following underground installed buried metal pipes is approved for use as a grounding electrode?

I. A water pipe, in direct contact with the earth for 8 ft.
II. A gas pipe, in direct contact with the earth for 30 ft.

A. I only
B. II only
C. both I and II
D. neither I nor II

8. For an overhead type motor fuel dispensing device located at a service station or a convenience store, the space within the dispenser enclosure shall be classified as a _____ location.

A. Class I, Division 2
B. Class I, Division 1
C. Class 2, Division 2
D. Class 2, Division 1

9. Disregarding exceptions, and assume the modification of the value you select is not necessary, determine the MAXIMUM trip setting permitted for the overload devices used to protect a 3-phase, 10 hp, 208-volt, continuous-duty motor with a FLA of 28 amperes and a temperature rise of 46°C marked on the motor nameplate.

A. 30.8 amperes
B. 38.5 amperes
C. 35.0 amperes
D. 32.2 amperes

10. The neutral conductor is ALWAYS:

A. Connected to the neutral point of an electrical system.
B. A grounding conductor.
C. A bonding conductor.
D. An ungrounded conductor.

11. The overcurrent protection for feeders and branch circuits that serve electric vehicle supply equipment, shall be sized at NOT less than _____ of the maximum load of the electric vehicle supply equipment.

A. 115%
B. 150%
C. 125%
D. 175%

12. Stationary ac motors require the _____ where installed in a Class I, Zone 2 atmosphere that is considered a hazardous or classified location.

A. motor disconnecting means shall be within 5 feet of the motor
B. frame of the motor shall be grounded
C. the wiring method to consist of rigid metal conduit (RMC)
D. motor disconnecting means to be unfused

13. Given: A rigid metal conduit (RMC) originates in an area that is unclassified, then passes through a Class I, Division 1 area, and finally terminates in a panelboard located in an unclassified area. The RMC is without any connections or fittings when passing through the Class I, Division 1 area or within a foot on either size of the boundary of the Class I, Division1 location. How many seal-off fittings are required in this conduit run?

A. none
B. one
C. two
D. three

14. Given: A 3-phase, 240-volt delta system is balanced with a 15 kVA load per phase (45,000 VA total load). What is the line current in amperes?

A. 249.3 amperes
B. 144.3 amperes
C. 120.4 amperes
D. 108.2 amperes

15. Where switches or circuit breakers are used as the main disconnecting means for a building service, they shall be installed such that the center of the grip of the operating handle of the switch or circuit breaker, when in its highest position, is NOT more than _____ above the floor or working platform.

A. 6 feet
B. 7 feet
C. 6 feet, 6 inches
D. 6 feet, 7 inches

16. The service equipment for a mobile home shall have an ampere rating of NOT less than _____ at 120/240-volts, single-phase.

A. 200 amperes
B. 60 amperes
C. 100 amperes
D. 150 amperes

17. Which of the following is NOT a requirement for an intersystem bonding termination?

A. It is provided with not less than three terminals.
B. It shall be connected to the meter enclosure only, with a minimum size 8 AWG conductor.
C. The terminals shall be listed for grounding and bonding.
D. The terminals shall be accessible for connection and inspection.

18. For 120-volt, 15- and 20-ampere branch circuits, the rating of any one (1) cord-and-plug connected utilization equipment not fastened in place shall NOT exceed _____ of the branch circuit ampere rating.

A. 80 percent
B. 70 percent
C. 60 percent
D. 50 percent

19. The National Electrical Code® requires ventilation of a battery room where batteries are being charged to prevent _____.
A. battery corrosion
B. electrostatic charge
C. deterioration of the building steel
D. an accumulation of an explosive mixture

20. Where a building has a service rated at 1,200 amperes and multiple driven ground rods are used as part of the grounding electrode system, what is the MINIMUM size copper conductor that may be used to bond the ground rods together?

A. 8 AWG
B. 6 AWG
C. 4 AWG
D. 2 AWG

21. All 15- and 20-ampere, 125 and 250-volt, nonlocking receptacles located in a wet location shall be listed _____ type.

A. weather proof
B. waterproof
C. weather-resistant
D. water-resistant

22. Where liquidtight flexible metal conduit (LFMC) is used to connect equipment where flexibility is necessary to minimize the transmission of vibration from equipment or to provide flexibility for equipment that requires movement after installation _____.

A. an equipment grounding conductor is not needed
B. an equipment grounding conductor should be installed outside the flexible metal conduit
C. the raceway must be used as the equipment grounding conductor.
D. an equipment grounding conductor shall be installed

23. Luminaires shall be installed so that adjacent combustible material is not subjected to temperatures in excess of _____.

A. 60°C
B. 75°C
C. 90°C
D. 110°C

24. A household gas furnace with a one (1) hp motor protected with a circuit breaker accessible to the user, does NOT require a disconnecting means if _____.

A. provided with a limit switch
B. provided with GFCI protection
C. the circuit breaker is rated for 20 amperes or less
D. located on the same floor level with the circuit breaker

25. In switchboards and panelboards, a 3-pole circuit breaker or fusible switch shall be considered _____.

A. as an independent circuit
B. as 3 overcurrent protection devices
C. a bi-directional breaker
D. a back-fed overcurrent device

END OF EXAM #8

MASTER ELECTRICIAN'S EXAM PREP GUIDE
EXAM #9

The following questions are based on the 2014 edition of the National Electrical Code® and are typical of questions encountered on most Master Electricians' Licensing Exams. On each question select the best answer from the choices given and review your answers with the answer key included in this book. Typically, the only material permitted for use on this type of exam is a calculator, scratch paper and a current edition of the NEC® book. Each question on this test has a value of 4 points; passing score is 70% therefore, in order to pass you need to get 18 of the 25 questions correct.

ALLOTTED TIME: 75 minutes

1. When calculating the service entrance conductors for a farm service, the second largest load of the total load, shall be computed at _____.

A. 90 percent
B. 80 percent
C. 75 percent
D. 65 percent

2. When used in a non-power limited fire alarm circuit (NPLFA), what is the MAXIMUM size overcurrent protective device that may be used for a size 18 AWG conductor?

A. 7 amperes
B. 10 amperes
C. 15 amperes
D. 8 amperes

3. Installation of information technology equipment remote disconnecting controls shall NOT be required for critical operations data systems when several conditions are in place including _____.

A. an emergency fire detection system
B. an approved fire suppression system suitable for the application
C. an engineer has given approval
D. when the equipment is installed in a room with a 3 hour fire rating

4. What is the term used for electrical equipment or materials to which a symbol has been attached, or other identifying mark of an organization that is acceptable to the authority having jurisdiction?

A. labeled
B. listed
C. rated
D. approved

5. Rooms or areas of dwelling units shall be protected by a listed arc-fault circuit interrupter (AFCI), combination type, installed to provide protection of the _____.

A. service
B. panelboard
C. feeder circuit
D. entire branch circuit

6. All receptacles located within at LEAST _____ of a therapeutic tub shall be provided with GFCI protection.

A. 10 feet
B. 5 feet
C. 6 feet
D. 15 feet

7. When applying the general method of calculations for a dwelling unit having four (4) or more fastened in place appliances, other than electric ranges, dryers, space heating equipment, or air-conditioning equipment, it shall be permissible to apply a demand factor of _____ when sizing the service conductors.

A. 50 percent
B. 60 percent
C. 75 percent
D. 65 percent

8. Branch circuits that supply electric signs shall be considered ____ loads for the purposes of calculations.

A. continuous
B. non-continuous
C. full-current
D. intermittent

9. Additional services shall be permitted for a single building or other structure sufficiently large to make two (2) or more services necessary if permitted by _____.

A. the registered design professional
B. qualified personnel
C. the engineer of record
D. special permission

10. Which of the following statements are true for transformers serving electric discharge lighting having a rating of more than 1,000 volts?

A. The transformers are not required to be accessible.
B. The transformers should be installed as near to the lamps as practicable.
C. The secondary voltage shall be a maximum of 16,000 volts.
D. The maximum secondary current rating shall not exceed 120 mil amperes.

11. Assuming the use of THWN copper conductors and terminations rated for 75°C, determine the MINIMUM feeder conductor size when given the following related information:

- 120-volt, single-phase system
- one (1) 30 ampere continuous load
- one (1) 5 ampere non-continuous load

A. 4 AWG
B. 8 AWG
C. 6 AWG
D. 10 AWG

12. As a general rule, all conductors of a multiwire branch circuit shall originate from the same panelboard, simultaneously disconnect all ungrounded conductors and supply only line-to- _____ loads.

A. neutral
B. ground
C. line
D. hot

13. In general, for newly installed grounded systems, where branch circuits or feeders supply separate buildings or structures, equipment grounding conductors are _____.

A. required
B. not required
C. required only on 3-phase systems
D. not required if a ground rod is installed

14. Given: An underground run of PVC conduit with size 4 AWG conductors is the wiring method used to supply an air-conditioning unit that is protected by an overcurrent protective device rated 60 amperes. What is the MINIMUM size copper equipment grounding conductor that must be installed in the PVC?

A. 10 AWG
B. 12 AWG
C. 6 AWG
D. 8 AWG

15. The service disconnecting means for each electrical service shall consist of NOT more than _____ switches or circuit breakers.

A. one
B. two
C. three
D. six

16. Utilization equipment weighing not more than 6 pounds is permitted to be supported to any box or plaster ring secured to a box, provided the equipment or its supporting yoke is secured with at LEAST two (2) _____ or larger screws.

A. No. 10
B. No. 8
C. No. 6
D. No. 12

17. Listed overcurrent protection devices for solar PV source circuits must be _____.

A. readily accessible
B. accessible
C. non-accessible to unqualified personnel
D. identified by orange in color

18. In general, for household electric ranges with a rating of 8¾ kW or more, the MINIMUM branch-circuit rating shall be _____.

A. 30 amperes
B. 40 amperes
C. 50 amperes
D. 45 amperes

19. Each doorway leading into a transformer vault from the building interior shall be provided with a tight-fitting door that has a minimum fire rating of three (3) hours. However, if the transformer vault is protected with an automatic sprinkler system, the construction rating of _____ shall be permitted.

A. 2 hours
B. 2½ hours
C. 1 hour
D. 1½ hours

20. Where a 240-volt, single-phase, 5 kW storage-type water heater is located in the basement of a dwelling, and the load-center panelboard is located outdoors, a disconnect in the basement for the water heater is _____.

A. required
B. not required
C. not permitted
D. permitted but not required

21. What is the MAXIMUM ampere rating permitted for a 125-volt, single-phase, receptacle outlet having a cord-and-plug connected motor load that does not have individual overload protection?

A. 20 amperes
B. 30 amperes
C. 25 amperes
D. 15 amperes

22. After all demand factors have been taken into consideration and calculations completed, a one family dwelling with a 120/240-volt, single-phase electrical system has a demand load of 35,000 VA. The MINIMUM size THWN copper ungrounded (line) conductors required for an underground installed service lateral is _____.

A. 1 AWG
B. 1/0 AWG
C. 2/0 AWG
D. 3/0 AWG

23. Which of the following shall be permitted in the dedicated electrical space above a switchboard or panelboard?

A. air-conditioning ducts
B. sprinkler protection
C. leak protection
D. water piping

24. Which of the following 3-phase systems would be allowed to be a high-impedance grounded neutral system where a resistor limits the ground-fault current to a low value?

A. 230-volts
B. 208Y/120-volts
C. 480-volts
D. 480Y/277-volts

25. Boxes shall be closed by suitable covers securely fastened in place. An underground metal box cover that weighs over _____ shall be considered meeting this requirement.

A. 75 pounds
B. 80 pounds
C. 90 pounds
D. 100 pounds

END OF EXAM #9

MASTER ELECTRICIAN'S EXAM PREP GUIDE
EXAM #10

The following questions are based on the 2014 edition of the National Electrical Code® and are typical of questions encountered on most Master Electricians' Licensing Exams. On each question select the best answer from the choices given and review your answers with the answer key included in this book. Typically, the only material permitted for use on this type of exam is a calculator, scratch paper and a current edition of the NEC® book. Each question on this test has a value of 4 points; passing score is 70% therefore, in order to pass you need to get 18 of the 25 questions correct.

ALLOTTED TIME: 75 minutes

1. At carnivals and fairs, service equipment shall not be installed in a location that is accessible to unqualified persons, UNLESS the equipment _____.

A. has a voltage to ground of not more than 125 volts
B. is provided with GFCI protection
C. is lockable
D. is installed at a height of more than 6 feet

2. Where the NEC® specifies that one equipment shall be "within sight from" or "within sight of" another equipment, the specified equipment is to be visible and NOT more than _____ from the other.

A. 50 feet
B. 100 feet
C. 125 feet
D. 200 feet

3. As a general rule, where a cable is installed parallel to framing members, the cable shall be installed so that the nearest edge of the cable is NOT less than _____ from the nearest edge of the framing member.

A. ¾ in.
B. 1 in.
C. 1¼ in.
D. 1½ in.

4. Generally, how many grounded conductors are permitted to be terminated under an individual terminal within a switchboard or panelboard where the equipment operates at less than 1,000 volts?

A. four
B. three
C. two
D. one

5. The service equipment provided for a mobile home shall be located in sight from and NOT more than _____ from the exterior wall of the mobile home it serves.

A. 50 feet
B. 30 feet
C. 75 feet
D. 100 feet

6. In regard to power sources for Class 2 and Class 3 circuits, a dry cell battery shall be considered an inherently limited Class 2 power source, provided the voltage is _____ or less and the capacity is equal to or less than that available from series connected No. 6 carbon zinc cells.

A. 30 volts
B. 24 volts
C. 12 volts
D. 18 volts

7. Where electrical boxes are installed in a wall having a combustible finish and located above a kitchen countertop they shall be installed _____.

A. recessed ¼ in.
B. recessed a minimum of ½ in.
C. projected out not less than ¼ in. from the finish surface
D. flush or projected from the finish surface

8. A single-phase, 125-volt, 15- or 20-ampere receptacle outlet shall be installed at each residential kitchen, breakfast room, or dining room countertop space that is at LEAST _____ or wider.

A. 12 inches
B. 24 inches
C. 36 inches
D. 20 inches

9. A one-family dwelling unit is to have the following fastened in place appliances installed:

   1,200 VA dishwasher
   4,000 VA water heater
   1,150 VA garbage disposer
     700 VA attic fan
   1,920 VA garage door opener

   The demand load, in VA, on the ungrounded (line) service entrance conductors for the listed appliances is _____ when applying the general method of calculations for dwelling units.

   A. 7,728 VA
   B. 6,728 VA
   C. 6,276 VA
   D. 8,970 VA

10. Nonmetallic cable trays shall be made of _____ material.

    A. fire-resistant
    B. waterproof
    C. fire-proof
    D. flame-retardant

11. Switches are to be located a horizontal distance of at LEAST _____ from the inside walls of an indoor placed spa or hot tub.

    A. 4 feet
    B. 5 feet
    C. 8 feet
    D. 10 feet

12. Direct buried cables installed under an open field vacant property must have a MINIMUM cover depth of _____ when the applied voltage is not more than 600 volts.

    A. 24 inches
    B. 18 inches
    C. 12 inches
    D. 30 inches

13. Shore power for boats docked in marinas and boatyards shall be provided by single receptacles that are of the locking- and grounding-type, mounted at least 12 inches above the deck surface, and rated NOT less than _____.

A. 50 amperes
B. 40 amperes
C. 30 amperes
D. 20 amperes

14. For electrical systems over 1000 volts, where pulls of conductors in junction boxes are being made, the length of the box shall NOT be less than _____ the outside diameter of the largest shielded or lead-covered conductor or cable entering the box.

A. 8 times
B. 12 times
C. 32 times
D. 48 times

15. Each grounding electrode plate of bare or conductively coated iron or steel material shall expose NOT less than _____ sq. ft. of surface to exterior soil.

A. 1
B. 1½
C. 2
D. 3

16. Installation of direct buried cables in an area that is subject to movement by frost or settlement of the soil shall be _____.

A. prohibited
B. of copper conductors only
C. placed with "S" loops or provide an adequate allowance for movement
D. placed on running boards of pressure-treated wood or of nonmetallic material

17. Busways shall be securely supported at intervals NOT exceeding _____ unless the raceway is otherwise designed and marked.

A. 6 feet
B. 8 feet
C. 4 feet
D. 5 feet

18. At LEAST _____ of free conductor, measured from the point in the box where it emerges from its raceway, shall be left at each junction box or device box for splices or connections to devices.

A. 4 inches
B. 6 inches
C. 8 inches
D. 12 inches

19. Where fixed wiring above bulk storage tanks is installed in PVC conduit, the PVC shall be _____.

A. Schedule 20
B. Schedule 40
C. Schedule 80
D. Schedule 100

20. Electrical installations which are controlled by lock(s) or other approved means, shall be considered to be accessible to _____.

A. personnel with a key
B. qualified persons only
C. personnel with authority
D. building inspectors and first responders

21. The size of an equipment grounding conductor is most dependent upon _____.

A. line voltage
B. conductor resistance
C. line inductance
D. available fault-current

22. The NEC® mandates expansion fittings for rigid PVC conduit shall be provided to compensate for thermal expansion. In an environment where the normal annual change in temperature is 100°F, and the length of the PVC is 100 feet, how much allowance for thermal expansion must be considered?

A. 4.06 inches
B. 6.08 inches
C. 3.04 inches
D. 8.11 inches

23. Where an enclosure housing a motor controller is located outdoors and subjected to exposure to heavy rain, sleet and snow, the enclosure must be listed as a _____ enclosure.

A. Type 1
B. Type 3
C. Type 4
D. Type 6

24. The MINIMUM clearance between luminaires installed in clothes closets and the nearest point of a closet storage space shall be _____ where surface-mounted incandescent or LED luminaires are installed.

A. 24 inches
B. 18 inches
C. 12 inches
D. 6 inches

25. For other than one- and two-family dwellings, at least one (1) 125-volt, single-phase, 15- or 20-ampere rated receptacle outlet shall be installed NOT more than _____ from the electrical service equipment.

A. 6 feet
B. 10 feet
C. 20 feet
D. 50 feet

END OF EXAM #10

MASTER ELECTRICIAN'S EXAM PREP GUIDE
EXAM #11

The following questions are based on the 2014 edition of the National Electrical Code® and are typical of questions encountered on most Master Electricians' Licensing Exams. On each question select the best answer from the choices given and review your answers with the answer key included in this book. Typically, the only material permitted for use on this type of exam is a calculator, scratch paper and a current edition of the NEC® book. Each question on this test has a value of 4 points; passing score is 70% therefore, in order to pass you need to get 18 of the 25 questions correct.

ALLOTTED TIME: 75 minutes

1. PVC conduit shall be securely fastened within _____ of each outlet, junction device, conduit body, or other conduit termination box.

A. 3 feet
B. 4 feet
C. 5 feet
D. 6 feet

2. A hazardous location where easily ignitible fibers or materials producing combustible flyings are handled, manufactured, or used, but where they are not likely to be in suspension in the air in quantities sufficient to produce ignitible mixtures is recognized as a _____ location in the NEC®.

A. Class I
B. Class II
C. Class III
D. Class IV

3. A copper-clad steel rod type grounding electrode shall be at LEAST _____ in diameter.

A. 3/8 in.
B. 1/2 in.
C. 5/8 in.
D. 3/4 in.

4. Given: A single-phase, 120/240-volt service of a single-family dwelling has a chain-link metal fence opposite exposed live parts of the service equipment. The required depth of the working space in front of the service equipment must be at LEAST _____.

A. 2 ft. 6 in.
B. 3 ft.
C. 3 ft. 6 in.
D. 4 ft.

5. Tap conductors for a recessed luminaire shall be in a suitable raceway or Type AC or MC cable having a length NOT to exceed _____.

A. 4 feet
B. 6 feet
C. 5 feet
D. 8 feet

6. Where exposed Type NM cable passes through a floor, the cable shall be protected from physical damage by an approved means extending at LEAST _____ above the floor.

A. 10 inches
B. 8 inches
C. 12 inches
D. 6 inches

7. When used as a direct buried feeder cable, which of the following wiring methods is permitted for use to supply a water well pump located 50 feet from a dwelling?

A. Type NM cable
B. Type AC cable
C. Type TC cable
D. Type UF cable

8. The supply to a portable switchboard on a stage shall be by means of listed extra-hard usage cords or cables. Single-conductor portable supply cable sets used for this purpose shall NOT be smaller than _____.

A. 2 AWG
B. 4 AWG
C. 6 AWG
D. 8 AWG

9. The MINIMUM clearance for overhead feeder conductors, less than 1,000 volts, that pass above commercial areas subject to truck traffic is _____.

A. 10 feet
B. 12 feet
C. 15 feet
D. 18 feet

10. The lead wire of a 208-volt electric space heating units shall be identified by _____ in color.

A. blue
B. yellow
C. orange
D. brown

11. Where the heating, air-conditioning or refrigeration equipment is installed on the roof of a commercial, industrial, or an apartment building, a single-phase, 125-volt, 15- or 20-ampere rated receptacle outlet ____.

A. is required to be located within 100 ft. from the equipment
B. may be connected to the line side of the equipment disconnecting means, provided the receptacle is equipped with GFCI protection
C. shall be located on the same level and within 25 ft. of the equipment
D. is permitted to be connected to the load side of the equipment disconnecting means, if within 10 ft. of the equipment and GFCI protected.

12. Given: An existing 150 kVA transformer with a 208Y/120-volt, 3-phase, secondary has a full-load current of 220 amperes per phase. What approximate additional single-phase load, per phase, may be added to the secondary side of the transformer?

A. 180 amperes
B. 196 amperes
C. 416 amperes
D. 334 amperes

13. The conductors in multiconductor portable cables, of over 600 volts nominal, used to connect mobile equipment and machinery, shall be at LEAST size _____ copper or larger and employ flexible stranding.

A. 14 AWG
B. 12 AWG
C. 10 AWG
D. 8 AWG

14. In metal raceways or enclosures, all conductors of feeders using a common neutral shall be enclosed within the same raceway or enclosure, with a MAXIMUM of _____ sets of 3-wire feeders permitted to utilize a common neutral.

A. two
B. three
C. four
D. five

15. Where a flat cable assembly, Type FC, is installed LESS than _____ above the floor level or fixed working platform, it shall be protected by a cover identified for the use.

A. 6 feet
B. 7 feet
C. 8 feet
D. 10 feet

16. On a 4-wire, 3-phase, wye circuit where more than _____ of the load consists of nonlinear loads such a fluorescent lighting, there are harmonic current present in the neutral conductor and the neutral conductor shall be considered to be a current-carrying conductor.

A. 50 percent
B. 30 percent
C. 25 percent
D. 10 percent

17. Where direct-buried conductors emerge from below grade and extend up a pole, the conductors must be protected by raceways up to a height of 8 feet above finished grade and in no case shall protection be required to exceed _____ below finished grade.

A. 18 inches
B. 12 inches
C. 24 inches
D. 36 inches

18. Given: After all demand factors have been taken into consideration, a small office building with a single-phase, 120/240-volt electrical system has a demand load of 35,000 watts. The MINIMUM size copper conductors with THW insulation required for the ungrounded (line) service entrance conductors is _____.

A. 3 AWG
B. 1/0 AWG
C. 2/0 AWG
D. 3/0 AWG

19. According to the NEC®, the ampacity of a conductor is the current, in amperes, that the conductor can carry continuously under the conditions of use without exceeding its _____.

A. voltage rating
B. power rating
C. temperature rating
D. insulation rating

20. Where a building or structure is supplied by more than one (1) service from the local utility company:

A. a fire pump shall be installed.
B. a permanent plaque shall be installed at each service disconnect location denoting all other services.
C. an optional standby system shall be installed.
D. all of the above shall be installed.

21. In Class I, Division 1 locations, all threaded conduit and fittings referred as National Standard Pipe Taper (NPT) thread that are entries into explosionproof equipment shall be made up with at LEAST _____ fully engaged threads.

A. five
B. three
C. four
D. six

22. Where the service entrance conductors for a commercial building or an industrial facility are size 350 kcmil aluminum with XHHW insulation, what MINIMUM size copper grounding electrode conductor is required?

A. 6 AWG
B. 4 AWG
C. 2 AWG
D. 1 AWG

23. Where a wall-mounted central vacuum system is cord-and-plug connected to a single-phase, 125-volt, 20-ampere receptacle located in an attached garage of a residence, the receptacle shall be provided with _____ protection.

A. only AFCI
B. only GFCI
C. both AFCI and GFCI
D. only LCDI

24. Underground installed PVC conduit shall not be permitted under a swimming pool or within _____ horizontally from the inside wall of the pool unless the PVC is supplying equipment associated with the pool.

A. 10 feet
B. 8 feet
C. 6 feet
D. 5 feet

25. Where a galvanized rigid metal conduit (RMC) is used as a driven or buried grounding electrode, it shall be a MINIMUM trade size _____ and not less than 8 ft. in length.

A. ½ in.
B. 1 in.
C. 1¼ in.
D. ¾ in.

END OF EXAM #11

MASTER ELECTRICIAN'S EXAM PREP GUIDE
EXAM #12

The following questions are based on the 2014 edition of the National Electrical Code® and are typical of questions encountered on most Master Electricians' Licensing Exams. On each question select the best answer from the choices given and review your answers with the answer key included in this book. Typically, the only material permitted for use on this type of exam is a calculator, scratch paper and a current edition of the NEC® book. Each question on this test has a value of 4 points; passing score is 70% therefore, in order to pass you need to get 18 of the 25 questions correct.

ALLOTTED TIME: 75 minutes

1. All of the following wiring methods are permitted to be present in a ceiling space used as a return-air plenum EXCEPT _____.

A. Type AC cable
B. PVC conduit
C. IMC conduit
D. Type MI cable

2. Cabinets housing overcurrent protective devices shall NOT be located _____.

A. over uneven surfaces
B. over stairway landings
C. over steps of a stairway
D. under a mezzanine

3. For the purpose of determining conductor fill in a device box, a three-way switch is counted as equal to _____ conductor(s), based on the largest conductor connected to the switch.

A. one
B. two
C. three
D. four

4. A transformer vault is required to be provided with a door sill or curb with a height of NOT less than _____.

A. 6 inches
B. 8 inches
C. 2 inches
D. 4 inches

5. Single-phase, 125-volt, 15- and 20-ampere receptacle outlets installed in floors of dwelling units shall not be counted as part of the required number of receptacle outlets, if they are located more than _____ from the wall.

A. 18 inches
B. 12 inches
C. 30 inches
D. 24 inches

6. Where practicable, overhead CATV coaxial cables attached to a building shall be separated from lightning conductors by at LEAST _____.

A. 2 feet
B. 4 feet
C. 6 feet
D. 5 feet

7. Grounding conductors and bonding jumpers shall NOT be connected by _____.

A. exothermic welding
B. pressure connectors
C. machine screw-type fasteners
D. sheet metal screws

8. Determine the MAXIMUM standard size time-delay fuses permitted for branch-circuit, short-circuit and ground-fault protection for a 50 hp, 3-phase, 460-volt, induction-type motor with a FLA rating of 61 amperes marked on the nameplate.

A. 100 amperes
B. 110 amperes
C. 115 amperes
D. 125 amperes

9. Each commercial occupancy accessible to pedestrians shall be provided with at least one sign outlet supplied by a branch circuit rated at LEAST _____.

A. 15 amperes
B. 20 amperes
C. 30 amperes
D. 40 amperes

10. The MAXIMUM number of size 14 AWG TW conductors permitted in a trade size 3/8 in. flexible metal conduit (FMC) without fittings inside the FMC is _____.

A. five
B. two
C. three
D. four

11. Class 1 power-limited conductors of MINIMUM size _____ shall be permitted to be used, provided they supply loads that do not exceed the ampacities give in 402.5 and are installed in a raceway, an approved enclosure, or a listed cable.

A. 18 AWG
B. 22 AWG
C. 28 AWG
D. 16 AWG

12. Luminaires mounted in the walls of a permanently installed swimming pool, shall be installed with the top of the luminaire lens NOT less than _____ below the normal water level of the pool, unless the luminaire is listed and identified for use at lesser depths.

A. 12 inches
B. 18 inches
C. 20 inches
D. 24 inches

13. A point on a wiring system at which current is taken to supply fixtures, receptacles, lamps, luminaires, heaters, motors and other utilization equipment is considered _____.

A. an outlet
B. a supply
C. a junction
D. a termination

14. A ground ring consisting of a size 2 AWG bare copper conductor encircling the building or structure is permitted for use as a grounding electrode however, the conductor must have a length of 20 feet or more and be buried below the earth's surface at a depth of NOT less than _____.

A. 24 inches
B. 18 inches
C. 36 inches
D. 30 inches

15. Apply the optional method of calculations for dwelling units and determine the demand load, in kW, on the ungrounded (line) service entrance conductors where an eight (8) unit multifamily condo has an 8 kW electric range in each unit.

A. 27.52 kW
B. 28.80 kW
C. 32.00 kW
D. 26.88 kW

16. In the patient bed location of a health care facility, each patient bed location shall be supplied by at least two (2) branch circuits, and the branch circuits ___.

A. should be provided with AFCI protection
B. shall not be part of a multiwire branch circuit
C. must have isolated equipment grounded conductors
D. shall supply only single receptacle outlets

17. Which of the following statements regarding vertically-installed circuit breakers, if any, are TRUE?

I. The breakers shall be closed (ON) when in the up position.
II. The breakers shall clearly indicate when they are ON or OFF.

A. I only
B. II only
C. both I and II
D. neither I nor II

18. Extreme _____ may cause PVC conduit to become brittle, and therefore more susceptible to damage from physical contact.

A. sunlight
B. corrosive conditions
C. heat
D. cold

19. According to the NEC®, if used to connect to equipment where flexibility is necessary after installation, trade size ¾ in. flexible metal conduit (FMC) will require additional support if the FMC exceeds _____ from the last point where the FMC is securely fastened.

A. 5 feet
B. 4 feet
C. 3 feet
D. 2 feet

20. In an aircraft storage hangar, the area that extends upward from the floor to a level _____ above the surface of aircraft wings, power plants and fuel tanks shall be classified as a Class I, Division 2 or Zone 2 location.

A. 5 feet
B. 6 feet
C. 8 feet
D. 10 feet

21. In residential outdoor areas where permanently installed swimming pools are located, suspended paddle fans installed above the pool or the area extending 5 feet horizontally from the inside walls of the pool, shall be installed at a height of NOT less than _____ above the maximum water level of the swimming pool.

A. 10 feet
B. 12 feet
C. 15 feet
D. 8 feet

22. For conductors of more than 1000 volts, multiconductor or multiplexed single-conductor cables having individual shielded conductors, the MINIMUM bending radius is _____ times the diameter of the individually shielded conductors or 7 times the overall diameter, whichever is greater.

A. 10
B. 15
C. 16
D. 12

23. Where equipment grounding conductors are installed in parallel in multiple metallic raceway, they shall be sized in accordance with _____ of the NEC®.

A. Table 250.66
B. Table 250.122
C. Table 310.15(B)(16)
D. Table 310.15 (B)(17)

24. Where chain-link metal fences are surrounding an electrical substation and located within a MINIMUM distance of _____ from the exposed electrical conductors or equipment, the fence shall be bonded to the grounding electrode system.

A. 20 feet
B. 25 feet
C. 16 feet
D. 22 feet

25. In the NEC®, an enclosure constructed so that moisture will not enter the enclosure under specified test conditions is referred to as _____.

A. weatherproof
B. watertight
C. water-repellant
D. water-resistant

END OF EXAM #12

MASTER ELECTRICIAN'S EXAM PREP GUIDE
FINAL EXAM #1

The following questions are based on the 2014 edition of the National Electrical Code® and are typical of questions encountered on most Master Electricians' Licensing Exams. Select the best answer from the choices given and review your answers with the answer key included in this book. Passing score on this exam is 75%. The exam consists of 100 questions valued at 1.0 point each, so you must answer 75 questions correct for a passing score. If you do not score at least 75%, try again and keep studying. GOOD LUCK.

ALLOTTED TIME: 5 hours

1. Given: After all demand factors have been taken into consideration for an office building, the demand load is determined to be 90,000 VA; the building has a 120/240-volt, single-phase electrical system. What MINIMUM size copper conductors with THHN/THWN insulation are required for the ungrounded service-lateral conductors?

A. 400 kcmil
B. 350 kcmil
C. 300 kcmil
D. 500 kcmil

2. Given: A commercial building is to be supplied from a transformer having a 480Y/277-volt, 3-phase primary and a 208Y/120-volt, 3-phase secondary. The secondary will have a balanced computed demand load of 416 amperes per phase. The transformer is required to have a MINIMUM kVA rating of _____.

A. 100 kVA
B. 150 kVA
C. 86 kVA
D. 200 kVA

3. Manhole covers shall be OVER _____ or otherwise require the use of tools to open.

A. 25 lbs.
B. 50 lbs.
C. 75 lbs.
D. 100 lbs.

4. The branch circuit conductors supplying one or more units of information technology equipment shall have an ampacity of NOT less than _____ of the connected load.

A. 80 percent
B. 100 percent
C. 115 percent
D. 125 percent

5. In regard to a 7½ hp, 480-volt, 3-phase ac motor with an 80 percent power factor and a full-load ampere rating of 19 amperes indicated on the nameplate, and a service factor of 1.15; when the initial setting of the overload device you have selected is not sufficient to carry the load, what is the MAXIMUM setting permitted for the overload protection?

A. 21.85 amperes
B. 23.75 amperes
C. 24.70 amperes
D. 26.60 amperes

6. Electrical services and feeders for recreational vehicle parks shall be calculated on the basis of NOT less than _____ per RV site equipped with both 20-ampere and 30-ampere supply facilities.

A. 9600 volt-amperes
B. 4800 volt-amperes
C. 3600 volt-amperes
D. 2400 volt-amperes

7. What MINIMUM voltage is required after 1½ hours to serve emergency lighting from a storage battery, when the normal source voltage of 120 volts is interrupted?

A. 60 volts
B. 90 volts
C. 105 volts
D. 120 volts

8. Determine the MAXIMUM ampere setting permitted for an overload protective device responsive to motor current, where used to protect a 20 hp, 240-volt, 3-phase, induction type ac motor with a temperature rise of 48 deg. C and a FLA of 54 amperes indicated on the nameplate.

A. 54.0 amperes
B. 70.2 amperes
C. 62.1 amperes
D. 75.6 amperes

9. In general, where a cable is installed parallel to framing members, the cable shall be installed so that the nearest edge of the cable is NOT less than _____ from the neatest edge of the framing member.

A. 3/4 in.
B. 1 in.
C. 1¼ in.
D. 1½ in.

10. Aluminum or steel cable trays shall be permitted to be used as equipment grounding conductors, provided _____ .

   I. the cable tray sections and fittings are identified as an equipment grounding conductor
   II. the cable tray sections and fittings are durably marked to show the cross-sectional area of the metal

A. I only
B. II only
C. neither I nor II
D. both I and II

11. When intermediate metal conduit (IMC) is threaded in the field, a standard cutting die with a _____ taper per ft. shall be used.

A. 3/8 in.
B. 1/2 in.
C. 3/4 in.
D. 1 in.

12. In regard to emergency systems, where internal combustion engines are used as the prime movers, they shall NOT be solely dependent on a public utility gas system for their fuel supply, unless _____ .

A. it is acceptable to the authority having jurisdiction
B. the gas system is listed and approved
C. the gas system and electrical utility are jointly owned and maintained
D. none of these apply

13. When a motor controller enclosure is installed outdoors and is subject to be exposed to sleet, it shall have a MINIMUM rating of _____, where the controller mechanism is required to be operable when ice covered.

A. Type 3
B. Type 3S
C. Type 3R
D. Type 3SX

14. Each operating room of a health care facility shall be provided with a MINIMUM of _____ hospital grade receptacles.

A. 12
B. 24
C. 36
D. 18

15. Ceiling-suspended luminaires (lighting fixtures) or paddle fans located _____ or more above the maximum water level of an indoor installed spa or hot tub shall NOT require GFCI protection.

A. 10 feet
B. 7½ feet
C. 8 feet
D. 12 feet

16. When flat conductor cable (FCC) is used for general-purpose branch circuits, the MAXIMUM rating of the circuits shall be _____ .

A. 20 amperes
B. 30 amperes
C. 15 amperes
D. 10 amperes

17. When sizing overcurrent protection for fire pump motors, the device(s) shall be selected or set to carry indefinitely the _____ of the motor.

A. starting current
B. full-load running current
C. locked-rotor current
D. full-load amperage as indicated on the nameplate

18. Under which, if any, of the following conditions is the neutral conductor to be counted as a current-carrying conductor?

  I. When it is only carrying the unbalanced current.
  II. When it is the neutral conductor of a 3-phase, wye-connected system that consist of nonlinear loads.

A. I only
B. II only
C. neither I nor II
D. both I and II

19. In general, all mechanical elements used to terminate a grounding electrode conductor or bonding jumper to a grounding electrode shall be accessible. Which of the following, if any, is/are an exception(s) to this rule?

  I. A connection to a concrete encased electrode.
  II. A compression connection to fire-proofed structural metal.

A. I only
B. II only
C. neither I nor II
D. both I and II

20. For other than listed low-voltage luminaires not requiring grounding, all electrical equipment within a fountain or within _____ of the inside wall of a fountain shall be grounded.

A. 5 feet
B. 6 feet
C. 8 feet
D. 10 feet

21. Fuses shall NOT be permitted to be connected in parallel where _____.

   I. they are factory assembled and listed as a unit
   II. they are installed by a technician on the jobsite

A. I only
B. II only
C. neither I nor II
D. both I and II

22. Each multiwire branch circuit shall be provided with a means that will _____ at the point where the branch circuit originates.

A. simultaneously disconnect all ungrounded conductors
B. not simultaneously disconnect all ungrounded conductors
C. simultaneously disconnect all grounded and ungrounded conductors
D. simultaneously disconnect all grounded, ungrounded and grounding conductors

23. When calculating the total load for a mobile home park before demand factors are taken into consideration, each individual mobile home lot shall be calculated at a MINIMMUM of _____.

A. 20,000 VA
B. 15,000 VA
C. 24,000 VA
D. 16,000 VA

24. A single electrode consisting of a ground rod, pipe, or plate that does not have a resistance to ground of 25 ohms or less, shall be supplemented by one (1) additional electrode. Which of the following listed is/are approved for this purpose?

A. a concrete-encased electrode
B. a ground ring
C. the metal frame of the building
D. all of these

25. What classified (hazardous) location(s), if any, does the NEC® permit flexible metal conduit (FMC) for connections to motors?

   I. Class I, Division 2
   II. Class II, Division 1

A. I only
B. II only
C. both I and II
D. Neither I nor II

26. At carnivals and fairs, service equipment shall not be installed in a location that is accessible to unqualified persons unless the equipment _____.

A. is lockable
B. is provided with GFCI protection
C. is installed at a height of 6 feet or greater
D. has a voltage to ground of not more than 125 volts

27. Nonmetallic surface extensions shall be permitted to be run in any direction from an existing outlet, but NOT within _____ of the floor level.

A. 1 foot
B. 1½ feet
C. 2 feet
D. 2 inches

28. The NEC® permits a building to have more than one service when:

   I. the load requirements of the building are at least in excess of 800 amperes.
   II. the building is separated by firewalls with a four-hour rating.

A. I only
B. II only
C. either I or II
D. neither I nor II

29. In the garage of a dwelling unit, a 125-volt, single-phase, 15 ampere, receptacle installed in the ceiling provided for the garage door opener must be _____ .

   I. a single receptacle
   II. GFCI protected for personnel

A. I only
B. II only
C. either I or II
D. neither I nor II

30. Underground installed service conductors that are not encased in concrete and buried 18 inches or more below grade level, shall have their location identified by a warning ribbon placed at LEAST _____ above the underground installation.

A. 6 inches
B. 8 inches
C. 12 inches
D. 18 inches

31. Outlets supplying permanently installed swimming pool pump motors from single-phase, 15- or 20-ampere, 120- or 240-volt branch circuits, shall be provided with GFCI protection _____ .

A. where installed outdoors
B. when cord-and-plug connected
C. when direct (hard-wired) connected
D. where any of the above conditions exist

32. The branch circuit conductors supplying a 240-volt, single-phase, 15 kW rated fixed electric space heater provided with a 10 ampere blower motor are required to have an ampacity of at LEAST _____ .

A. 63 amperes
B. 78 amperes
C. 91 amperes
D. 109 amperes

33. A commercial kitchen is to contain the following listed cooking related equipment:

* one - 14 kW range
* one - 5.0 kW water heater
* one - 0.75 kW mixer
* one - 2.5 kW dishwasher
* one - 2.0 kW booster heater
* one - 2.0 kW broiler

Determine the demand load, in kW, after applying the demand factors for the kitchen equipment.

A. 19.00 kW
B. 26.25 kW
C. 18.38 kW
D. 17.06 kW

34. When two (2) ground rods are used to form the entire grounding electrode system of a building, the grounding conductor that bonds the two rods together shall NOT be required to be larger than size _____ copper, regardless of the size of the service-entrance conductors.

A. 8 AWG
B. 6 AWG
C. 4 AWG
D. 2 AWG

35. A kitchen with a total demand load of 54,000 VA is to be added to an existing church. The electrical system is 208Y/120-volts, 3-phase. What MINIMUM size THWN copper feeder conductors are required for the kitchen addition?

A. 1 AWG
B. 1/0 AWG
C. 2/0 AWG
D. 3/0 AWG

36. A feeder at a school welding shop is to supply the following listed transformer arc welders all with a 50 percent duty cycle.

   * two (2) with 60 amperes rated primary current
   * two (2) with 50 amperes rated primary current
   * two (2) with 40 amperes rated primary current

The feeder is required to have an ampacity of at LEAST _____.

A. 213 amperes
B. 196 amperes
C. 182 amperes
D. 176 amperes

37. The National Electrical Code® requires ventilation of a battery room where batteries are being charged to prevent:

A. battery corrosion.
B. electrostatic charge.
C. deterioration of the building steel.
D. an accumulation of an explosive mixture.

38. What is the MAXIMUM balanced demand load, in VA, permitted to be connected to a new service of a commercial building, given the following conditions?

   I. The service is 208Y/120 volts, 3-phase, with a 600 ampere rated main circuit breaker.
   II. The maximum load must not exceed 80 percent of the ampere rating of the main circuit breaker.

A. 57,600 VA
B. 99,840 VA
C. 172,923 VA
D. 178,692 VA

39. Determine the MAXIMUM standard size overcurrent protection required for the primary and secondary side of a transformer, when primary and secondary overcurrent protection is to be provided, given the following related information.

* 150 kVA rating
* Primary - 480 volt, 3-phase, 3-wire
* Secondary - 208Y/120 volt, 3-phase, 4-wire

A. Primary - 500 amperes, Secondary - 500 amperes
B. Primary - 450 amperes, Secondary - 600 amperes
C. Primary - 500 amperes, Secondary - 450 amperes
D. Primary - 450 amperes, Secondary - 500 amperes

40. Openings around electrical penetrations of a wall of a designated information technology room are required to be _____ .

A. insulated
B. airtight
C. firestopped
D. sound proof

41. When buried raceways pass under a driveway, the MINIMUM cover requirements _____ .

A. decrease if installed in rigid metal conduit (RMC).
B. do not change in regard to wiring methods used.
C. shall be increased for direct burial cables.
D. can be increased, decreased, or remain the same, depending on the wiring method used.

42. For capacitors over 1000 volts, a means shall be provided to reduce the residual voltage to _____ after the capacitor is disconnected from the source of power.

A. 50 volts or less within 1 minute
B. 50 volts or less within 5 minutes
C. 24 volts or less within 5 minutes
D. 12 volts or less within 1 minute

43. Where used outside of a, building, aluminum or copper-clad aluminum grounding electrode conductors shall not be terminated WITHIN_____ of the earth.

A. 18 inches
B. 24 inches
C. 3 feet
D. 6 feet

44. Where installed for a commercial occupancy, determine the MINIMUM size THWN copper conductors required from the terminals of a 3-phase, 277/480-volt, 4-wire, 200 kW generator to the first distribution device(s) containing overcurrent protection. Assume the design and operation of the generator does NOT prevent overloading.

A. 250 kcmil
B. 300 kcmil
C. 400 kcmil
D. 500 kcmil

45. Enclosures containing circuit breakers, switches and motor controllers located in Class II, Division 2 locations, shall be _____ or otherwise identified for the location.

A. gastight
B. vapor-proof
C. dusttight
D. stainless steel

46. Information technology equipment is permitted to be connected to a branch circuit by flexible cord-and-attachment plug cap, if the cord does NOT exceed _____ in length.

A. 6 feet
B. 8 feet
C. 10 feet
D. 15 feet

47. Where required, conduit seals installed in Class I, Division 1 & 2 locations shall have the minimum thickness of the sealing compound not less than the trade size of the sealing fitting and, in no case less than _____.

A. 1/2 in.
B. 5/8 in.
C. 3/4 in.
D. 1 in.

48. Given: A one-family dwelling to be built will have 4,000 sq. ft. of livable space, a 600 sq. ft. garage, a 400 sq. ft. open porch, a 2,000 sq. ft. unfinished basement (adaptable for future use), three (3) small-appliance branch-circuits and a branch circuit for the laundry room. Determine the demand load, in VA, on the ungrounded service-entrance conductors for the
general lighting and receptacle loads using the standard method of calculation for a one-family dwelling.

A. 10,350 VA
B. 9,825 VA
C. 7,350 VA
D. 24,000 VA

49. Determine the MINIMUM size Type SOW flexible cord that may be used to supply a 30 hp, 3-phase, 480-volt, continuous-duty, ac motor from the motor controller to the motor terminations. Assume voltage-drop and elevated ambient temperature are not considerations.

A. 4 AWG
B. 6 AWG
C. 8 AWG
D. 10 AWG

50. Portable structures for fairs, carnivals and similar events shall not be located under or within a MINIMUM of _____ horizontally of conductors operating in excess of 600 volts.

A. 22½ feet
B. 15 feet
C. 10 feet
D. 12 feet

51. Flexible cord and cables shall be permitted to be attached to building surfaces _____.

A. under no circumstances
B. where concealed
C. where used as a substitute for the fixed wiring of a structure
D. where the length of the cord or cable from a busway plug-in device to a suitable tension "take-up" support device does not exceed 6 feet

52. In regard to outside branch circuits of overhead spans of open individual conductors for 1000 volts or less up to 50 feet in length, the NEC® mandates the conductors to be NOT less than _____ copper in size

A. 12 AWG
B. 10 AWG
C. 8 AWG
D. 6 AWG

53. The ampacity requirements for a disconnecting means of x-ray equipment shall be based on _____ of the input required for the momentary rating of the equipment, if greater than the long-term rating.

A. 125 percent
B. 115 percent
C. 80 percent
D. 50 percent

54. The MINIMUM spacing required between live bare metal parts in feeder circuits of 480-volt industrial control panels and bare metal parts of the enclosure is _____.

A. 1/2 in.
B. 3/4 in.
C. 1 in.
D. 1¼ in.

55. AFCI protection is required for all 15- and 20-ampere, 120-volt branch circuits supplying outlets located in _____ .

A. boat houses
B. recreational vehicles
C. all guest rooms and suites of hotels
D. guest rooms and guest suites of hotels that are provided with permanent provisions for cooking

56. All swimming pool electric water heaters shall have the heating elements subdivided into loads not exceeding 48 amperes and protected at NOT over _____ .

A. 45 amperes
B. 50 amperes
C. 55 amperes
D. 60 amperes

57. In regard to emergency and legally required standby systems, transfer switches shall be _____ and approved by the authority having jurisdiction.

A. manual
B. automatic
C. nonautomatic
D. red in color

58. Where Type SE service-entrance cable is used for interior wiring as a substitute for Type NM cable for branch circuits and feeders, where installed in thermal insulation, the ampacity shall be in accordance with the _____ conductor temperature rating.

A. 40°C
B. 60°C
C. 75°C
D. 90°C

59. Power distribution blocks shall be permitted in pull and junction boxes having a volume over _____ for connections of conductors where installed in boxes, provided the power distribution blocks do not have uninsulated live parts exposed within the box, whether or not the box cover is exposed.

A. 50 cu. in.
B. 75 cu. in.
C. 100 cu. in.
D. 1650 cu. in.

60. Where a receptacle outlet is removed from an underfloor raceway, the conductors supplying the outlet shall be _____ .

A. capped with an approved insulating material
B. taped off with red colored tape
C. marked and identified
D. removed from the raceway

61. What is the MINIMUM dimension required by the NEC® for a working space containing live parts on both sides of the equipment that will require examination and maintenance of the equipment when energized and operating at 480-volts between conductors?

A. 4 feet
B. 3 feet
C. 6 feet
D. 5 feet

62. Where a mobile home park has 25 mobile home lots calculated at 15,000 VA each, determine the MINIMUM required ampacity required for the ungrounded service-entrance conductors.

A. 400 amperes
B. 380 amperes
C. 820 amperes
D. 782 amperes

63. A 3-phase, 150 kVA transformer with a 208Y/120-volt secondary has an existing load of 212 amperes on each of the ungrounded phases. What is the MAXIMUM load, in amperes, that may be added to each of the ungrounded secondary phases?

A. 416 amperes
B. 180 amperes
C. 204 amperes
D. 250 amperes

64. In regard to an isolated grounding type receptacle, the reason the insulated isolated grounding conductor is not bonded to the outlet box is _____ .

A. for the reduction of electrical noise
B. to insure the circuit breaker will trip in the event of a ground-fault
C. to prevent the circuit breaker from tripping in the event of a ground-fault
D. for the reduction of voltage-drop

65. Where a central vacuum assembly is located in a storage closet adjacent to the laundry room of a dwelling, accessible non-current-carrying metal parts of the assembly likely to be energized shall be _____ .

A. isolated
B. insulated
C. GFCI protected
D. connected to an equipment grounding conductor

66. Type CMP communications cable of NOT more than _____ in length shall be permitted in ducts used for environmental air if they are directly associated with the air distribution system.

A. 8 feet
B. 6 feet
C. 4 feet
D. 2 feet

67. The disconnecting switch or circuit breaker for electric signs and outline lighting systems shall open all _____ conductors simultaneously on multi-wire branch circuits supplying the sign or outline lighting system.

A. grounded and ungrounded
B. grounded, ungrounded and grounding
C. grounding, ungrounded and bonding
D. ungrounded

68. In an industrial establishment, what is the MAXIMUM length of 200 ampere rated busway that may be tapped to a 600 ampere rated busway, without additional overcurrent protection?

A. 10 feet
B. 25 feet
C. 50 feet
D. 75 feet

69. Where constant wattage heating cables are installed in concrete floors, the cables shall NOT exceed _____ per linear foot per cable.

A. 30 watts
B. 54 watts
C. 16½ watts
D. 37 watts

70. In general, the NEC® does not mandate the maximum number of circuit breakers a panelboard may contain. An exception to this rule is _____, which is limited to no more than 42 overcurrent protection devices.

A. a delta-connected panelboard
B. a split-bus panelboard
C. a 3-phase panelboard
D. panelboards containing overcurrent protection devices rated only 30 amperes or less

71. When water reaches the height of the established electrical datum plane for an irrigation pond, the service equipment must _____.

A. be installed in a NEMA 6 enclosure
B. float
C. be installed in a NEMA 6P enclosure
D. disconnect

72. In health care facilities, essential electrical systems shall have a MINIMUM _____.

A. capacity of 200 gallons of fuel for the auxiliary generator
B. of two independent sources of power
C. of 1 hour back-up time
D. capacity of 150 kVA

73. Lampholders shall be constructed, installed, or equipped with shades or guards so that combustible material is not subjected to temperatures in EXCESS of _____.

A. 130 degrees F
B. 140 degrees F
C. 162 degrees F
D. 194 degrees F

74. Pendant conductors having a length of at LEAST _____ or more, shall be twisted together where not cabled in a listed assembly.

A. 3 feet
B. 4 feet
C. 5 feet
D. 6 feet

75. For nonshielded conductors of over 1000 volts, the conductors shall NOT be bent to a radius of less than _____ times the overall conductor material.

A. six
B. eight
C. ten
D. twelve

76. At least one structural member of a building or structure that is direct contact with the earth for at LEAST _____ or more, with or without concrete encasement shall be permitted to be used as a grounding electrode.

A. 20 feet
B. 8 feet
C. 10 feet
D. 6 feet

77. The circuit supplying an autotransformer-type dimmer installed in theaters and similar places shall NOT exceed _____ between conductors.

A. 480 volts
B. 277 volts
C. 250 volts
D. 150 volts

78. At least one 125-volt, single-phase 15- or 20-ampere rated receptacle outlet shall be installed within 18 inches of the top of a show window of a retail store for each _____ of show window area measured horizontally.

A. 8 linear ft.
B. 10 linear ft.
C. 12 linear ft.
D. 15 linear ft.

79. Each luminaire installed in Class III, Divisions 1 and 2 locations shall be clearly marked to show the maximum wattage of the lamps that shall be permitted without exceeding an exposed surface temperature of _____ under normal conditions of use.

A. 329° F
B. 165° F
C. 144° F
D. 125° F

80. Conductors supplying a continuous-rated, varying-duty motor shall have an ampacity of NOT less than _____ of the motor nameplate current rating.

A. 125 percent
B. 140 percent
C. 150 percent
D. 200 percent

81. Where located in Class I, Division 1 locations, transformers containing oil or a liquid that will burn shall be _____.

A. enclosed in a fence
B. installed in vaults only
C. identified for use in Class I locations
D. installed in a fire-resistant room

82. Receptacles or receptacle cover plates supplied from the essential electrical system in a hospital, shall be identified by _____ .

A. brown in color
B. white in color
C. distinctive color or marking
D. an orange triangle

83. What is the MAXIMUM standard size circuit breaker that may be used for overcurrent protection of size 4/0 AWG THWN copper conductors that are not serving a motor load?

A. 200 amperes
B. 225 amperes
C. 230 amperes
D. 250 amperes

84. A multiwire branch circuit supplying a motor fuel dispensing pump, shall be provided with a switch that will disconnect _____ .

A. only one ungrounded supply conductor
B. all of the ungrounded supply conductors only
C. only the neutral (grounded) conductor
D. the grounded conductor and all of the ungrounded supply conductors

85. The depth of the working space in front of a 120-volt, single-phase, fire alarm control panel (FACP) is required to be at LEAST _____.

A. 2½ feet
B. 3 feet
C. 3½ feet
D. 4 feet

86. Where an air conditioning unit is supplied with size 6 AWG CU conductors and protected by a 60 ampere circuit breaker, the MINIMUM size CU equipment grounding conductor permitted for this installation is _____.

A. 12 AWG
B. 10 AWG
C. 8 AWG
D. 6 AWG

87. Which of the following is NOT required to be marked on the nameplate of a transformer?

A. overcurrent protection
B. manufacturer
C. kVA rating
D. voltage

88. When combination surface nonmetallic raceways are used for both signaling and for power and lighting circuits, the different systems shall be _____.

A. prohibited
B. run in the same compartment
C. run in separate compartments
D. maintain a spacing of at least ½ in.

89. Where explosionproof equipment is provided with metric threaded entries, which of the following methods is approved to adapt the entries from metric threads to NPT threads?

A. Approved adapters from metric threads to NPT threads shall be used.
B. Tap the metric threaded entries to NPT threads.
C. Thread the conduit with metric threads.
D. All of these are approved methods.

90. An indoor located 100 kVA, dry-type transformer with a 4,160 volt primary is required to have a clearance of at LEAST _____ from combustible material.

A. 6 inches
B. 10 inches
C. 12 inches
D. 8 inches

91. A clearance of NOT less than _____ must be maintained from the maximum water level of a permanently installed swimming pool and messenger-supported *triplex* service-drop conductors of 0-750 volts.

A. 10 feet
B. 14½ feet
C. 19 feet
D. 22½ feet

92. Where an apartment complex has a calculated connected lighting load of 205.4 kVA, what is the DEMAND load, in kVA, on the ungrounded service-entrance conductors where applying the standard (general) method of calculation? Given: Each dwelling unit in the complex has cooking facilities provided.

A. 58.9 kVA
B. 60.2 kVA
C. 16.5 kVA
D. 65.3 kVA

93. What is the MINIMUM permitted sill height of a transformer vault doorway?

A. 2 inches
B. 4 inches
C. 6 inches
D. 8 inches

94. For the purpose of sizing branch circuits for fixed storage-type water heaters with a capacity of 120 gallons or less, the water heater shall be considered _____ .

A. a continuous load
B. an intermittent load
C. a noncontinuous load
D. a short-time load

95. When supplying a 36,000 VA, 240-volt, single-phase load in an area where the ambient temperature reaches 119º F, determine the MINIMUM size 75ºC rated copper conductors required to supply the load.

A. 1/0 AWG
B. 2/0 AWG
C. 3/0 AWG
D. 4/0 AWG

96. Color coding shall be permitted to identify intrinsically safe conductors where they are colored _____ and where no other conductors of the same color are used.

A. light blue
B. orange
C. yellow
D. purple

97. What is the MINIMUM bend radius of trade size 4 in. rigid metal conduit (RMC) where the bend is not made with a one-shot or full-shoe bender?

A. 16 inches
B. 18 inches
C. 24 inches
D. 30 inches

98. Where exceptions are not to be applied, determine the MINIMUM required length of a junction box that has a trade size 3½ in. conduit containing four (4) size 250 kcmil conductors, pulled through the box for a 90º angle pull.

A. 21 inches
B. 24 inches
C. 28 inches
D. 34 inches

99. An approved method of protection for equipment installed in Class I, Zone 0, hazardous locations is _____ .

A. purged and pressurized
B. encapsulation
C. powder filling
D. oil immersion

100. Cables operating at over 600 volts and those operating at 600 volts or less, are permitted to be installed in a common cable tray without a fixed barrier, where the cables operating at over 600 volts are _____ .

A. Type MI
B. Type AC
C. Type CT
D. Type MC

END OF FINAL EXAM #1

MASTER ELECTRICIAN'S EXAM PREP GUIDE
FINAL EXAM #2

The following questions are based on the 2014 edition of the National Electrical Code® and are typical of questions encountered on most Master Electricians' Licensing Exams. Select the best answer from the choices given and review your answers with the answer key included in this book. Passing score on this exam is 75%. The exam consists of 100 questions valued at 1.0 point each, so you must answer 75 questions correct for a passing score. If you do not score at least 75%, try again and keep studying. GOOD LUCK.

ALLOTTED TIME: 5 hours

1. For individual dwelling units with single-phase, 120/240-volt electrical systems of not over 400 amperes, the NEC® permits the service conductors to have an ampacity NOT less than _____ of the service rating.

A. 80%
B. 83%
C. 75%
D. 70%

2. Where multiple driven ground rods, driven pipes or buried plate grounding electrodes are installed to meet the rules set forth by the NEC®, the electrodes shall NOT be spaced less than _____ apart.

A. 6 feet
B. 8 feet
C. 4 feet
D. 5 feet

3. When an ac general-use snap switch is used as a controller for a single-phase, 2 hp, 240-volt, ac motor, the switch is required to have a rating of at LEAST_____.

A. 10 amperes
B. 15 amperes
C. 20 amperes
D. 30 amperes

4. Conductors shall be permitted to be tapped to feeder conductors without overcurrent protection at the tap where the length of the tap conductors does not exceed 25 feet. However, the tap conductors are to have an ampacity of NOT less than _____ of the ampacity of the feeder conductors to which they are tapped.

A. one-forth
B. one-half
C. three-quarters
D. one-third

5. For other than service conductors, to provide a reliable bonding connection, for circuits over _____ to ground, the electrical continuity of rigid metal conduit (RMC) or intermediate metal conduit (IMC) that enclose conductors shall be ensured with two locknuts, one inside and one outside of the enclosures.

A. 480 volts
C. 300 volts
D. 250 volts
D. 125 volts

6. Which of the following listed is NOT a requirement for an intersystem bonding termination?

A. Consist of not less than three (3) terminals.
B. Connected to the meter enclosure only with a minimum size 8 AWG conductor.
C. Terminals shall be listed for grounding and bonding.
D. Be accessible for connection and inspection.

7. Polyvinyl chloride conduit (PVC) larger than trade size _____ shall not be used.

A. 4 inch
B. 5 inch
C. 4½ inch
D. 6 inch

8. Where lighting track is installed in a continuous row, each individual section of NOT more than _____ in length, shall be securely supported.

A. two feet
B. four feet
C. six feet
D. five feet

9. Flat cable assemblies (Type FC) shall be permitted for use as:

A. feeder circuits.
B. branch circuits not exceeding 30 amperes.
C. branch circuits not exceeding 20 amperes.
D. feeder or branch circuits not to exceed 50 amperes.

10. Where a building or structure is supplied with a 3-phase, 480Y/277-volt electrical system, each disconnecting means rated at LEAST _____ or more shall be provided with ground-fault protection.

A. 800 amperes
B. 1,200 amperes
C. 1,000 amperes
D. 1,500 amperes

11. Exposed power-limited fire alarm (PLFA) circuit conductors shall be protected from physical damage up to _____ above the floor.

A. 6 feet
B. 8 feet
C. 10 feet
D. 7 feet

12. A fused disconnecting means for a 3-phase, 480-volt motor shall have an ampere rating of NOT less than _____ of the full-load current rating of the motor.

A. 115 percent
B. 125 percent
C. 150 percent
D. 175 percent

13. An optical fiber cable is a factory assembly or field assembly of one or more optical fibers having a/an _____ covering.

A. conductive
B. nonconductive
C. overall
D. metallic

14. Where multiple driven ground rod electrodes make up the entire grounding electrode system for a building or structure having a 480Y/277-volt, 1,200 ampere rated service, what is the MINIMUM size copper conductor required to bond the ground rods together?

A. 8 AWG
B. 6 AWG
C. 4 AWG
D. 1/0 AWG

15. Where conduits or other raceways enter floor-standing switchboards, panelboards or switchgear from the bottom, the conduits or raceways, including their end fittings, shall not rise more than _____ above the bottom of the enclosure.

A. 4 inches
B. 6 inches
C. 2 inches
D. 3 inches

16. For 120-volt, 15-and 20-ampere branch circuits, the rating of any one cord-and-plug connected utilization equipment not fastened in place, shall NOT exceed _____ of the rating of the branch circuit.

A. 80%
B. 50%
C. 25%
D. 75%

17. In motion picture studios, television studios and similar locations, each receptacle of dc plugging boxes shall be rated NOT less than how many amperes?

A. 15 amperes
B. 20 amperes
C. 25 amperes
D. 30 amperes

18. Where sizes 1/0 AWG through 4/0 AWG single conductor cables are installed in ladder type cable tray, the MAXIMUM allowable rung spacing for the ladder type cable tray shall be _____.

A. 6 inches
B. 9 inches
C. 10 inches
D. 12 inches

19. Type UF cable is NOT permitted to be used _____.

A. as a substitute for Type NM cable
B. in an attic space
C. as service-entrance conductors
D. as single conductor cables

20. When applying the general method of calculations for dwelling units, the permitted demand factor, in percent, on the feeder and service conductors for five (5) household clothes dryers is _____.

A. 85%
B. 75%
C. 70%
D. 60%

21. The MINIMUM height (headroom) of working spaces about service equipment, switchboards, switchgear, panelboards, motor control centers and similar equipment of 600-volts or less is _____ or the height of the equipment, whichever is greater.

A. 72 inches
B. 78 inches
C. 84 inches
D. 96 inches

22. As per the NEC®, plate grounding electrodes shall be installed NOT less than _____ below the surface of the earth.

A. 12 inches
B. 18 inches
C. 24 inches
D. 30 inches

23. Size 14 AWG branch circuit tap conductors that serve individual outlets other than receptacles, are permitted to be tapped from 20-ampere rated branch circuit conductors when the _____.

A. load on the tap conductors is not more than 10 amperes
B. load on the size 14 AWG conductors is not more than 8 amperes
C. size 14 AWG conductor length is not more than 18 inches
D. conductor length is limited to 36 inches

24. The branch-circuit, short-circuit and ground-fault protection for a hermetic motor-compressor shall have a rating or setting NOT exceeding _____ of the motor-compressor rated-load current or branch-circuit selection, whichever is greater, where the protection specified is sufficient for the starting current of the motor and modifications are not necessary.

A. 150 percent
B. 175 percent
C. 125 percent
D. 225 percent

25. Where an electrical equipment room houses large equipment that contains overcurrent protective devices or switching devices, and the equipment is 600-volts or less, rated 1,200-amperes or more and over 6 feet wide, for the purposes of entering and exiting the working space, two (2) entrances are required, one at each end. The doors are required to be not less than 6½ ft. high and NOT less than _____ wide.

A. 2 ft.
B. 2½ ft.
C. 3 ft.
D. 3½ ft.

26. Given: A trade size Schedule 40 PVC conduit is run horizontally out of the side of a panelboard for 50 feet, then turns at a 90° angle vertically for 40 feet where it enters the building through a LB. How many expansion fittings are required for this installation?

A. one
B. two
C. three
D. four

27. As a general rule, luminaires and lampholders shall have no live parts exposed to contact, an exception to this rule is where cleat-type lampholders are located at LEAST _____ or more above the floor, they shall be permitted to have exposed terminals.

A. 12 feet
B. 10 feet
C. 7 feet
D. 8 feet

28. What MINIMUM size 75°C copper feeder conductors are required to supply the following listed 3-phase, 230-volt, continuous-duty, ac motors?

• one (1) 15 hp wound-rotor
• one (1) 7½ hp induction-type

A. 6 AWG THHN
B. 4 AWG THHN
C. 4 AWG THWN
D. 2 AWG THW

29. Wiring located above heated ceilings shall be spaced at not less than 2 inches above the heated ceiling and shall be considered as operating at an ambient temperature of _____.

A. 50°C
B. 86°F
C. 60°C
D. 75°C

30. In general, cables or raceways shall be permitted to be laid in notches of wood studs where the cable or raceway at those points is protected by a steel plate at LEAST _____ thick to cover the area of the wiring.

A. 1/16 in.
B. 1/8 in.
C. 1/4 in.
D. 3/8 in.

31. According to the National Electrical Code®, what would cause excessive objectionable current flow in the equipment grounding conductor when servicing an appliance branch circuit?

A. High load resistance.
B. Excessive resistance of the neutral conductor.
C. Excessive resistance of the grounding conductor.
D. Multiple connections between the neutral and grounding conductors.

32. Where conductors are installed in conduits 12 inches above a rooftop and exposed to direct sunlight, you are to apply an ambient temperature adder of _____ for the purposes of calculating the allowable ampacity of the conductors.

A. 25°F
B. 30°F
C. 40°F
D. 50°F

33. The NEC® recommended the MAXIMUM total voltage drop on both feeders and branch circuit conductors is _____.

A. 2%
B. 3%
C. 4%
D. 5%

34. For other than single-family dwellings, an emergency disconnect switch must be provided for spas and hot tubs NOT less than _____ away from the spa or hot tub and must be readily accessible to users.

A. 6 feet
B. 10 feet
C. 5 feet
D. 12 feet

35. When normal power is lost, legally required standby systems must be able to supply standby power in at LEAST _____ or less.

A. 60 seconds
B. 10 seconds
C. 30 seconds
D. 2 minutes

36. Where conduit or tubing nipples having a length not to exceed 24 inches are installed between boxes, cabinets and similar enclosures, the nipples shall be permitted to be filled not to exceed _____ of their total cross-sectional area.

A. 40%
B. 60%
C. 70%
D. 75%

37. Receptacles supplying power to freestanding-type office furnishings shall NOT be more than _____ from the furnishing that it is connected to it.

A. 6 feet
B. 3 feet
C. 1 foot
D. 8 feet

38. A type of fuse NOT permitted for new installations and shall be used only for replacements in existing installations is a/n _____ fuse.

A. Edison-base
B. Class K
B. Class CC
D. time-delay

39. Given: An equipment disconnecting means is mounted at a height of 6 feet on a remote wall in an aircraft storage and maintenance hangar. The disconnect switch is 10 feet away from any aircraft fuel tanks. The disconnect switch is located in a _____ area.

A. Class II, Division 1
B. Class I, Division 2
C. Class I, Division 1
D. unclassified

40. Given: A 120/240-volt, single-phase service has a metal chain link fence opposite exposed live parts of the service equipment. The required depth of clear working space in front of the service equipment must be at LEAST _____.

A. 2 ft. 6 in.
B. 3 ft.
C. 3 ft. 6 in.
D. 4 ft.

41. Remote disconnecting controls shall NOT be required for critical operations data systems when _____.

A. an approved fire suppression system suitable for the application is in place
B. wiring is under raised floors
C. a smoke detection system is in place
D. wiring is grouped and identified

42. Given: A retail jewelry store has two (2) large show windows having a length of 15 feet each. One show window is on each side of the entry door. How many single-phase, 125-volt, 15- or 20-ampere rated receptacles must be provided for the show window lighting?

A. one per window
B. two per window
C. three per window
D. four per window

43. All emergency systems switchboards and panelboards shall be provided with _____ protection.

A. AFCI
B. LCDI
C. GFCI
D. surge

44. What is the MINIMUM wire bending space required at the top and bottom of a panelboard that has one (1) size 3/0 AWG conductor connected to each busbar in the panelboard?

A. 6½ inches
B. 8 inches
C. 7½ inches
D. 6 inches

45. Given: A six (6) foot high chain-link fence topped with razor-wire, used to deter access by persons who are not qualified, encloses an outdoor installation of electrical apparatus rated 12 kV. The razor-wire shall be at LEAST_____ in height to comply with the NEC® standards.

A. 24 inches
B. 18 inches
C. 12 inches
D. 6 inches

46. When used as service entrance conductors, size 250 kcmil Type IGS cable has an allowable ampacity of _____.

A. 215 amperes
B. 225 amperes
C. 119 amperes
D. 205 amperes

47. Where a fused disconnect switch is used as the disconnecting means for an air-conditioning unit, the disconnect switch shall have an ampere rating of at LEAST _____ of the nameplate rated-load current of the equipment or branch-circuit selection current, whichever is greater.

A. 100%
B. 115%
C. 150%
D. 175%

48. Metal plugs or plates used to close unused openings in nonmetallic enclosures shall be recessed at LEAST _____ from the outer surface of the enclosure.

A. 1/2 in.
B. 1/8 in.
C. 1/16 in.
D. 1/4 in.

49. In the bedroom of a residence, any wall space having a width of _____ or more (including space measured around corners) and unbroken along the floor line by doorways or similar openings or fixed obstructions shall have a 125-volt, 15- or 20-ampere receptacle installed.

A. 6 feet
B. 10 feet
C. 4 feet
D. 2 feet

50. As a general rule, cables and conductors of Class 2 and Class 3 circuits shall NOT be placed in any _____ with the conductors of electric light and power circuit conductors unless, they are separated by a barrier.

A. device box
B. cable tray
C. manhole
D. device box, cable tray or manhole

51. Given: An induction-type, 3-phase, continuous-duty, ac motor has the following related information marked on the nameplate:
FLA -54 amperes
Temperature rise - 50°C
Your task is to select the MAXIMUM size overload devices, in amperes, that is responsive to motor to protect the motor from overload. Assume the value you select will allow the motor and start without tripping and modification of this value is not necessary.

A. 62.1 amperes
B. 67.5 amperes
C. 54.0 amperes
D. 75.6 amperes

52. The connection between the grounded circuit conductor and the equipment grounding conductor at the electrical service is recognized as the _____ in the NEC®.

A. main bonding jumper
B. grounding electrode conductor
C. equipment bonding jumper
D. neutral conductor

53. In guest rooms and guest suites of hotels and motels, at LEAST _____ 125-volt, single-phase, 15- or 20-ampere receptacle(s) is/are required to be readily accessible.

A. one
B. two
C. three
D. four

54. Where a 225-ampere rated panelboard is equipped with snap switches rated for 30-amperes or less, the MAXIMUM overcurrent protection permitted for the panelboard has a rating of _____.

A. 225 amperes
B. 180 amperes
C. 200 amperes
D. 250 amperes

55. Given: A 3-phase, 480-volt, squirrel-cage, Design B, 50 hp motor has a nameplate FLA rating of 59 amperes. The MAXIMUM initial standard size non-time delay fuses permitted for use as branch-circuit, short-circuit and ground-fault protective devices for the motor is _____.

A. 125 amperes
B. 180 amperes
C. 225 amperes
D. 200 amperes

56. As a general rule, all fixed metal parts such as metal piping, metal fences, and metal awnings in the proximity of a permanently installed swimming pool are required to be bonded. An exception to this rule is when the metal parts are located at a horizontal distance at least greater than _____ from the inside walls of the pool they shall not be required to be bonded to the equipotential bonding grid.

A. 6 feet
B. 10 feet
C. 5 feet
D. 12 feet

57. The rating of a cord-and-plug connected room air-conditioner unit shall NOT exceed _____ where the unit is connected to a single receptacle supplied by a 30-ampere dedicated branch circuit.

A. 24 amperes
B. 20 amperes
C. 30 amperes
D. 15 amperes

58. When exceptions are not a consideration, when attached to a building, final spans of outside overhead conductors, not over 1,000 volts, shall have a clearance of NOT less than ____ from windows designed to be opened, doors, porches balconies, stairs and fire escapes.

A. 2 feet
B. 3 feet
C. 4 feet
D. 5 feet

59. A trade size 1 in. listed liquidtight flexible metal conduit (LFMC) is approved for use as an equipment grounding conductor where the circuit conductors contained in the LFMC are protected by overcurrent devices rated NOT more than _____ amperes.

A. 20 amperes
B. 60 amperes
C. 30 amperes
D. 50 amperes

60. Legally required standby luminaires (unit equipment), provided for legally required standby illumination systems, are permitted to be cord-and-plug connected provided the flexible cord does NOT exceed _____ in length.

A. 18 inches
B. 2 feet
C. 3 feet
D. 4 feet

61. In regard to electrified track parking spaces, upon loss of the normal power from the local utility company or other electric supply systems, means shall be provided where energy _____.

A. cannot be fed through a TRU
B. can be fed with a two-wire cord
C. can be fed with an ungrounded receptacle
D. cannot be back-fed through the truck supply equipment

62. According to the NEC®, handholes in metal or nonmetallic poles supporting luminaires shall not be required for poles _____ or less in height above finished grade, if the pole is provided with a hinged base.

A. 5 feet
B. 10 feet
C. 15 feet
D. 20 feet

63. A junction box with a flat blank cover and no clamps will contain the following conductors:

- six – size 14 AWG THHN
- eight – size 12 THWN
- three – size 10 THW

The junction box is required to have a volume, in cubic inches, of _____.

A. 24.0 cubic inches
B. 29.5 cubic inches
C. 35.0 cubic inches
D. 37.5 cubic inches

64. A hazardous location where ignitible flammable gases, flammable vapors, or combustible liquid-produced vapors may be present in the air is a _____ location.

A. Class I
B. Class II
C. Class III
D. Class IV

65. Determine the MAXIMUM standard size overcurrent protection permitted for a 480-volt transformer having primary full-load current rating of 40 amperes where primary protection only is required.

A. 60 amperes
B. 50 amperes
C. 80 amperes
D. 100 amperes

66. All single-phase, 120-volt, 15- and 20-ampere branch circuits supplying outlets or devices installed in residential kitchens or similar rooms shall be protected by a listed arc-fault circuit-interrupter of the _____ type.

A. individual
B. series connected
C. combination
D. parallel

67. Outdoor installed spas and hot tubs are permitted to be cord-and-plug connected with a flexible cord NOT longer than _____ where protected by a ground-fault circuit interrupter.

A. 10 feet
B. 15 feet
C. 8 feet
D. 12 feet

68. Luminaires installed in fountains shall be protected by a ground-fault circuit interrupter and operate at a voltage NOT to exceed _____ between conductors.

A. 150 volts
B. 120 volts
C. 250 volts
D. 25 volts

69. Which of the following is NOT required to be marked on the nameplate of a motor?

A. manufacturer's name
B. full-load current
C. rated temperature rise
D. overcurrent protection

70. What MINIMUM size ungrounded (phase) THWN copper service entrance conductors are required for a 208Y/120-volt, 3-phase commercial service with a demand load of 72,000 VA?

A. 260 kcmil
B. 2/0 AWG
C. 3/0 AWG
D. 4/0 AWG

71. Refer to the previous question and determine the required trade size of rigid metal conduit (RMC) for use as a service riser to enclose the conductors.

A. 2 in.
B. 2½ in.
C. 1½ in.
D. 3 in.

72. The ampacity adjustment factors shown in Table 310.15(B)(3)(a), shall only be required to be applied to conductors in a metal wireway, where the number of current-carrying conductors exceeds _____ at any cross-section of the wireway.

A. 4
B. 20
C. 30
D. 25

73. Every panelboard circuit and circuit modification shall be:

A. marked before installing.
B. legibly identified at the panelboard to its use.
C. copper branch circuit conductors only.
D. a maximum of three (3) 2-pole, 30 ampere branch circuits.

74. Where a vertical raceway contains three (3) size 3/0 AWG copper conductors, the conductors shall be supported at intervals NOT greater than _____ with an additional support at the top of the conduit run.

A. 80 feet
B. 60 feet
C. 30 feet
D. 40 feet

75. In general, 4 in. wide underfloor raceways shall have a covering of wood or concrete NOT less than _____ above the raceway.

A. 1/2 in.
B. 3/4 in.
C. 1 in.
D. 1¼ in.

76. Branch circuit conductors within 3 inches of a ballast of a fluorescent or HID luminaire shall have an insulation temperature rating of NOT less than _____.

A. 90°F
B. 75°C
C. 110°C
D. 90°C

77. The service conductors between the terminals of the service equipment and a point usually outside the building, clear of building walls, where joined by splice or tap to the service drop or overhead service conductors, are recognized as _____.

A. service lateral conductors
B. service drop conductors
C. service entrance conductors
D. none of these

78. All 15- and 20-ampere, 125-volt and 250-volt nonlocking receptacles located in damp or wet locations shall be a listed _____ type.

A. weather-resistant
B. watertight
C. water-resistant
D. weatherproof

79. In the lubrication pit area of a commercial garage where ventilation is not provided, the pit below floor level shall be a _____ location that extends up to the floor level.

A. Class I, Division 1
B. Class I, Division 2
C. Class II, Division 1
D. Class II, Division 2

80. What is the MAXIMUM number of times a grounding electrode conductor is permitted to be spliced by the use of split-bolt connectors?

A. one
B. two
C. three
D. none

81. What is the general lighting demand load on the ungrounded (phase) conductors, in VA, of an industrial commercial (loft) building having dimensions of 100 ft. by 300 ft.

A. 60,000 VA
B. 75,000 VA
C. 90,000 VA
D. 105,000 VA

82. In health care facilities, a patient care vicinity shall be permitted to have an optional patient equipment grounding point. An equipment bonding jumper NOT small than _____ shall be used to connect the grounding terminal of all grounding-type receptacles to the patient equipment grounding point.

A. 14 AWG
B. 12 AWG
C. 10 AWG
D. 8 AWG

83. Given: Type UF cable is to be used for direct buried residential branch circuits of 120-volts. The conductors are GFCI protected and overcurrent protection is rated 20-amperes; the UF cable does not cross under any driveways or concrete. What is the MINIMUM required burial depth of the cable?

A. 6 inches
B. 18 inches
C. 24 inches
D. 12 inches

84. _____ is NOT permitted to be installed in theaters and similar locations unless it is encased in concrete.

A. Electrical metallic tubing (EMT)
B. Flexible metal conduit (FMC)
C. Schedule 40 PVC
D. Rigid metal conduit (RMC)

85. When a 240-volt, single-phase residential branch circuit using copper Type NM cable is used to supply an 8 kW rated counter-mounted cooking unit and a wall-mounted oven rated 6 kW, what MINIMUM size NM cable is required?

A. 6/3 AWG with ground
B. 8/3 AWG with ground
C. 4/3 AWG with ground
D. 10/3 AWG with ground

86. The entire area of an aircraft maintenance and storage hangar, including any adjacent and communicating areas not suitably cut off from the hangar, shall be classified as a Class I, Division 2 or Zone 2 location up to a level of _____ above the floor.

A. 18 inches
B. 24 inches
C. 12 inches
D. 30 inches

87. What is the MAXIMUM number of size 4 AWG THHN copper conductors permitted by the NEC® that may be installed in a trade size 1¼ in. electrical metallic tubing (EMT) 18 inch long nipple?

A. 10
B. 11
C. 12
D. 13

88. Luminaires installed over highly combustible material shall be of the _____ type and located 8 ft. above the floor or guarded.

A. totally enclosed
B. fire-retardant
C. incandescent
D. unswitched

89. Arc-fault circuit protection for 120-volt, single-phase, 15- and 20-ampere branch circuits supplying outlets and devices shall be provided for various areas and rooms in a dwelling. However, which one of the following areas of a dwelling does NOT require AFCI protection for the branch circuits?

A. closets
B. hallways
C. laundry area
D. bathrooms

90. When doing conduit fill calculations, for cables that have elliptical cross-sections, the cross-sectional area calculation shall be based on using the _____ diameter ellipse as a circular diameter.

A. major
B. minor
C. total
D. circular

91. Where circuit breakers are used as switches in 120-volt and 277-volt fluorescent lighting circuits they shall be listed and marked with _____ on the circuit breaker.

I. SWD
II. HID

A. I only
B. II only
C. either I or II
D. both I and II

92. Determine the MINIMUM number of 120-volt, 15-ampere general-lighting branch circuits required for a 15,000 sq. ft. multifamily dwelling unit.

A. 20
B. 25
C. 15
D. 30

93. Wiring located above heated ceilings shall be spaced at not less than 2 inches above the heated ceiling and shall be considered as operating at an ambient temperature of _____.

A. 50°C
B. 86°F
C. 60°C
D. 75°C

94. Unless approved for a higher voltage, surface nonmetallic raceways are NOT approved where the voltage is _____ or more between conductors.

A. 120 volts
B. 150 volts
C. 300 volts
D. 277 volts

95. At marinas and boatyards, the electrical datum plane, in land areas subject to tidal fluctuation, is a horizontal plane _____ above the highest high tide under normal circumstances.

A. 1 foot
B. 2 feet
C. 3 feet
D. 4 feet

96. Given: A feeder circuit using aluminum conductors is installed in PVC conduit and protected by a 500-ampere rated circuit breaker. What is the MINIMUM size aluminum conductor permitted for use as the equipment grounding conductor.

A. 3 AWG
B. 2 AWG
C. 2/0 AWG
D. 1/0 AWG

97. Bends in liquidtight flexible nonmetallic conduit (LFNC) shall be made so that the conduit will not be damaged and the internal diameter of the conduit will not be reduced. Bends can be made _____.

A. manually without auxiliary equipment
B. with conduit benders specifically identified for the purpose
C. full shoe benders only
D. one shot benders only

98. Where an information technology equipment room houses electronic computer/data processing equipment, the disconnecting means for the equipment shall be:

A. at readily accessible locations in case of fire.
B. locked and protected from unqualified personnel.
C. located as near as practicable to the main service disconnect.
D. not required if the equipment room is provided with a fire suppression system.

99. When size 500 kcmil copper conductors with THWN insulation are used as service entrance conductors, the MAXIMUM standard size circuit breaker permitted for use as overcurrent protection has a rating of ____.

A. 350 amperes
B. 400 amperes
C. 375 amperes
D. 300 amperes

100. The disconnecting means for transport refrigerated units (TRUs) located in electrified truck parking spaces of a truck plaza, shall be readily accessible and NOT more than _____ from the receptacle it controls.

A. 36 inches.
B. 24 inches
C. 30 inches
D. 48 inches

END OF FINAL EXAM #2

NOTES

MASTER ELECTRICIAN'S EXAM PREP GUIDE
PRACTICE EXAM #1
ANSWER KEY

ANSWER	REFERENCE	NEC PG. #
1. C	690.42,IN	pg. 633
2. B	110.31	pg. 42
3. B	820.15	pg. 730
4. C	430.109(C)(2)	pg. 344

15 amperes x 80% = 12 amperes

5. C	220.14(I)	pg. 69

120 volts x 20 amps = 2,400 VA (circuit)
2,400 VA (circuit) ÷ 180 VA (one receptacle) = 13 outlets

6. B	110.26(D)	pg. 41
7. A	240.24(B)(1)	pg. 101
8. B	Table 310.15(B)(16)	pg. 161
	Table 310.15(B)(2)(a)	pg. 158
	Table 310.15(B)(3)(a)	pg. 160

Size 250 kcmil THWN copper ampacity before derating = 255 amperes
255 amps x .82 (temp. correction) x .8 (adjustment factor) = 167.28 amperes

9. D	Table 430.72(B)	pg. 339
10. D	240.83(B)	pg. 103
11. C	210.8(A)(7)	pg. 54
	210.12(A)	pg. 56

12. C   310.15(B)(3)(c)   pg. 158
                  Table 310.15(B)(3)(c)   pg. 160
                  Table 310.15(B)(2)(a)   pg. 158
                  Table 310.15(B)(16)   pg. 161

   outdoor ambient temperature = 100 deg. F
   adder (3" above roof)   + 40 deg. F
                        TOTAL   140 deg. F (for derating)

   Size 8 AWG THWN ampacity (before derating) = 50 amperes
   50 amperes x .58 (temp. correction) = 29 amperes

13. D   Table 310.104(A)   pg. 175

14. A   645.15   pg. 587

15. B   Table 220.12   pg. 68

   12,000 sq. ft. x 3 VA = 36,000 VA (building)
   120 volts x 15 amps = 1,800 VA (1 circuit)

   $\dfrac{36{,}000 \text{ VA (building)}}{1{,}800 \text{ VA (1 circuit)}}$ = 20 circuits

16. C   700.12(A)   pg. 655

17. A   230.6(1)   pg. 84

18. B   513.3(B)   pg. 440

19. D   Chapter 9, Table 8   pg. 766
                  Voltage-drop formula

   VD = $\dfrac{2KID}{CM}$ VD = $\dfrac{2 \times 12.9 \times 90 \text{ amps} \times 225 \text{ ft.}}{52{,}620 \text{ CM}}$ = 9.92 volts dropped

20. D   525.32   pg. 495

21. D   551.73   pg. 524

22. C   511.12   pg. 440

23. B   Table 430.52, Note 1   pg. 335

24. C   Table 408.5   pg. 287

25. C   250.102(D)   pg. 124
                  250.122(C)   pg. 130
                  Table 250.122   pg. 131

###

MASTER ELECTRICIAN'S EXAM PREP GUIDE
PRACTICE EXAM #2
ANSWER KEY

ANSWER	REFERENCE	NEC PG.#
1. D	408.5	pg. 287
2. A	700.12(B)(2)	pg. 655
3. C	540.13	pg. 500
4. D	424.20(A)(3)	pg. 310
5. B	800.100(D)	pg. 715
6. D	314.28(A)(1)	pg. 190

    3 in. (largest conduit) x 8 = 24 inches

7. B	220.103	pg. 76
	Table 220.103	pg. 76
	Single-phase current formula	

    18,000 VA x 100% = 18,000 VA
    16,000 VA x 75% = 12,000 VA
    10,000 VA x 65% =   6,500 VA
        Demand = 36,500 VA ÷ 240 volts = 152 amperes

8. C	680.58	pg. 619
9. D	514.11(B)	pg. 448
10. A	312.6(B)(2)	pg. 181
	Table 312.6(B)	pg. 183

11. D   Table 430.250   pg. 351
                          430.22   pg. 329
                          Table 310.15(B)(2)(a)   pg. 158
                          Table 310.15(B)(16)   pg. 161

25 hp motor FLC = 74.8 amperes x 125% = 93.5 amperes
93.5 amps /.75 (temperature correction) = 124.6 amperes

*NOTE: The wire size needs to be increased because of the elevated ambient temperature. Size 1 AWG THWN conductors with an allowable ampacity of 130 amperes should be selected.

12. B   430.4, Exception   pg. 324

13. D   Table 310.104(A)   pg. 175

14. D   Table 220.55 & Note 1   pg. 72

19 kW − 12 kW = 7 kW x 5% = 35% increase in Column C
17 kW (4 appliances in Col. C) x 135% = 22.95 kW demand

15. B   700.21   pg. 657

16. C   690.31(C)(1)   pg. 630

17. B   551.71   pg. 524

18. D   517.19(C)(1)   pg. 467

19. B   3-Phase Current Formula
                          Table 450.3(B)   pg. 362
                          240.6(A)   pg. 96 & 97

$$I = \frac{kVA \times 1000}{208 \times 1.732} \quad\quad I = \frac{25 \times 1{,}000}{208 \times 1.732} = \frac{25{,}000}{360.25} = 69.3 \text{ amperes}$$

69.3 amperes x 125% = 86.62 amperes

*NOTE: You are permitted to go up to the next standard size OCP device which has a rating of 90 amperes.

20. B   250.122(F)   pg. 130

21. B   410.154   pg. 301

22. C	Table 430.250	pg. 351
	430.24(1)&(2)	pg. 330
	Table 310.15(B)(16)	pg. 161

40 hp FLC = 52 amps x 100% = 52 amperes
50 hp FLC = 65 amps x 100% = 65 amperes
60 hp FLC = 77 amps x 125% = <u>96 amperes</u>
         Total = 213 amperes

Size 4/0 AWG THWN conductors with an ampacity of 230 amperes should be selected.

23. C	517.35(A)	pg. 472

24. A	511.3(C)(2)(a)	pg. 438

25. C	Chapter 9, Table 8	pg. 766
	3-phase wire size formula

*NOTE: 3% of 480 volts = .03 x 480 = 14.4 (voltage drop permitted)

$$CM = \frac{1.732 \times K \times I \times D}{VD \text{ permitted}}$$

$$CM = \frac{1.732 \times 21.2 \times 100 \text{ amps} \times 390 \text{ ft.}}{14.4 \text{ volts}} = 99{,}446 \text{ CM}$$

Size 1/0 AWG conductors with a CMA of 105,600 should be selected.

##

MASTER ELECTRICIAN'S EXAM PREP GUIDE
PRACTICE EXAM #3
ANSWER KEY

ANSWER	REFERENCE	NEC PG.#
1. B	700.8	pg. 653
2. D	370.23	pg. 235
	240.4(B)(1),(2),&(3)	pg. 95
	240.6(A)	pg. 96 & 97
3. C	240.21(B)&(B)(2)(1)	pg. 98
4. A	Chapter 9, Table 5	pg. 763
	Chapter 9, Table 4	pg. 757

250 kcmil THWN – 0.3970 sq. in. x 1 = 0.3970 sq. in.
400 kcmil THWN – 0.5863 sq. in. x 3 = <u>1.7589 sq. in.</u>
Total = 2.1559 sq. in.

A trade size 3 in. FMC with a permitted fill area of 2.827 sq. in. @ 40% fill should be selected.

5. D	517.18(A)&(B)	pg. 466
6. B	250.24(C)(1)	pg. 111
	Table 250.102(C)(1)	pg. 124
7. C	210.19(A)(1)(a)	pg. 57
	210.11(A)	pg. 55

400 kVA x 1,000 = 400,000 VA
400,000 VA x 125% (continuous load) = 500,000 VA (bldg.)

120 volts x 20 amperes = 5,540 VA (one circuit)

<u>500,000 VA (bldg. lighting)</u> = 90.2 = 91 lighting circuits
     5,540 VA (one circuit)

*NOTE: Circuits need only to be installed to serve the connected load.

8. B	404.8(B)	pg. 279
9. C	300.4(E)	pg. 144
10. D	517.13(B), Exception 2	pg. 465

11. C   680.23(B)(2)(b)   pg. 610

12. B   445.13   pg. 360

13. B   502.10(A)(3)   pg. 402

14. B   Table 514.3(B)(1)   pg. 446

15. C   695.14(D)   pg. 651

16. C   Table 310.15(B)(16)   pg. 161
                      Table 310.15(B)(2)(a)   pg. 158
                      Table 310.15(B)(3)(a)   pg. 160

Size 750 kcmil AL ampacity (before derating) = 435 amperes
435 amps x 1.04 (temp. correction) x .8 (adjustment factor) = 361.92 amperes

17. B   424.66(B)(2)   pg. 313

18. C   324.10(A)   pg. 196

19. C   Single-Phase Current Formula
                      Table 310.15(B)(16)   pg. 161

I = P ÷ E   I = 23,600 VA ÷ 240 volts = 98.33 amperes

   Size 1 AWG AL USE cable with an ampacity of 100 amperes should
   be selected.

20. A   220.43(B)   pg. 70

21. D   Table 220.42   pg. 70

Total lighting equals 205,400 VA
1st. 3000 VA @ 100 %   = 3,000 VA
next 117,000 VA @ 35%   = 40,950 VA
remainder [205.4 kVA - 120 kVA] = 85,400 VA @ 25% = 21,350 VA
                                     Total demand = 65,300 VA

22. A   Chapter 9, Table 5   pg. 761 & 763
                      Chapter 9, Table 4   pg. 757

Size 10 AWG THHW = .0243 sq. in. x 24 = 0.5832 sq. in.
Size 10 AWG THHN = .0211 sq. in. x 10 = 0.2110 sq. in.
Size 12 AWG THHN = .0133 sq. in. x 14 = 0.1865 sq. in.
                              Total   = 0.9807 sq. in.

2 in. EMT with a 40% allowable fill of 1.342 sq. in. should be selected.

23. A Table 220.54 pg. 71
Single-phase current formula

Demand = 35% minus .5% for each dryer exceeding 23
40 dryers − 23 = 17 (exceeding 23) x .5% = 8.5%
35% - 8.5% = 26.5% demand

40 dryers x 6 kW = 240 kW x 26.5% (demand) = 63.6 kW
63.6 kW x 1000 = 63,600 watts

I = P ÷ E   I = 63,600 watts ÷ 240 volts = 265 amperes

24. D 440.22(A) pg. 355 & 356

25. D 220.14(H)(2) pg. 69
645.5(A) pg. 585
210.19(A)(1)(a) pg. 57

90 ft. x 180 VA per ft. x 125% = 20,250 VA (multioutlet assembly)

20 amps x 120 volts = 2,400 VA (one circuit)

$\dfrac{20{,}250 \text{ VA (total load)}}{2{,}400 \text{ VA (one circuit)}}$ = 8.43 = 9 circuits

##

MASTER ELECTRICIAN'S EXAM PREP GUIDE
PRACTICE EXAM #4
ANSWER KEY

ANSWER	REFERENCE	NEC PG.#
1. D	760.43	pg. 690
2. D	310.15(B)(3)(c), Exception	pg. 158
3. A	700.12	pg. 654
4. C	517.71(A), Exception	pg. 478
5. A	620.61(B)(1)	pg. 566
6. C	Table 300.50	pg. 154
7. C	551.71	pg. 524
8. A	430.6 & 6(A)(1)	pg. 324
	Table 430.250	pg. 351
	430.22	pg. 329
	Table 400.5(A)(1), Column A	pg. 269

FLC of motor = 52 amperes x 125% = 65 amperes
   Size 2 AWG SO cord with an ampacity of 80 amperes should be selected.

| 9. B | Table 430.250 | pg. 351 |

63 amperes x 1.1 (power factor) = 69.3 amperes

10. D	682.11	pg. 621
11. D	700.12(F)(3)	pg. 656
12. C	368.17(B), Exception	pg. 232
13. B	Table 310.15(B)(16)	pg. 161
	240.4(B)(3)	pg. 95
	240.6(A)	pg. 96 & 97

Size 4/0 AWG AL conductors rated @ 75 deg. C ampacity = 180 amperes
Next standard size OCP is rated at 200 amperes.
*NOTE: Sec. 240.4(F) requires secondary OCP on delta-wye transformers.

14. C   332.24(1)   pg. 202

15. C   322.10(3)   pg. 195

16. A   Table 300.5   pg. 145

17. A   430.6(A)(2)   pg. 324
                       430.32(A)(1)   pg. 332

   FLA of motor = 18 amps x 115% = 20.7 amperes

18. D   430.32(C)   pg. 333

   FLA of motor = 18 amps x 130% = 23.4 amperes

19. B   450.3(B)   pg. 361
                       Table 450.3(B)   pg. 362
                       240.6(A)   pg. 96 & 97

$$I = \frac{kVA \times 1{,}000}{E \times 1.732} = \frac{50 \times 1{,}000}{480 \times 1.732} = \frac{50{,}000\ VA}{831.36} = 60.2\ \text{amperes}$$

   60.2 amperes x 250% = 150.5 amperes

20. A   220.14(I)   pg. 69
                       220.44   pg. 70
                       Table 220.44   pg. 70

   150 receptacles x 180 VA = 27,000 VA
   1st. 10,000 VA @ 100%   = 10,000 VA
   (remainder) 17,000 VA @ 50%   = 8,500 VA
                       TOTAL DEMAND   = 18,500 VA

21. A   314.16(B)(4)   pg. 185
                       Table 314.16(A)   pg. 186

   [masonry box] 9 (Size 12 AWG conductors permitted per gang)
                 - 2 conductors (switch)
                   7 wires per box x 3 gang = 21 conductors

22. C   502.15(2)   pg. 403

23. D   800.25   pg. 710

24. D   680.32   pg. 615

25. C   450.13(B)   pg. 365
##

MASTER ELECTRICIAN'S EXAM PREP GUIDE
PRACTICE EXAM #5
ANSWER KEY

ANSWER	REFERENCE	NEC PG.#
1. A	502.130(A)(3)	pg. 405
2. B	680.74	pg. 620
3. C	760.130(B)(2)	pg. 692
4. C	410.10(F)	pg. 293
5. C	450.9	pg. 364 & 365
6. C	210.52(G)(1)	pg. 62
7. A	Table 680.8(A)	pg. 607
8. C	Table 310.15(B)(16)	pg. 161
	Table 310.15(B)(2)(a)	pg. 158
	Table 310.15(B)(3)(a)	pg. 160

$$\frac{200 \text{ amperes (load)}}{.75 \text{ (temp. cor.)} \times .8 \text{ (adj. factor)}} = \frac{200}{.6} = 333 \text{ amperes}$$

Size 400 kcmil conductors with an ampacity of 335 amperes should be selected from Table 310.15(B)(16).

9. C	314.16(B)(1)&(5)	pg. 185
	Table 314.16(B)	pg. 186

6 AWG ungrounded conductors	- 3 x 5.00 cu. in.	= 15.00 cu. in.
6 AWG grounded conductors	- 3 x 5.00 cu. in.	= 15.00 cu. in.
8 AWG grounding conductor	- 1 x 3.00 cu. in.	= 3.00 cu. in.
12 AWG ungrounded conductors	- 3 x 2.25 cu. in.	= 6.75 cu. in.
12 AWG grounded conductors	- 3 x 2.25 cu. in.	= 6.75 cu. in.
12 AWG grounding conductor	- 1 x -0- cu. in.	= -0- cu. in.
	TOTAL	= 46.50 cu. in.

10. B	680.21(A)(3)	pg. 608
11. B	518.4(A)	pg. 482
12. C	511.7(B)(1)(b)	pg. 439

13. C	430.6(A)(1)	pg. 324
	Table 430.250	pg. 351
	Table 430.52	pg. 335

FLC of 10 hp motor = 30.8 amperes x 250% = 77 amperes

14. C	450.42	pg. 367
15. C	626.31(C)	pg. 576
16. B	342.30(A)(2)	pg. 210
17. A	500.7(A)	pg. 387
18. D	690.31(D)	pg. 631
19. C	430.6(A)(1)	pg. 324
	Table 430.250	pg. 351
	430.52(C)(1),Exception2(c)	pg. 335
	240.6(A)	pg. 96 & 97

FLC of 50 hp motor = 65 amperes x 400% = 260 amperes

20. D	250.30(A)	pg. 112
21. A	517.32(H)	pg. 471
22. A	504.10(A)	pg. 411
23. B	250.24(C)(3)	pg. 111
24. A	3-phase Current Formula	

$$I = \frac{kVA \times 1{,}000}{E \times 1.732} = \frac{150 \times 1{,}000}{480 \times 1.732} = \frac{150{,}000}{831.36} = 180.32 \text{ amperes}$$

25. C	Table 300.5, Column 1	pg. 145

###

MASTER ELECTRICIAN'S EXAM PREP GUIDE
PRACTICE EXAM #6
ANSWER KEY

ANSWER	REFERENCE	NEC PG.#
1. C	250.64(E)(1) 250.106	pg. 120 pg. 126
2. B	320.108	pg. 195
3. D	501.125(A)(2)	pg. 398
4. B	504.80(C)	pg. 413
5. A	90.5(A)	pg. 24
6. C	280.3	pg. 139
7. A	Article 100 – Definitions	pg. 32
8. D	250.36(1)-(3)	pg. 116
9. A	440.22(A)	pgs. 355 & 356
10. D	513.3(A)	pg. 440
11. B	250.102(E)(2)	pg. 125
12. C	320.30(B)	pg. 194
13. B	Table 110.26(A)(1)	pg. 40
14. D	300.6(A)	pg. 146
15. C	348.30(A)	pg. 214
16. A	645.5(G)	pg. 586
17. B	310.15(B)(3)(A)	pg. 157
18. C	220.14(I)	pg. 69
19. C	300.5(D)(4)	pg. 146
20. D	Article 100 – Definitions	pg. 33
21. A	392.56	pg. 251
22. B	500.100(A)(1)	pg. 397

23. C   Table 310.15(B)(16)   pg. 161
               334.80   pg. 205

   The overcurrent protection is to be not less than the ampacity of the conductors.

24. B   Table 220.12   pg. 68
               Article 100 – Definitions   pg. 29
               230.42(A)(1)   pg. 87

   100 ft. x 300 ft. = 30,000 sq. ft. x 2 VA = 60,000 VA
   60,000 VA x 125% (continuous load) = 75,000 VA demand load

25. D   250.92(B)(1)-(4)   pg. 122

##

MASTER ELECTRICIAN'S EXAM PREP GUIDE
PRACTICE EXAM #7
ANSWER KEY

ANSWER	REFERENCE	NEC PG.#
1. A	250.24(C)	pg. 110
2. D	240.83(C)	pg. 103
3. A	422.16(B)(1)(2)	pg. 304
4. C	600.5(B)(2)	pg. 544
5. A	Table 344.30(B)(2)	pg. 212
6. D	210.52(C)(5)	pg. 62
7. D	Table 220.12 230.42(A)(1)	pg. 68 pg. 87

20 ft. x 30 ft. = 600 sq. ft. per office x 3.5 VA = 2,100 VA
2,100 VA x 4 offices = 8,400 VA x 125% (continuous load) = 10,500 VA demand

8. B	225.6(A)(1)	pg. 76
9. A	314.23(F), Ex. 2(b)-(e)	pg. 188
10. B	406.3(D)	pg. 281
11. B	550.10(A), Exception 1	pg. 505
12. D	378.22	pg. 239
13. D	430.103	pg. 343
14. C	250.118(6)(c)	pg. 128
15. A	406.12(A) 210.52	pg. 285 pg. 60
16. C	334.12(B)(4)	pg. 204
17. B	Table 110.28	pg. 43

18. A 3-phase current formula
I = VA ÷ E x 1.732

$$I = \frac{7{,}200 \text{ VA}}{208 \times 1.732} = \frac{7{,}200}{360} = 200 \text{ amperes}$$

19. D 430.2 pg. 323

20. C Trade knowledge

120 volts x 20 amperes = 2,400 VA (one circuit)

$$\frac{9{,}600 \text{ VA (load)}}{2{,}400 \text{ VA (ckt.)}} = 4 \text{ circuits}$$

21. B Table 250.122 pg. 131

22. C 230.70(A)(2) pg. 89

23. A Table 300.5, Column 2 pg. 145

24. B 392.22(A)(1)(b) pg. 249
Table 392.22(A), Column 1 pg. 250

25. D 314.16(C)(1) pg. 186

##

MASTER ELECTRICIAN'S EXAM PREP GUIDE
PRACTICE EXAM #8
ANSWER KEY

ANSWER	REFERENCE	NEC PG.#
1. D	200.6(A)&(B) 250.119 310.110(C)	pgs. 49 & 50 pg. 129 pg. 179
2. D	250.52(A)(1)	pg. 117
3. B	411.3	pg. 302
4. A	590.6(A)(3)	pg. 541
5. C	Article 100 –Definitions	pg. 30
6. D	680.43(B)(1)(a)	pg. 616
7. D	250.52(A)(1) 250.52(B)(1)	pg. 117 pg. 117
8. B	Table 514.3(B)(1)	pg. 445
9. D	430.32(A)(1)	pg. 332

Nameplate FLA rating – 28 amperes x 115% = 32.2 amperes

10. A	Article 100 – Definitions	pg. 32
11. C	625.40	pg. 569
12. B	430.242(3)	pg. 348
13. A	501.15(A),Ex.1	pg. 393
14. D	3-phase current formula I = P ÷ E x 1.732	

$$I = \frac{45{,}000 \text{ VA}}{240 \times 1.732} = \frac{45{,}000}{416} = 108.2 \text{ amperes}$$

15. D	240.24(A) 404.8(A)	pg. 100 pg. 279

16. C	550.32(C)	pg. 513
17. B	250.94(1)-(6)	pg. 123
18. A	210.23(A)(1)	pg. 59
19. D	480.9(A)	pg. 374
20. B	250.66(A)	pg. 120
21. C	406.9(A)	pg. 284
22. D	250.118(6)(e)	pg. 128
23. C	410.11	pg. 293
24. A	422.34	pg. 306
25. B	408.54	pg. 289

##

MASTER ELECTRICIAN'S EXAM PREP GUIDE
PRACTICE EXAM #9
ANSWER KEY

ANSWER	REFERENCE	NEC PG.#
1. C	Table 220.103	pg. 76
2. A	760.43	pg. 690
3. B	645.10(B)(4)	pg. 587
4. A	Article 100 – Definitions	pg. 31
5. D	210.12(A)(1)	pg. 56
6. C	680.62(E)	pg. 619
7. C	220.53	pg. 70
8. A	600.5(B)	pg. 543
9. D	230.2(B)(2)	pg. 84
10. B	410.144(B)	pg. 301
11. B	215.2(A)(1)(a) Table 310.15(B)(16)	pg. 64 pg. 161

    30 amp continuous load x 125%   = 37.5 amperes
    5 amp non-continuous load x 100% = <u>5.0 amperes</u>
                         Total load   = 42.5 amperes

    Size 8 AWG THWN conductors with an ampacity of 50 amperes should be selected from Table 310.15(B)(16).

12. A	210.4(C)	pg. 52
13. A	250.32(B)(1)	pg. 114
14. A	250.122(A) Table 250.122	pg. 130 pg. 131
15. D	230.71(A)	pg. 90
16. C	314.27(D),Ex.	pg. 190
17. B	690.9(D)	pg. 627

18. B	210.19(A)(3)	pg. 57
19. C	450.43(A),Ex.	pg. 367
20. A	422.31(B)	pg. 305
21. D	430.42(C)	pg. 334
22. A	Single-phase current formula I = P ÷ E	
	310.15(B)(7)(1)	pg. 160
	Table 310.15(B)(16)	pg. 161

$$I = \frac{36,000 \text{ VA}}{240 \text{ volts}} = 145.8 \text{ amperes} \times .83 = 121 \text{ amperes}$$

Size 1 AWG THWN CU conductors with an ampacity of 130 amperes should be selected from Table 310.15(B)(16).

23. B	110.26(E)(1)(a)&(c)	pg. 41
24. C	250.36	pg. 116
25. D	314.72(E)	pg. 193

##

MASTER ELECTRICIAN'S EXAM PREP GUIDE
PRACTICE EXAM #10
ANSWER KEY

ANSWER	REFERENCE	NEC PG.#
1. C	525.10(A)	pg. 494
2. A	Article 100 - Definitions	pg. 31
3. C	300.4(D)	pg. 144
4. D	408.41	pg. 289
5. B	550.32(A)	pg. 512
6. A	725.121(A)(5)	pg. 677
7. D	314.20	pg. 187
8. A	210.52(C)(1)	pg. 61
9. B	220.53	pg. 76

    1,200 VA dishwasher
    4,000 VA water heater
    1,150 VA garbage disposer
       700 VA attic fan
    <u>1,920 VA</u> garage door opener
    8,970 VA connected load x 75% (demand factor) = 6,728 VA demand load

10. D	392.100(F)	pg. 254
11. B	680.43(C)	pg. 616
12. A	Table 300.5, Column 1	pg. 145
13. C	555.19(A)(4)	pg. 539
14. D	314.71(A)	pg. 192
15. C	250.52(A)(7)	pg. 117
16. C	300.5(J),(IN.)	pg. 146
17. D	368.30	pg. 233

18. B	300.14	pg. 148
19. C	515.7(A)	pg. 448
20. B	110.31	pg. 42
21. D	250.4	pg. 108
22. A	Table 352.44	pg. 218
23. B	Table 110.28	pg. 43
24. C	410.16(C)(1)	pg. 293
25. D	210.64	pg. 63

##

MASTER ELECTRICIAN
PRACTICE EXAM #11
ANSWER KEY

ANSWER	REFERENCE	NEC PG.#
1. A	352.30(A)	pg. 217
2. C	500.5(D)	pg. 385
3. C	250.52(A)(5)(b)	pg. 117
4. B	Table 110.26(A)(1)	pg. 40
5. B	410.117(C)	pg. 298
6. D	334.15(B)	pg. 204
7. D	340.10(1)	pg. 208
	334.12(B)(4)	pg. 204
	340.12(2)	pg. 193
	336.12(4)	pg. 206
8. A	520.53(H)(2)	pg. 488
9. D	225.18(4)	pg. 78
10. A	424.35(2)	pg. 311
11. C	210.63	pg. 63
12. B	3-phase current formula	

$$I = \frac{power}{E \times 1.732} \quad I = \frac{150 \times 1000}{208 \times 1.732} = \frac{150,000}{360} = 416 \text{ amperes FLC}$$

416 amperes (available FLC) − 220 amperes (existing load) = 196 amperes

13. B	400.31(A)	pg. 273
14. B	215.4(A)	pg. 65
15. C	322.10(3)	pg. 195
16. A	310.15(B)(5)(c)	pg. 158

17. A   300.5(D)(1)   pg. 46

18. B   Single-phase current formula
                 I = P ÷ E
                 Table 310.15(B)(16)   pg. 161

$$I = \frac{35{,}000 \text{ VA}}{240 \text{ volts}} = 145.8 \text{ amperes}$$

Size 1/0 THW CU conductors with an ampacity of 150 amperes should be selected from Table 310.15(B)(16).

19. C   Article 100 – Definitions   pg. 27

20. B   230.2(E)   pg. 84

21. A   500.8(E)(1)   pg. 390

22. C   250.66   pg. 120
                 Table 250.66   pg. 121

23. B   210.8(A)(2)   pg. 54

24. D   680.10   pg. 607

25. D   250.52(A)(5)(a)   pg. 117

##

MASTER ELECTRICIAN'S EXAM PREP GUIDE
PRACTICE EXAM #12
ANSWER KEY

ANSWER	REFERENCE	NEC PG.#
1. B	300.22(C)(1)	pg. 152
2. C	240.24(F)	pg. 101
3. B	314.16(B)(4)	pg. 185
4. D	450.43(B)	pg. 367
5. A	210.52(A)(3)	pg. 60
6. C	820.44(E)(3)	pg. 731
7. D	250.8(A)	pg. 109
8. D	430.6(A)(1)	pg. 324
	Table 430.250	pg. 351
	Table 430.52	pg. 335
	430.52(C)(1), Exception 1	pg. 335
	240.6(A)	pg. 96

FLC of motor = 65 amperes x 175% = 113.75 amperes
The next standard size fuses with a rating of 125 amperes should be selected.

9. B	600.5(A)	pg. 543
10. D	Table 348.22	pg. 213

3 - #14 TW + 1 #14 TW equipment grounding conductor = 4 - #14 TW

11. A	725.49(A)	pg. 676
12. B	680.23(A)(5)	pg. 609
13. A	Article 100 – Definitions	pg. 32
14. D	250.53(F)	pg. 118

15. A	Table 220.84	pg. 74

8 kW x 8 units = 64 kW x 43% (demand factor) = 27.52 kW demand

16. B	517.18(A)	pg. 466
17. C	240.81	pgs. 102 & 103
18. D	352.10, IN.	pg. 216
19. C	348.30, Exception 2(1)	pg. 214
20. A	513.3(C)(1)	pg. 440
21. B	680.22(B)(1)	pg. 608
22. D	300.34	pg. 152
23. B	250.122(A)&(F)	pg. 130
24. C	250.194(A)	pg. 139
25. B	Article 100 – Definitions	pg. 35

##

MASTER ELECTRICIAN'S EXAM PREP GUIDE
FINAL EXAM #1
ANSWER KEY

ANSWER	REFERENCE	NEC PG.#

1. D   300.5(B)   pg. 144
              Table 310.104(A)   pg. 176
              Table 310.15(B)(16)   pg. 161
              Single-phase Current Formula

   I = P ÷ E   I = 90,000 VA ÷ 240 volts = 375 amperes

   Size 500 kcmil THHN/THWN conductors with an ampacity of 380 amperes should be selected from Table 310.15(B)(16).

2. B   3-phase Power Formula
              VA = I x E x 1.732

   VA = 416 amperes x 208 volts x 1.732 = 149,866 VA
   149,866 VA ÷ 1,000 = 149.8 kVA

3. D   110.75(D)   pg. 48

4. D   645.5(A)   pg. 585

5. D   430.6(A)(2)   pg. 324
              430.32(A)(1)   pg. 332
              430.32(C)   pg. 333

   19 amperes x 140% = 26.60 amperes

6. A   551.73(A)   pg. 524

7. C   700.12(A)   pg. 655

   120 volts x 87.5% = 105 volts

8. B   430.6(A)(2)   pg. 324
              430.32(C)   pg. 333

   54 amperes x 130% = 70.2 amperes

9. C	300.4(D)	pg. 144
10. D	392.60(B)(1)&(3)	pg. 252
11. C	342.28	pg. 210
12. A	700.12(B)(3), Exception	pg. 655
13. B	Table 110.28	pg. 43
14. C	517.19(C)(1)	pg. 467
15. D	680.43(B)(1)(a)	pg. 616
16. A	324.10(B)(2)	pg. 196
17. C	695.5(B)	pg. 648
18. B	310.15(B)(5)(a)&(c)	pg. 158
19. D	250.68(A), Exceptions 1&2	pg. 121
20. A	680.54(1)	pg. 618
21. B	240.8	pg. 97
22. A	210.4(B)	pg. 52
23. D	550.31(1)	pg. 512
24. D	250.53(A)(2) 250.52(A)(2)-(A)(8)	pg. 118 pg. 117
25. A	501.10(B)(2)(2) 502.10(A)(2)	pg. 392 pg. 402
26. A	525.10(A)	pg. 494
27. D	382.15(A)	pg. 241
28. D	230.2(A),(B),&(C)	pg. 84
29. B	210.8(A)(2)	pg. 54
30. C	300.5(D)(3)	pg. 146
31. D	680.21(C)	pg. 608

32. C   424.3(B)   pg. 308
                               210.19(A)(1)(a)   pg. 57
                               Single-Phase Current Formula

$$I = \frac{kW \times 1{,}000}{\text{volts}} \quad I = \frac{15 \times 1{,}000}{240} = \frac{15{,}000}{240} = 62.5 \text{ amperes (heater)}$$

       62.5 amperes (heater)
    +10.0 amperes (blower)
       72.5 amperes x 125% = 91 amperes

33. A   220.56   pg. 71
                               Table 220.56   pg. 71

    14.00 kW - range
     5.00 kW - water heater
     0.75 kW - mixer
     2.50 kW - dishwasher
     2.00 kW - booster heater
     2.00 kW - broiler
    26.25 kW - total connected load x 65% = 17.06 kW

*NOTE: However the NEC® states the demand shall not be less than the two largest pieces of equipment. 14.00 kW + 5.00 kW = 19 kW demand

34. B   250.66(A)   pg. 120

35. B   3-phase current formula
                               Table 310.15(B)(16)   pg. 161

$$I = \frac{54{,}000 \text{ VA}}{208 \times 1.732} = \frac{54{,}000}{360.25} = 149.89 \text{ amperes}$$

       Size 1/0 THWN conductors with an ampacity of 150 amperes should be selected from Table 310.15(B)(16).

36. D   Table 630.11(A)   pg. 577
                               630.11(B)   pg. 577

   60 amperes x .71 = 43 amperes x 100% = 43 amperes
   60 amperes x .71 = 43 amperes x 100% = 43 amperes
   50 amperes x .71 = 36 amperes x 85% = 31 amperes
   50 amperes x .71 = 36 amperes x 70% = 25 amperes
   40 amperes x .71 = 28 amperes x 60% = 17 amperes
   40 amperes x .71 = 28 amperes x 60% = 17 amperes
                                        TOTAL   = 176 amperes

37. D   480.9(A)   pg. 374

38. C   3-phase Power Formula
                              P = I x E x 1.732

P = 600 amperes x 208 volts x 1.732 x 80% = 172,923 VA

39. B   3-phase Current Formula
                            450.3(B)   pg. 361
                            Table 450.3(B)   pg. 362
                            240.6(A)   pg. 96 & 97

(Primary)
$I = \dfrac{kVA \times 1{,}000}{E \times 1.732}$ $I = \dfrac{150 \times 1{,}000}{480 \times 1.732} = \dfrac{150{,}000}{831.36}$ = 180 amps x 250% = 450 amps

(Secondary)
$I = \dfrac{kVA \times 1{,}000}{E \times 1.732}$ $I = \dfrac{150 \times 1{,}000}{208 \times 1.732} = \dfrac{150{,}000}{360.25}$ = 416 amps x 125% = 520 amps

*NOTE: For the secondary you are permitted to go up to the next standard size overcurrent device which has a rating of 600 amperes.

40. C   645.3(A)   pg. 585
                            300.21   pg. 151

41. B   Table 300.5   pg. 145

42. B   460.28(A)   pg. 371

43. A   250.64(A)   pg. 119

44. B   3-phase Current Formula
                            445.13   pg. 360
                            Table 310.15(B)(16)   pg. 161

$I = \dfrac{kW \times 1{,}000}{volts \times 1.732}$ $I = \dfrac{200 \times 1{,}000}{480 \times 1.732} = \dfrac{200{,}000}{831.36}$ = 240.56 amperes (FLC)

241 amperes x 115% = 277 amperes (required ampacity of conductors)

       Size 300 kcmil THWN conductors with an allowable ampacity of 285 amperes should be selected.

45. C   502.115(B)   pg. 404

46. D   645.5(B)(1)   pg. 586

47. B   501.15(C)(3)   pg. 394

48. A   220.12   pg. 67 & 68
        Table 220.12   pg. 68
        220.52(A)&(B)   pg. 70
        Table 220.42   pg. 70

4,000 sq. ft. + 2,000 sq. ft. = 6,000 sq. ft. x 3 VA = 18,000 VA
three small appliance circuits @ 1,500 VA each   = 4,500 VA
one laundry circuit @ 1,500 VA   = 1,500 VA
                    Total connected load   = 24,000 VA

1st 3,000 VA @ 100%   3,000 VA
24,000 VA - 3,000 VA = 21,000 VA (remainder) @ 35% =   7,350 VA
                    Total demand load   = 10,350 VA

49. A   430.6 & .6(A)(1)   pg. 324
        430.22   pg. 329
        Table 430.250   pg. 351
        Table 400.5(A)(1), Column A   pg. 269

FLC of 30 HP motor = 40 amperes x 125% = 50 amperes

Size 4 AWG SOW cord with an allowable ampacity of 60 amperes should be selected from Table 400.5(A)(1).

50. B   525.5(B)(2)   pg. 494

51. D   400.8(4), Exception   pg. 271
        368.56(B)(2)   pg. 233

52. B   225.6(A)(1)   pg. 76

53. D   517.72(A)   pg. 478

54. C   409.106   pg. 291
        Table 430.97(D)   pg. 342

55. D   210.18   pg. 57
        210.12(A)   pg. 56

56. D   680.9   pg. 606

57. B   700.5(A)   pg. 653
        701.5(A)   pg. 658

58. B   338.10(B)(4)(a)   pg. 207

59. C   314.28(E)   pg. 191

60. D   390.8   pg. 246

61. A   Table 110.26(A)(1), Condition 3   pg. 40

62. A　　　　　　　　550.30 & .31(1)　　　　　pg. 512
　　　　　　　　　　　Table 550.31　　　　　　　pg. 512
　　　　　　　　　　　Single-phase current formula

　　25 lots x 16,000 VA (minimum)　= 400,000 VA
　　　　　　　　　　　　　　　　　　　X .24　　(demand factor)
　　　　　　　　　　　　　　　　　　96,000 VA (demand load)

　　I = power　　I = 96,000 VA　= 400 amperes
　　　　Volts　　　　240 volts

63. C　　　　　　　　3-phase current formula

　　I = kVA x 1000　I = 150 x 1000　= 150,000　= 416 amperes (FLA)
　　　　E x 1.732　　　 208 x 1.732　　 360.25　 - 212 amperes (existing load)
　　　　　　　　　　　　　　　　　　　　　　　　= 204 amperes (additional load)

64. A　　　　　　　　250.146(D)　　　　　　　pg. 133

65. D　　　　　　　　422.15(C)　　　　　　　　pg. 304

66. C　　　　　　　　800.113(B)(1)　　　　　　pg. 715

67. D　　　　　　　　600.6　　　　　　　　　　pg. 544

68. C　　　　　　　　368.17(B), Exception　　　pg. 232

69. C　　　　　　　　424.44(A)　　　　　　　　pg. 312

70. B　　　　　　　　408.36, Exception 2　　　 pg. 288

71. D　　　　　　　　682.11　　　　　　　　　 pg. 621

72. B　　　　　　　　517.35(A)　　　　　　　　pg. 472

73. D　　　　　　　　410.97　　　　　　　　　 pg. 297

74. A　　　　　　　　410.54(C)　　　　　　　　pg. 295

75. B　　　　　　　　300.34　　　　　　　　　 pg. 152

76. C　　　　　　　　250.52(A)(2)(1)　　　　　pg. 117

77. D　　　　　　　　520.25(C)　　　　　　　　pg. 483

78. C　　　　　　　　210.62　　　　　　　　　 pg. 63

79. A　　　　　　　　503.130(A)　　　　　　　 pg. 409

80. D	430.22(E) Table 430.22(E)	pg. 329 pg. 329
81. B	500.100(A)(1)	pg. 397
82. C	517.30(E)	pg. 470
83. D	Table 310.15(B)(16) 240.4(B)(2)&(3) 240.6(A)	pg. 161 pg. 95 pg. 96
84. D	514.11(A)	pg. 448
85. B	Table 110.26(A)(1)	pg. 40
86. B	Table 250.122	pg. 131
87. A	450.11(A)	pg. 365
88. C	388.70	pg. 245
89. A	500.8(E)(2)	pg. 390
90. C	450.21(A)	pg. 365
91. D	Table 680.8(A)	pg. 607
92. D	Table 220.42	pg. 70

205.4 kVA x 1,000 = 205,400 VA

first 3,000 VA @ 100% = 3,000 VA
3,001 to 120,000 VA @ 35% = 117,000 VA @ 35% = 40,950 VA
Remainder 205,400 VA − 120,000 VA = 85,400 VA @ 25% = 21,350 VA
Demand = 65,300 VA

$$\frac{65,300 \text{ VA}}{1,000} = 65.3 \text{ kVA}$$

93. B	450.43(B)	pg. 367
94. A	422.13	pg. 304
95. C	Single-phase current formula Table 310.15(B)(16) Table 310.15(B)(2)(a)	 pg. 161 pg. 158

$$I = \frac{power}{volts} \quad I = \frac{36,000 \text{ VA}}{240 \text{ volts}} = 150 \text{ amperes load}$$

$$\text{required ampacity} = \frac{150 \text{ amperes}}{.75 \text{ (temp. cor.)}} = 200 \text{ amperes}$$

96. A   504.80(C)   pg. 413

97. C   Chapter 9, Table 2   pg. 756

98. A   314.28(A)(2)   pg. 190

   3.5 inches (conduit) x 6 = 21 inches

99. B   505.8(G)   pg. 418

100. D   392.20(B)(1)   pg. 249

##

MASTER ELECTRICIAN'S EXAM PREP GUIDE
FINAL EXAM #2
ANSWER KEY

ANSWER	REFERENCE	NEC PG.#
1. B	310.15(B)(7)	pg. 160
2. A	250.53(B)	pg. 118
3. B	Table 430.248 404.14(A)(3)	pg. 350 pg. 280

    15 Ampere switch x 80% = 12 amperes
    FLC of motor – 12 amperes x 125% = 15 amperes

ANSWER	REFERENCE	NEC PG.#
4. D	240.21(B)(2)(1)	pg. 98
5. C	250.97, Exception 2	pg. 123
6. B	250.94(1)-(6)	pg. 123
7. D	352.20(B)	pg. 216
8. B	410.154	pg. 301
9. B	322.10(1)	pg. 195
10. C	230.95 240.13	pg. 92 pg. 97
11. D	760.130(B)(1)	pg. 692
12. A	430.110(A)	pg. 344
13. C	770.2	pg. 699
14. B	250.66(A)	pg. 120
15. D	408.5	pg. 287
16. A	210.23(A)(1)	pg. 59
17. D	530.14	pg. 497

18. B		392.10(B)(1)(a)	pg. 247
19. C		340.10(1)-(4)	pg. 208
		340.12(1)	pg. 208
20. A		Table 220.54	pg. 71
21. B		110.26(A)(3)	pg. 40

6½ ft. = 78 in.

22. D	250.53(H)	pg. 118
23. C	210.19(A)(4)(c)	pg. 58
24. B	440.22(A)	pgs. 355 & 356
25. A	110.26(C)(2)	pg. 41
26. B	352.44	pg. 217
27. D	410.5, Exception	pg. 292
28. C	430.6(A)(1)	pg. 325
	Table 430.250	pg. 351
	430.24(1)&(2)	pg. 331
	Table 310.15(B)(16)	pg. 161

15 hp FLC – 42 amperes x 125% = 52.5 amperes
7½ hp FLC – 22 amperes x 100% = 22.0 amperes
                                                                74.5 amperes

Size 4 AWG THWN conductors with an ampacity of 85 amperes should be selected from Table 310.15(B)(16).

29. A	424.36	pg. 311
30. A	300.4(A)(2)	pg. 143
31. D	250.6(B)	pg. 108
32. B	Table 310.15(B)(3)(c)	pg. 160
33. D	210.19(A), FPN #4	pg. 57
34. C	680.41	pg. 615
35. A	701.12(A)	pg. 659
36. B	Chapter 9, Note 4 to Tables	pg. 756
37. C	605.9(B)	pg. 551

38. A.	240.51(B)	pg. 102
39. D	513.3(B)	pg. 440
40. B	Table 110.26(A)(1)	pg. 40
41. A	645.10(B)	pg. 587
42. B	210.62	pg. 63

One receptacle is required for each 12 ft. of show window or major fraction Thereof. Therefore, two receptacles are required for each 15 ft. of show window.

43. D	700.8	pg. 653
44. A	Table 312.6(B), Column 1	pg. 183
45. C	110.31	pg. 42
46. C	Table 362.80	pg. 198
47. B	440.12(A)(1)	pg. 354
48. D	110.12(A)	pg. 37
49. D	210.52(A)(2)(1)	pg. 60
50. D	725.136(A)	pg. 680
51. A	430.32(A)(1)	pg. 334

FLA of motor – 54 amperes x 115% = 62.1 amperes

52. A	Article 100 – Definitions	pg. 28
53. B	210.60(B)	pg. 63
54. C	408.36(A)	pg. 288
55. D	430.6(A)	pg. 325
	Table 430.250	pg. 351
	Table 430.52	pg. 335
	430.52(C)(1), Exception 1	pg. 335
	240.6(A)	pgs. 96 & 97

FLC of motor – 65 amperes x 300% = 195 amperes
The next standard size non-time delay fuses are rated 200 amperes.

56. C	680.26(B)(7), Exception 2	pg. 613

57. A	440.62(B)	pg. 359

30 amperes x 80% = 24 amperes

58. B	225.19(D)(1)	pg. 79
59. B	250.118(6)(c)	pg. 128
60. C	701.12(G)	pg. 660 & 661
61. D	626.26	pg. 576
62. D	410.30(B)(1), Exception 2	pg. 294
63. D	Table 314.16(B)	pg. 186

Size 14 AWG – 6 wires x 2.00 cu. in. = 12.0 cu. in.
Size 12 AWG - 8 wires x 2.25 cu. in. = 18.0 cu. in.
Size 10 AWG - 3 wires x 2.50 cu. in. = 7.5 cu. in.
                       Total = 37.5 Cu. in.

64. A	500.5(B)	pg. 384
65. B	450.3(B)	pg. 361
	Table 450.3(B)	pg. 362
	240.6(A)	pg. 96

Primary current – 40 amperes x 125% = 50 amperes

66. C	210.12(A)(1)	pg. 56
67. B	680.42(A)(2)	pg. 615
68. A	680.51(B)	pg. 617
69. D	430.7(A)(1)-(5)	pg. 325
70. C	3-phase current formula	
	Table 310.15(B)(16)	pg. 161

$$I = P \div E \times 1.732 \quad I = \frac{72{,}000 \text{ VA}}{208 \times 1.732} = \frac{72{,}000}{360.25} = 199.8 \text{ amperes}$$

Size 3/0 AWG THWN conductors with an allowable ampacity of 200 amperes should be selected.

71. B	Annex C, Table C.8	pg. 819
72. C	376.22(B)	pg. 238
73. B	408.4(A)	pg. 287

74. A		Table 300.19(A)	pg. 150
75. B		390.4(A)	pg. 246
76. D		410.68	pg. 297
77. C		Article 100 – Definitions	pg. 34
78. A		406.9(A)	pg. 284
79. B		511.3(C)(3)(b)	pg. 438
80. D		250.64(C)	pg. 119
81. B		Table 220.12	pg. 68
		Article 100 – Definitions	pg. 29
		230.42(A)(1)	pg. 87

100 ft. x 300 ft. = 30,000 sq. ft. x 2 VA = 60,000 VA
60,000 VA x 125% (continuous load) = 75,000 VA

82. C		517.19(D)	pg. 467
83. D		Table 300.5, Column 4	pg. 145
84. C		520.5(A)	pg. 483
85. B		334.80	pg. 205
		Table 220.55, Notes 1 & 2	pg. 72
		Single-phase current formula	
		Table 310.15(B)(16)	pg. 161

8 kW + 6 kW = 14 kW (treat as one range)
14 kW – 12 kW = 2 kW x 5% = 10% increase in column C
8 kW (column C) x 110% = 8.8 kW

$$I = P \div E \quad I = \frac{8.8 \text{ kW} \times 1000}{240 \text{ volts}} = \frac{8800}{240} = 36.7 \text{ amperes}$$

Size 8 AWG conductors with an ampacity of 40 amperes should be selected from the 60°C column of Table 310.15(B)(16).

86. A		513.3(B)	pg. 440
87. B		Chapter 9, Table 4	pg. 757
		Chapter 9, Table 5	pg. 763
		Note 7 to Chapter 9 Tables	pg. 756

$$\frac{0.897 \text{ sq. in (conduit)}}{0.0824 \text{ sq. in. (wire)}} = 10.8 = 11 \text{ wires}$$

88. D	410.12	pg. 293
89. D	210.12(A)	pg. 56
90. A	Chapter 9, Note 9 to Tables	pg. 756
91. C	240.83(D)	pg. 103
92. B	Table 220.12	pg. 68

15,000 sq. ft. x 3 VA = 45,000 VA (load)
120 volts x 15 amperes = 1,800 VA (one circuit)

$$\frac{45,000 \text{ VA (load)}}{1,800 \text{ VA (1 ckt.)}} = 25 \text{ (15 ampere general lighting circuits)}$$

93. A	424.36	pg. 311
94. C	388.12(3)	pg. 245
95. B	555.2(1)	pg. 537
96. D	Table 250.122	pg. 131
97. A	356.24	pg. 224
98. A	645.10(A)(1)	pg. 587
99. B	Table 310.15(B)(16)	pg. 161
	240.4(B)	pg. 94
	240.6(A)	pgs. 96 & 97
100. C	626.31(B)	pg. 576

##

Glossary

Adjustable-trip circuit breakers: Circuit breakers whose trip setting can be changed by adjusting the ampere rating, trip time characteristics, or both, within a particular range.

Aluminum wire: An electrical conductor composed of aluminum metal.

Ambient temperature: The surrounding temperature present in a specific area.

American Wire Gauge (AWG): Standard used to identify the size of a wire.

Ampacity: The maximum current, in amperes that a conductor can carry continuously, under the conditions of use without exceeding its temperature rating.

Ampere: The unit of current measurement. The amount of current that will flow through a one ohm resistor when one volt is applied.

Appliance: Utilization equipment, installed to perform one or more functions, such as clothes washing, air conditioning, cooking, etc.

Appliance branch circuit: A branch circuit that supplies energy to one or more outlets to which appliances are to be connected.

Arc-Fault Circuit Interrupter (AFCI): A device intended to provide protection from the effects of arc faults by recognizing characteristics unique to arcing and by functioning to de-energize the circuit when an arc fault is detected.

Automatic: Performing a function without the necessity of human intervention.

Balanced load: The load of an electrical system, in which two or more branches are balanced and symmetrical with respect to voltage and intensity of current.

Ballast: An electrical circuit component used with discharge lighting luminaires to provide the voltage necessary to strike the mercury arc within the lamp, and then to limit the amount of current that flows through the lamp. (Examples of discharge lighting luminaires are fluorescent and HID lighting fixtures.)

Bare conductor: A conductor with no insulation or covering of any type.

Bonded (Bonding): Connected to establish electrical continuity and conductivity.

Bonding conductor: The conductor that connects the non-current carrying parts of electrical equipment, cable raceways or other enclosures to the approved system ground conductor.

Bonding jumper: A conductor used to assure the required electrical connection between metal parts of an electrical system.

Bonding jumper, System: The connection between the grounded circuit conductor and the supply-side bonding jumper, or the equipment grounding conductor, or both, at a separately derived system.

Box: A metallic or nonmetallic electrical enclosure used to house utilization equipment and devices, the support of luminaires and pulling or terminating conductors.

Branch circuit: That portion of a wiring system beyond the final overcurrent protection device protecting the circuit and the outlet(s).

Branch circuit, Multiwire: A branch circuit that consists of two or more ungrounded conductors that have a voltage between them, and a grounded conductor that has equal voltage between it and each ungrounded conductor of the circuit and that is connected to the neutral or grounded conductor of the system.

Branch-circuit rating: The ampere rating or setting of the overcurrent device protecting the conductors.

Building: A stand-alone structure or a structure which is separated from adjoining structures by fire walls.

Buried cable: A cable laid directly in the ground without being enclosed or protected in an electrical conduit.

Bus: A conductor, or group of conductors, that serve as a common connection for two or more circuits.

Busway: A sheet metal enclosure that contains factory assembled aluminum or copper busbars which are supported on insulators.

Cable: One or more insulated or non-insulated wires used to conduct electrical current.

Cable assembly: A flexible assembly containing multiconductors with a protective outer sheath.

Cablebus: An assembly of insulated conductors and terminations in an enclosed, ventilated protective metal housing.

Cable tray system: An assembly of sections and associated fittings which form a rigid structural system used to support cables and raceways.

Carrying capacity: The MAXIMUM current strength, in amperes, that a conductor can safely carry continuously. (See ampacity)

Celsius: A unit of measurement, in degrees, for temperature at which the freezing point is 0° and the boiling point is 100°. It is commonly represented by the letter "C".

Circuit: A complete path over which an electric current can flow.

Circuit breaker: A device which opens and closes circuits by nonautomatic means and opens circuits automatically when a predetermined overcurrent exists.

Circuit voltage: The greatest effective difference of potential between any two conductors in a given circuit.

Circular mil (CM): A measurement of the cross-sectional area of a conductor. The area of one circular mil equals .001 inches in diameter.

Circular mil foot: A unit of conductor size, equal to a portion of the conductor having a cross-sectional area of one circular mil and length of one foot.

Clamp: A device intended to secure raceways, tubing or cables.

Commercial equipment: Equipment intended to be used on commercial, industrial or institutional premises, such as schools, hotels, office buildings, manufacturing facilities, libraries and other public buildings.

Computer: An electronic machine which, by means of stored instructions and information, performs rapid, often complex calculations or compiles, correlates and selects data.

Conductor: A wire that is used to transmit the flow of electrons in an electrical circuit. Copper wire is the most common used today in the electrical industry.

Conduit: A metallic or nonmetallic pipe or tubing used to enclosed conductors.

Connected load: The sum of the rating(s) of the load consuming equipment, connected to an electrical system or any part thereof.

Contactor: An electrically operated switch, usually by a coil or solenoid. The switch contains one or more sets of contacts which controls one or more circuits.

Continuous duty: Operation at a substantially constant load for an indefinitely long time.

Continuous load: A load in which the MAXIMUM current may continue for three hours or more.

Controller: A device, or group of devices, which serves to govern in some predetermined manner the electric power delivered to the apparatus to which it is connected.

Control panel: A panel containing switches and other protective, controlling and measuring devices for electrical equipment, motors, and/or machinery.

Copper: A brownish-red, malleable, ductile, metallic element that is an excellent conductor of electricity and heat. The most common element used for conductors in the electrical industry.

Copper Wire: An electrical conductor composed of copper metal.

Cord: A small cable, very flexible, and substantially insulated to withstand wear. There is no sharp dividing line in respect to size between a cord and a cable, and likewise no sharp dividing line in respect to the character of insulation between a cord and a stranded wire.

Cord-and-plug connected appliance: An appliance to be connected to the power source by means of a supply cord.

Cord-connected unit: A unit intended for connection to the power source by means of a supply cord to prevent vibration or enable the unit to be moved.

Cross-section: A cutting or piece of something cut off at right angles to an axis. The cross-sectional area is 100% of the cross-section.

Current: The flow of electricity in a circuit, measured in amperes. Represented by the letter "I" or "A".

Current transformer (CT): An instrument transformer with a primary winding in series with a current-carrying conductor and secondary winding connected to a meter or device which is actuated by conductor current and current changes.

Demand factor: The ratio of the MAXIMUM demand of a system, or part of a system, to the total connected load of a system or the part of the system under consideration. All the loads of a system are usually never used all at the same time due to the many uses of the power.

Device box: A box which houses an electrical device(s), such as receptacles and switches.

Device: Electrical components, such as receptacles, switches and dimmers, that are designed to carry and/or control electric energy as its principle function, but not use electricity.

Disconnecting means: A device, or group of devices, by which the circuit conductors are disconnected from their source of supply.

Double pole: Switch or device connected to both lines of a circuit or controlling both lines of a circuit.

Dry location: A location not normally subject to dampness or wetness. A location classified as dry may be temporarily subject to dampness or wetness, as in the case of a building under construction.

Duty cycle: The time interval occupied by a device on intermittent duty in starting, running, stopping and idling.

Dwelling: A structure that contains eating, living and sleeping space and permanent provisions for cooking and sanitation.

Dwelling unit: A dwelling with one or more rooms used by one or more people for housekeeping.

Effectively grounded: Grounded with sufficient low impedance and current-carrying capacity to prevent hazardous voltage build-ups.

Efficiency: The ratio of output power to input power, expressed as a percentage.

Electrical discharge luminaire: A luminaire (lighting fixture) that utilizes a ballast for the operation of the lamp.

Electrical metallic tubing (EMT): A lightweight tubular steel raceway used to enclosed conductors.

Electric circuit: The complete path of an electric current.

Electric power production and distribution network: Power production, distribution, and utilization equipment and facilities, such as electric utility systems that deliver electric power to the connected loads, that are external to and not controlled by an interactive system.

Electric sign: A fixed, stationary, or portable self-contained, electrically illuminated, utilization equipment with words or symbols designed to convey information or attract attention.

Electrode: A conducting substance through which electric current enters or leaves.

Enclosed: Surrounded by a case, housing, fence or walls which will prevent persons from accidentally contacting energized parts.

Enclosure: The case or housing of equipment or other apparatus which provides protection from live or energized parts.

Equipment: A general term including devices, luminaires, appliances, materials, machinery, apparatus, etc. used in conjunction with electrical installations.

Equipment bonding jumper: A conductor that connects two or more parts of the equipment grounding conductor.

Equipment grounding conductor: An electrical conductor that provides a low-impedance path between electrical equipment and enclosures and the system grounded conductor and grounding electrode conductor.

Explosionproof equipment: Equipment enclosed in a case that is capable of withstanding an explosion of a specified gas or vapor that may occur within it and of preventing the ignition of a specified gas or vapor surrounding the enclosure by sparks, flashes, or explosion of the gas or vapor within, and that operated at such an external temperature that a surrounding flammable atmosphere will not be ignited thereby.

Fahrenheit: A unit of measurement, in degrees, for temperature at which the freezing point is 32° and the boiling point is 212°. It is commonly represented by the letter "F".

Fault: An electrical defect.

Fault current: Any current that travels an unwanted path, other than the normal operating path of an electrical system.

Feeder: All circuit conductors between the service equipment or the source of a separately derived system and the final branch circuit overcurrent device.

Feeder neutral load: The maximum unbalanced load between any of the ungrounded conductors and the grounded conductor of a feeder.

Fished: A means of installing electrical wiring in existing inaccessible hollow spaces of buildings with a minimum damage to the building finish.

Fixed appliance: An appliance which is fastened in place or otherwise secured at a specific location.

Fixed equipment: Equipment intended to be permanently connected electrically and not easily moved.

Flexible cord: An assembly of two or more insulated conductors, with or without braids, contained within an overall outer covering and used for the connection of equipment to a power source.

Flexible metal conduit (FMC): A raceway consisting of metal strips which are formed into a circular cross-sectional raceway, which is used to enclose conductors.

Fluorescent light: A method of lighting which makes use of ultraviolet energy to activate a fluorescent material coated inside of the bulb's surface.

Full-load amperes (FLA): The amount of current, in amperes, in an electrical circuit when the load is operating in a full-capacity condition.

Full-load current (FLC): The current required by a motor to produce the full-load torque at the motor's rated speed.

Fuse: A protective device with a fusible element that opens the circuit by melting when subjected to excessive current.

Galvanizing: The process of coating metals with zinc to prevent corrosion.

Ganged switch box: A box containing more than one switch.

General lighting: Lighting designed to provide a substantially uniform level of illumination throughout an area, exclusive of any provision for special local requirements.

General-purpose branch circuit: A branch circuit that supplies a number of outlets for lighting and appliances.

General-use snap switch: A form of general-use switch constructed so that it can be installed in device and/or outlet boxes.

General-use switch: A switch for use in general distribution and branch circuits. The ampere rated switch is capable of interrupting its rated current at its rated voltage.

General-use receptacle: 125-volt, single-phase, 15-or-20 ampere receptacles connected to a branch-circuit supplying two or more receptacles provided for the purpose of supplying cord-and-plug connected loads. Not provided for specific loads such as small appliances or laundry equipment.

Generator: A device that is used to convert mechanical energy to electrical energy.

Grade: The final level or elevation of the earth at a given location.

Ground: A conducting connection between electrical circuits or equipment and the earth.

Grounded (Grounding): Connected to the earth or a conducting body connected to the earth.

Grounded circuit: A circuit in which one conductor or point (usually the neutral) is intentionally grounded, either solidly or through a grounding device.

Grounded conductor: A conductor that has been intentionally grounded.

Ground-fault: An unintentional connection between an ungrounded conductor and any grounded raceway, box, enclosure, fitting, etc.

Ground-fault circuit interrupter: An electrical device which protects personnel by detecting hazardous ground faults and quickly disconnects power from the circuit.

Grounding: The connection of all exposed non-current carrying metal parts to the earth.

Grounding conductor: A conductor used to connect equipment or the grounded circuit of a wiring system to a grounding electrode or electrodes.

Grounding electrode: A conducting object through which a direct connection to earth is established.

Grounding electrode conductor: The conductor used to connect the system grounded conductor and/or the equipment to a grounding electrode or to a point on the grounding electrode system.

Handhole enclosure: An enclosure for use in underground systems, provided with an open or closed bottom, and sized to allow personnel to reach into, but not enter, for the purpose of installing, operating, or maintaining equipment or wiring or both.

Health care facility: A location, either a building or a portion of a building, which contains occupancies such as, hospitals, nursing homes, limited or supervisory care facilities, clinics, medical and dental offices and either ambulatory facilities.

Hermetic refrigerant motor-compressor: A combination of a compressor and motor enclosed in the same housing, having no external shaft or shaft seals, with the motor operating in the refrigerant.

Hickey (fitting): A fitting used to mount a lighting fixture in an outlet box or on a pipe or stud. It has openings through which fixture wires may be brought out of the fixture stem.

HID lamp: A high-intensity discharge lamp.

High-intensity discharge (HID) luminaire: A luminaire (lighting fixture) that generates light from an arc lamp contained within an outer tube.

Horsepower (hp): A unit of power equal to 746 watts that describes the output of electric motors.

Hybrid system: A system comprised of multiple power sources. These power sources may include photovoltaic, wind, micro-hydro generators, engine-driven generators, and others, but do not include electrical production and distribution network systems. Energy storage systems, such as batteries, do not constitute a power source for the purpose of this definition.

Identified: Recognized as suitable for the use, purpose, etc.

Illumination: The supplying of light or lighting up a given area. The density of light flux projected on a surface, measured in footcandles (FC).

Impedance: The total opposition to the flow of current in an ac circuit.

Incandescent lamp: A lamp in which the light is produced by a filament of conducting material contained in a vacuum and heated to incandescence by an electric current.

Individual branch circuit: A branch circuit that supplies only one unit of utilization equipment.

Induction: The process by which an electrical conductor becomes electrified when near a charged body and becomes magnetized.

Information Technology Equipment (ITE): Equipment and systems rated 600 volts or less, normally found in offices or other business establishments and similar environments classified as ordinary locations, that are used for creation and manipulation of data, voice, video, and similar signals that are not communications equipment as defined in the NEC®.

Instantaneous: A qualifying term used in giving properties and characteristics of apparatus indicating that no delay is purposely introduced in its action. Done in an instant.

Instantaneous-trip circuit breakers: Circuit breakers with no delay between the fault or overload sensing element and the tripping action of the device.

Insulated: Separated from other conducting surfaces by a dielectric substance or air space permanently offering a high resistance to the passage of current and to disruptive discharge through the substance or space.

Insulated conductor: A conductor covered with a material identified as electrical insulation.

Intensity of current: The strength of an electric current. It is the quantity of electricity that flows past any point in a circuit in one second, and is measured by a unit called the ampere. Represented by the letter "I".

Interactive system: A solar photovoltaic system that operates in parallel with and may deliver power to an electrical production and distribution network. For the purpose of this definition, an energy storage subsystem of a solar photovoltaic system, such as a battery, is not another electrical production source.

Intermittent duty: Operation for alternate intervals of (1) load and no load; or (2) load and rest; or (3) load, no load, and rest. A requirement of operation or service consisting of alternate periods of load and rest so apportioned and regulated that the temperature rise at no time exceeds that specified for the particular class of apparatus under consideration.

Intermittent load: A load in which the MAXIMUM current does not continue for three hours.

Interrupt: To stop a process in such a way that it can be resumed.

Interrupting rating: The maximum rating, in amperes, of an overcurrent protective device (OCPD).

Intersystem bonding termination: A device that provides a means for connecting bonding conductors for communications systems to the grounding electrode system.

Inverse-time circuit breakers: Circuit breakers with an intentional delay between the time when the fault or overload is sensed and the time when the circuit breaker operates. The greater the overload the less time the circuit breaker takes to trip. Conversely, the smaller the overload the more time the circuit breaker takes to trip.

Inverter: Equipment that is used to change voltage level or waveform, or both, of electrical energy. Commonly, an inverter [also known as a power conditioning unit (PCU) or power conversion system (PCS)] is a device that changes dc input to an ac output. Inverters may also function as battery chargers that use alternating current from another source and convert it into direct current for charging batteries.

Junction box: A box in which splices, taps or terminations are made.

kcmil: One thousand circular mils. Conductor sizes from 250 kcmil through 2,000 kcmil are expressed in this manner.

Kilo: A prefix often used with a physical unit to designate a quantity one thousand times as great. Designated by the letter "K".

Kilo-volt amperes (kva): One thousand (1,000) volt amperes.

Kilowatt (kw): One thousand (1,000) watts.

Lamp: A light source. Reference is to a light bulb, rather than a lamp.

Lampholders: Devices designed to accommodate a lamp for the purpose of illumination.

Lighting outlet: An outlet intended for the direct connection of a lampholder, a lighting fixture (luminaire) or pendant cord terminating in a lampholder.

Lighting outlets: Outlets that provide power for lighting fixtures (luminaires).

Lighting track: An assembly consisting of an energized track and luminaire units which can be positioned along the track.

Liquidtight flexible metal conduit (LFMC): A flexible metal raceway of circular cross-section with an outer liquidtight, non metallic, sunlight-resistant jacket over an inner helically-wound metal strip.

Liquidtight flexible nonmetallic conduit (LFNC): A flexible nonmetallic raceway of circular cross-section with an outer jacket which is resistant to oil, water, sunlight, corrosion, etc. The inner core varies based on intended use.

Load: The amount of electric power used by any electrical unit or appliance at any given moment.

Location, damp: Partially protected locations under canopies, marquees, roofed open porches and like locations and interior locations subject to moderate degrees of moisture, such as some basements, barns and cold storage warehouses.

Location, dry: A location not normally subject to dampness or wetness. A location classified as dry may be temporarily subject to dampness or wetness, as in the case of a building under construction.

Location, wet: Installations underground or in concrete slabs or masonry, in direct contact with the earth and locations subject to saturation with water or other liquids, such as vehicle washing areas and locations exposed to weather and unprotected.

Locked rotor: The condition when a motor is loaded so heavily that the shaft can not turn.

Locked rotor current: The steady-state current taken from the line with the rotor locked and with rated voltage applied to the motor.

Luminaire: A complete lighting fixture consisting of the lamp or lamps, reflector or other parts to distribute the light, lamp guards and lamp power supply.

Main bonding jumper: The connection at the service equipment that bonds together the equipment grounding conductor, the grounded conductor and the grounding electrode conductor.

MAXIMUM: The greatest value in any given group. A value greater than any which precedes or follows it in succession of values.

Metal wireway: A sheet metal raceway with a hinged or removable cover that houses and protects wires and cables laid in place after the wireway has been installed.

Mil: One thousandths of an inch (0.001").

Mobil home: A transportable factory assembled structure or structures constructed on a permanent chassis for use as a dwelling. A mobile home is not constructed on a permanent foundation but is connected to the required utilities. The term "mobile home" does not include manufactured homes.

Module: A complete, environmentally protected unit consisting of solar cells, optics, and other components, exclusive of tracker, designed to generate dc power when exposed to sunlight.

Motor: A device for converting electrical energy into mechanical energy.

Motor branch circuit: The point from the last fuse or circuit breaker in the motor circuit out to the motor.

Motor control center: An assembly of one or more enclosed sections with a common power bus and primarily containing motor control units.

Motor Efficiency: The effectiveness of a motor to convert electrical energy in to mechanical energy. The more efficient a motor is the less current it draws. Conversely, the less efficient a motor is the more current it draws.

Motor starter: An electrically operated switch (contactor) that includes overload protection.

Multiconductor cable: It consists of a number of individually insulated wires, either solid or stranded, which may or may not be grouped together within an outer covering. Sometimes an outer sheath of aluminum or steel is placed over the cable.

Multifamily dwelling: A dwelling with three or more dwelling units.

Multioutlet assembly: A metal raceway with factory-installed conductors and attachment plug receptacles. Usually surface mounted.

Multiwire branch-circuit: A branch circuit with two or more ungrounded conductors having a potential difference between them, and is connected to the neutral or grounded conductor of the system.

Nameplate: A plaque giving the manufacturer's name, current rating and voltage of a transformer, generator, motor, appliance, etc.

Neutral: Neither positive nor negative; having zero potential; having electrical potential intermediate between the potentials of other associated parts of the circuit, positive with reference to some parts, negative with reference to others.

Nipple: A short piece of conduit or tubing having a length not exceeding 24 inches.

Noncoincidental loads: Loads that are not on at the same time.

Nonlinear load: A load where the wave shape of the steady-state current does not follow the wave shape of the applied voltage. Examples of nonlinear loads are electronic equipment, such as computers and HID and fluorescent lighting.

Nonmetallic-sheathed cable (NM): A factory assembly of two or more insulated conductors having an outer sheath of moisture-resistant, flame-retardant, non-metallic material.

Non-time delay fuses: Fuses that may detect an overcurrent and open the circuit without any delay.

Ohm: The unit of measurement of electrical resistance. One ohm of resistance will allow one ampere of current to flow through a pressure of one volt.

Ohm's Law: A law which describes the mathematical relationship between voltage, current and resistance.

One-family dwelling: A dwelling with one dwelling unit.

Outlet: Any point in the electrical system where current supplies utilization equipment.

Overcurrent: Any current in excess of that for which the conductor or equipment is rated. It may result from overload, short circuit, or ground fault.

Overload: Operation of equipment in excess of normal, full-load rating, or of a conductor in excess of its rated ampacity that, when it persists for a sufficient length of time, would cause damage or dangerous overheating. A fault, such as a short circuit or ground fault, is not an overload.

Overload protection: A device that prevents overloading a circuit or motor such as a fuse or circuit breaker.

Panelboard: A single panel or group of assembled panels with buses and overcurrent devices, which may have switches to control light, heat or power circuits.

Parallel conductors: Two or more conductors that are electrically connected at both ends to form a single conductor.

Pendants: Hanging luminaires (lighting fixtures), that use flexible cords to support the lampholder.

Permanently-connected appliance: A hard-wired appliance that is not cord-and-plug connected.

Permanently installed swimming pool: A pool constructed in ground or partially above ground and designed to hold over 42 inches of water and all indoor pools regardless of depth.

Phase: Used in ac terminology, refers basically to time. Usually the phase position is defined by specifying the number of electrical degrees between the phase and the reference position. The number of electrical degrees that two quantities are out of phase is called the phase angle.

Phase conductor: The conductors other than the neutral conductor.

Phase converter: An electrical device that converts single-phase power to three-phase power.

Phase-to-ground voltage: The maximum voltage between any two phases of an electrical distribution system.

Portable appliance: An appliance which is actually moved or can be easily moved from one place to another in normal use.

Power (watts): A basic unit of electrical energy, measured in watts. Power is usually expressed as the letter "P" or "W".

Power (volt- amperes): The apparent power in an ac circuit or electrical system. Represented by the letters "VA".

Power factor: The ratio of the voltage and current, or volt-amperes that do useful work in an ac circuit or equipment, to the total voltage and current, volt-amperes, flowing in the circuit. Power factor is usually expressed as "pf."

Premises wiring: Basically all interior and exterior wiring installed on the load side of the service point or the source of a separately derived system.

Primary: The part of a motor or transformer having windings that are connected to the power supply line.

Primary current: The current in the primary of a transformer.

Primary winding: The coil of a transformer which is energized from a source of alternating voltage and current. The input side.

Pull box: A box used as a point to pull or feed electrical conductors in the raceway system.

Rated current: The load, in amperes, that a circuit breaker is intended to carry continuously without opening of the circuit.

Raceway: A metal or nonmetallic channel for enclosing and protecting conductors.

Receptacle outlets: Outlets that provide power for cord-and-plug connected equipment.

Recreational vehicle: A vehicular type unit which is self-propelled or is mounted on or pulled by another vehicle and is primarily designed as temporary living quarters for camping, travel or recreational use.

Resistance: That property of a conductor by which it opposes the flow of an electric current, resulting in the generation of heat in the conducting material. Usually measured in ohms. Resistance is usually represented by the letter "R".

Rigid metal conduit (RMC): A conduit used to enclose conductors, made of metal with a galvanized protective coating.

Rigid nonmetallic conduit (RNC): A conduit made of materials other than metal, usually polyvinyl chloride (PVC).

Secondary current: The current induced in the secondary of a transformer or induction coil.

Separately derived system: A premises wiring system whose power is derived from a source of electric energy or equipment other than a service. Examples of separately derived systems are transformers, generators and storage batteries. Such systems have no direct connection from circuit conductors of one system to circuit conductors of another system, other than connections through the earth, metal enclosures, metallic raceways, or equipment grounding conductors.

Series circuit: A circuit supplying energy to a number of loads connected in series. The same current passes through each load in completing its path to the source of supply.

Service: The conductors and equipment for delivering electric energy from the serving utility to the wiring system of the premises served.

Service conductors: The conductors from the service point or other source of power to the service disconnecting means.

Service drop: The overhead service conductors that extend from the last pole of the utility supply system to the service-entrance conductors at the building or structure.

Service-entrance cable (SE): A single or multiconductor assembly with or without an overall covering.

Service-entrance conductors: Conductors that connect the service equipment for the building or structure with the electrical utility supply conductors.

Service equipment: All of the necessary equipment to control the supply of electrical power to a building or a structure.

Service lateral: The underground service conductors that connect the utility's electrical distribution system with the service-entrance conductors.

Service mast: An assembly consisting of a service raceway, guy wires or braces, service head and any fittings necessary for the support of service drop conductors.

Sheath: The final outer protective coating applied to a cable.

Short circuit: The unintentional connection of two ungrounded conductors that have a potential difference between them. The condition that occurs when two ungrounded conductors (hot wires), or an ungrounded and grounded conductor of a circuit, come in contact with each other.

Short circuit protection: Any automatic current-limiting system that enables a power supply to continue operating at a limited current. and without damage, into any output overload including short-circuits.

Show window: Any window used or designed to be used for the display of goods, products, services, or advertising material. Usually visible by the general public from street or floor level.

Single phase: A term applied to a simple alternating current of uniform frequency as distinguished from polyphase currents.

Single-phase circuit: An ac circuit consisting of two or three intentionally interrelated conductors.

Solar cell: The basic photovoltaic device that generates electricity when exposed to light.

Solar photovoltaic system: The total components and subsystems that, in combination, convert solar energy into electric energy suitable for connection to a utilization load.

Spa (hot tub): An indoor or outdoor hydromassage pool or tub that is not designed to have the water discharged after each use.

Special permission: The written approval of the authority having jurisdiction.

Splice: A joint used for connecting conductors together.

Stationary appliance: A cord-connected appliance that is intended to be fastened in place or located in a dedicated space.

Switch: A device, with a current and voltage rating, used to open or close an electrical circuit.

Switchboard: A single panel or group of assembled panels with buses, overcurrent devices and instruments.

Temperature rise: The amount of heat that an electrical component produces above the ambient temperature.

Thermal protection: Refers to an electrical device which has inherent protection from overheating. Typically in the form of a bimetal strip which bends when heated to a certain point.

Three-phase circuit: a combination of circuits energized by ac that differ in phase by one third of a cycle, which is 120 degrees.

Three-phase power: A combination of three alternating currents (usually denoted as a, b and c) in a circuit with their voltages displaced 120 degrees or one third of a cycle.

Three-phase transformer: A combination in one unit of three single phase transformers with separate electric circuits, but having certain magnetic circuits in common. There are three magnetic circuits through the core and the fluxes in the various circuits are displaced in phase.

Time delay fuse: Fuses designed to provide a time interval upon detection of an overload, before blowing. This type of fuse is used primarily for overcurrent protection for motors.

Transformer: An electrical device that contains no moving parts, which converts or "transforms" electrical power at one voltage or current to another voltage or current.

Transformer vault: An isolated enclosure either above or below ground, with fire-resistant walls, ceiling and floor, for unattended transformers.

True power: The actual power used in an electrical circuit measured in watts or kilowatts. Represented by the letter "P" or the letter "W".

Unfinished basement: The portion of area of a basement which is not intended as a habitable room, but is limited to storage areas, work areas, etc.

Ungrounded: A system, circuit or apparatus without an intentional connection to ground except through potential indicating or measuring devices or other very high impedance devices.

Uninterruptible power supply: A power supply used to provide alternating current power to a load for some period of time in the event of a power failure.

Utilization equipment: Any electrical equipment which uses electrical energy for electronic, mechanical, heating, lighting, or similar purposes.

Ventilated: Provided with a means to permit circulation of air sufficient to remove an excess of heat, fumes or vapors.

Volt: The practical unit of electric pressure. The pressure which will produce a current of one ampere against a resistance of one ohm.

Voltage: The greatest root-mean-square (effective) difference of potential between any two conductors or the circuit concerned.

Voltage drop: The drop of pressure in an electric circuit due to the resistance of the conductor. This loss exists in every circuit. It is directly proportional to the length of the conductor, and is inversely proportional to its cross-sectional area.

Voltage, nominal: A nominal value assigned to a circuit or system for the purpose of conveniently designating its voltage class (e.g., 120/240-volts, 480Y/277-volts, 600-volts). The actual voltage at which a circuit operates can vary from the nominal within a range that permits satisfactory operation of equipment.

Voltage-to-ground: The difference of potential between a given conductor and ground.

Volt-ampere: the volt-ampere is the apparent power in an ac circuit. Represented by the letters "VA".

Wall mounted oven: An oven for cooking purposes designed for mounting in or on a wall or other surface and consisting of one or more heating elements.

Watt: The practical unit of power, being the amount of energy expended per second by an unvarying current of one ampere under a pressure of one volt.

Weatherproof: So constructed or protected that exposure to the weather will not interfere with successful operation.

Wireway: A metallic or nonmetallic trough with a hinged or removable cover designed to house and protect conductors and cables.

Wye connection: A connection that has one end of each coil connected together and the other end of each coil left open for external connections.

APPENDIX A
State Licensing Offices

Alabama
Electrical Contractors Board
2777 Zelda Road
Montgomery, AL 36106
(344) 420-7232
aecb.state.al.us

Alaska
Division of Occupational Licensing
Construction Contractor Section
P.O. Box 110806
Juneau, AK 99811-0806
(907)465-2550
dced.state.ak.us/occ/

Arizona
Registrar of Contractors
1700 W Washington Street, Suite 105
Phoenix, AZ 85007-2812
(602) 542-1525
azroc.gov

Arkansas
Board of Electrical Examiners
10421 W Markham Street
Little Rock, AR 72205
(501) 682-4549
Fax (501) 682-1765
labor.ar.gov/divisions/Documents/
electrician_app.pdf

California
Department of Consumer Affairs
Contractors State License Board
9821 Business Park Drive
Sacramento, CA 95827
(916) 255-3900 (800) 321-2752
cslb.ca.gov/

Colorado
State Electrical Board
1560 Broadway, Suite 110
Denver, CO 80202
(303) 894-7855 Fax (303) 894-7885
dora.state.co.us

Connecticut
Department of Consumer
Protection License Services
165 Capital Avenue, Room 147
Hartford, CT 06106
(860) 713-7240
state.ct.us/dcp

Delaware
Division of Professional Regulation
Board of Electrical Examiners
861 Silver Lake Blvd., Suite 203
Dover, DE 19904
(302) 744-4500 Fax (302) 739-2711
dpr.delaware.gov/boards/electrician/
index.shtml

Florida
Dept. of Business and Professional Regulation
Electrical Contractors' Licensing Board
1940 North Monroe Street
Tallahassee, FL 32399-0071
(850)487-1395 Fax (850) 488-8748
myfloridalicense.com/dbpr/

Georgia

Kansas

State Construction Industry
Licensing Board
Division of Electrical Contractors
237 Coliseum Drive
Macon, GA 31217-3858
(478) 207-2440 Fax (478) 207-1425
sos.state.ga.us/plb/

Hawaii
Department of Commerce and
Consumer Affairs
Board of Electricians and Plumbers
Division of Professional and Vocational
Licensing
P.O. Box 3469
Honolulu, HI 96801
(808) 586-3000
hawaii.gov/dcca/pvl/boards/electrician

Idaho
Division of Building Safety
Electrical Bureau, Licensing Section
1090 E Watertower
Meridian, ID 83642
(208) 334-3950 Fax (877) 810-2840
dbs.idaho.gov/

Illinois
The State of Illinois does not issue State Contractor's Licenses. Licensing is done on a local level. Look in the telephone directory under "Town of," "City of," or "County of."
Idfpr.com

Indiana
The State of Indiana does not issue State Contractor's Licenses. Licensing is done on a local level. Look in the telephone directory under "Town of," "City of," or "County of."
in.gov/pla

The State of Kansas does not issue State Contractor's Licenses. Licensing is done on a local level. Look in the telephone directory under "Town of," "City of," or "County of."
kansas.gov

Kentucky
Department of Housing, Buildings and Construction
Electrical Licensing
101 Sea Hero Road, Suite 100
Frankfort, KY 40601
(502) 573-2002
dhbc.ky.gov/

Louisiana
Licensing Board of Contractors
2525 Quail Drive
Baton Rouge, LA 70808
(225) 765-2301 (800) 256-1392
1s1bc.louisiana.gov

Maine
Electricians' Examining Board
35 State House Station
Augusta, ME 04333-0035
(207) 624-8603 Fax (207) 624-8637
state.me.us/pfr/olr/

Maryland
Board of Master Electricians
500 N Calvert Street, Room 302
Baltimore, MD 21202
(410) 230-6270
dllr.state.md.us/license/master_elec

Massachusetts
Division of Professional Licensure
Board of State Examiners
Of Electricians
1000 Washington Street, Suite 710
Boston, MA 02118
(617) 727-9931
mass.gov

Iowa
Must be registered with the state.

Licensing is done on a local level. Look in the telephone directory under "Town of," "City of," or "County of."
iowaworkforce.org/labor/contractor.htm

Michigan
Department of Labor
Electrical Administrative Board
7150 Harris Dr.
P.O. Box 30254
Lansing, MI 48909
(517) 241-9320 Fax (517) 241-9308
michigan.gov/lara

Minnesota
Electrical Licensing and Inspection
443 Lafayette Rd N.
St. Paul, MN 55155
(651) 284-5005 Fax (651) 284-5743
dli.mn.gov/main.asp

Mississippi
Contractor Licensing Board
2679 Crane Ridge Dr., Suite C
Jackson, MS 39216
(601) 354-6161
msboc.us

Missouri
The State of Missouri does not issue State Contractor's Licenses. Licensing is done on a local level. Look in the telephone directory under "Town of," "City of," or "County of."
mo.gov/

Montana
State Electrical Board
301 South Park, 4th Floor
P.O. Box 200513
Helena, MT 59620-0513
(406) 841-2309-Fax
dli.mt.gov/

Nebraska
State Electrical Division
800 S 13th Street, Suite 100
P.O. Box 95066
Lincoln, NE 68509-5066

Nevada
State Contractors Board
2310 Corporate Circle, Suite 200
Henderson, NV 89074
(702) 486-1100 Fax (702) 486-1190
nvcontractorsboard.com/

New Hampshire
Electricians' Licensing Board
Office of the State Fire Marshall
110 Smokey Bear Blvd.
Concord, NH 03301-0646
(603) 223-4289
nh.gov/jtboard/electricians.htm

New Jersey
Board of Examiners of Electrical Contractors
124 Halsey Street, 6th Floor
P.O. Box 45006
Newark, NJ 07101
(973) 504-6401
state.nj.us/lps/ca/electric/

New Mexico
Construction Industries Division
2550 Cerillos Rd., 3rd Floor
Santa Fe, NM 87505
(505) 476-4700 Fax (505) 476-4685
rld.state.nm.us/construction/

New York
The State of New York does not issue State Contractor's Licenses. Licensing is done on a local level. Look in the telephone directory under "Town of," "City of," or "County of."
dos.ny.gov

North Carolina
State Board of Examiners of Electrical Contractors
3101 Industrial Dr., Suite 206

(402) 471-3550 Fax (402) 471-4297
electrical.state.ne.us

North Dakota
State Electrical Board
1929 N. Washington Street, Suite A-1
Bismarck, ND 58507
(701) 328-9522 Fax (701) 328-9524
ndseb.com

Ohio
Construction Industry Licensing Board
6606 Tussing Road
P.O. Box 4009
Reynoldsburg, OH 43068-9009
(614) 644- 2223 Fax (614) 644-2618
com.ohio.gov/dico/ocilb/

Oklahoma
Occupational Licensing Service
Electrical Division
2401 NW 23rd St., Suite 2F
Oklahoma City, OK 73107-1299
(405) 521-6550
ok.gov/cib

Oregon
Department of Consumer and
Business Services
Building Codes Division-Licensing
1535 Edgewater Street, N.W.
Salem, OR 97304
(503) 378-4133 Fax (503) 378-2322
oregonbcd.org

Pennsylvania
The State of Pennsylvania does not
Issue State Contractor's Licenses.
Licensing is done on a local level.
Look in the telephone directory
Under "Town of," "City of," or "County of."
dli.state.pa.us

Rhode Island
Department of Labor & Training
Division of Professional Regulation
1511 Pontiac Avenue
P.O. Box 20247
Cranston, RI 02920-0943

P.O. Box 18727
Raleigh NC 27619
(919) 733-9042 (800) 392-6102
Fax (800) 691-8399
ncbeec.org

South Carolina
Contractors Licensing Board
P.O. Box 11329
Columbia, SC 29211
(803) 896-4300
llr.state.sc.us/POL/Contractors/

South Dakota
State Electrical Commission
308 S. Pierre Street
Pierre, SD 57501
(605) 773-3573 (800)233-7765
Fax (605) 773-6213
dol.sd.gov/bdcomm/electric/

Tennessee
Board of Licensing Contractors
500 James Robertson Parkway
4th Floor
Nashville, TN 37243
(615) 741-8307 Fax (615) 532-2868
tn.gov/regboards/contractors/

Texas
Department of Licensing and Regulation
P.O. Box 12157
Austin, TX 78711
(800) 803-9202 (TX)
Fax (512) 463-9468 (no applications)
license.state.tx.us/electricians/elec.htm

Utah
Division of Occupational and Professional
Licensing
160 East 300 South
P.O. Box 146741
Salt Lake City, UT 84114-6741
(801) 530-6628 Fax (801) 530-6511
dopl.utah.gov/

Vermont
State Electricians Licensing Board
1311 US Route 302, Suite 600
Barre, VT 05641
(802) 479-7561

(401) 462-8000 Fax (401) 462-8872
dlt.ri.gov/

Virginia
Board for Contractors
9960 Maryland Dr., Suite 400
Richmond, VA 23233-1066
(804) 367-8511 Fax (804) 430-1033
dpor.virginia.gov/boards/contractors

Washington
Department of Labor and Industries
Electrical Section
P.O. Box 44000
Olympia, WA 98504-4000
(360) 902-5800
lni.wa.gov/TradesLicensing/
Electrical/default.asp

West Virginia
State Fire Marshal
Electrician's Licensing Section
1207 Quarrier Street, 2nd Floor
Charleston, WV 25301
(304) 558-2191 Fax (304) 558-2537
firemarshal.wv.gov/rldivision/pages/
electricallicensing.aspx

Wisconsin
Safety and Building Division
201 West Washington Avenue
P.O. Box 7970
Madison, WI 53707-7970
(608) 266-1018
dsps.wi.gov/so/sb-homepage.html

Wyoming
Department of Fire Prevention
And Electrical Safety
Herschler Bldg., 122 W. 25th St.,
1-West
Cheyenne, WY 82002
(307) 777-7288 Fax (307) 777-7119
wyofire.state.wy.us/

firesafety.vermont.gov/boards/electrical

APPENDIX B

NEMA Classifications

NEMA 1 – Enclosures constructed for indoor use to provide a degree of protection to personnel against incidental contact with the enclosed equipment and to provide a degree of protection against falling dirt.

NEMA 2 – Same as NEMA 1 including protection against dripping and light splashing of liquids.

NEMA 3 – Enclosures constructed for either indoor or outdoor use to provide a degree of protection to personnel against incidental contact with the enclosed equipment; to provide a degree of protection against falling dirt, rain, sleet, snow, and windblown dust; and that will be undamaged by the external formation of the ice on the enclosures.

NEMA 3R – Same as NEMA 3 excluding protection against windblown dust.

NEMA 3S – Enclosures constructed for either indoor or outdoor use to provide a degree of protection to personnel against incidental contact with the enclosed equipment; to provide a degree of protection against falling dirt, rain, sleet, snow, and windblown dust; and in which the external mechanism(s) remain operable when ice laden.

NEMA 4 – Enclosures constructed for either indoor or outdoor use to provide a degree of protection to personnel against incidental contact with the enclosed equipment; to provide a degree of protection against falling dirt, rain, sleet, snow, windblown dust, splashing water, and hose-directed water; and that will be undamaged by the external formation of ice on the enclosure.

NEMA 4X – Same as NEMA 4 including protection against corrosion.

NEMA 5 – Enclosures constructed for indoor use to provide a degree of protection to personnel against incidental contact with the enclosed equipment; to provide a degree of protection against falling dirt; against settling airborne dust, lint, fibers, and flyings; and to provide a degree of protection against dripping and light splashing of liquids.

NEMA 6 – Enclosures constructed for either indoor or outdoor use to provide a degree of protection to personnel against incidental contact with the enclosed equipment; to provide a degree of protection against falling dirt; against hose-directed water and the entry of water during occasional temporary submersion at a limited depth; and that will be undamaged by the external formation of ice on the enclosure.

NEMA 6P – Same as NEMA 6 including protection against the entry of water during prolonged submersion at a limited depth.

NEMA 7 – Enclosures are for indoor use in locations classified as Class I, Groups A, B, C, or D, and shall be capable of withstanding the pressures resulting from an internal explosion of specified gases, and contain such an explosion sufficiently that an explosive gas-air mixture existing in the atmosphere surrounding the enclosure will not be ignited. Enclosed heat generating devices shall not cause external surfaces to reach temperatures capable of igniting explosive gas-air mixtures in the surrounding atmosphere. Enclosures shall meet explosion, hydro-static, and temperature design tests.

NEMA 9 – Enclosures are intended for indoor use in locations classified as Class II, Groups E, F, or G, and shall be capable of preventing the entrance of dust. Enclosed heat generating devices shall not cause external surfaces to reach temperatures capable of igniting or discoloring dust on the enclosure or igniting dust-air mixtures in the surrounding atmospheres. Enclosures shall meet dust penetration and temperature design test, an aging of gaskets (if used).

NEMA 12 – Enclosures constructed (without knockouts) for indoor use to provide a degree of protection to personnel against incidental contact with the enclosed equipment; to provide a degree of protection against falling dirt; against circulating dust, lint, fibers, and flyings; and against dripping and light splashing of liquids.

NEMA 12K – Same as NEMA 12 including enclosures constructed with knockouts.

NEMA 13 – Enclosures constructed for indoor use to provide a degree of protection to personnel against incidental contact with the enclosed equipment; to provide a degree of protection against falling dirt; against circulating dust, lint, fibers, and flyings; and against the spraying, splashing, and seepage of water, oil, and non-corrosive coolants.

Hazardous Location Basics

Definitions:

Hazardous location [NEC®-500] – An area where the possibility of explosion and fire is created by the presence of flammable gases, vapors, dusts, fibers or flyings.

Class I [NEC®-500.5(B)] – Those areas in which flammable gases or vapors are or may be present in the air in qualities sufficient to produce explosive or ignitible mixtures.

Class II [NEC®-500.5(C)] – Those areas made hazardous by the presence of combustible dust.

Class III [NEC®-500.5(D)] – Those areas that are hazardous because of the presence of easily ignitable fibers or flyings, but in which such fibers or flyers are not likely to be in suspension in the air in quantities sufficient to produce ignitible mixtures.

Division 1 [NEC®-500.5(B)(1), 500.5(C)(1), 500.5(D)(1)] – Division One in the normal situation, the hazard would be expected to be present in everyday production operations or during frequent repair and maintenance activity.

Division 2 [NEC®- 500.5(B)(2), 500.5(C)(2), 500.5(D)(2)] – Division Two in the abnormal situation, material is expected to be confined within closed containers or closed systems and will be present only through accidental rupture, breakage, or unusual faculty operation.

Groups [NEC®-500.6(A)(1,2,3,4) & 500.6(B)(1,2,3)] – The gases of vapors of Class I locations are broken into four groups by the code. A, B, C, and D. These materials are grouped according to the ignition temperature of the substance, its explosion pressure and other flammable characteristics.

Class II – dust locations – groups E, F, and G. These groups are classified according to the ignition temperature and the conductivity of the hazardous substance.

Seals [NEC®-501.15 & 502.15] – Special fittings that are required either to prevent the passage of hot gasses in the case of an explosion in a Class I area or the passage of combustible dust, fibers, or flyings in a Class II or III area.

Articles 500 through 504 (2011 NEC®) – Explains in detail the requirements for the installation of wiring of electrical equipment in hazardous locations. These articles along with other applicable regulations, local governing inspection authorities, insurance representatives, and qualified engineering/technical assistance should be your guides to the installation of wiring or electrical equipment in any hazardous or potentially hazardous location.

Typical Class I Locations:

- Petroleum refineries, and gasoline storages and dispensing areas.
- Industrial firms that are flammable liquids in dip tanks for parts cleaning or other operations.
- Petrochemicals companies that manufacture chemicals from gas and oil.
- Dry cleaning plants where vapors from cleaning fluids can be present.
- Companies that have spraying areas where they coat products with paint or plastics.
- Aircraft hangars and fuel servicing areas.
- Utility gas plants and operations involving storage and handling of liquefied petroleum gas or natural gas.

Typical Class II Locations:

- Grain elevators, flour and feed mills.
- Plants that manufacture, use, or store magnesium or aluminum powders.
- Plants that have chemical or metallurgical processes of plastics, medicines, and fireworks, etc.
- Producers of starch or candies.
- Spice-grinding plants, sugar plants, and cocoa plants.
- Coal preparation plants and other carbon-handling or processing areas.

Typical Class III Locations:

- Textile mills, cotton gins, cotton seed mills, and flax processing plants.
- Any plant that shapes, pulverizes, or cuts wood and creates sawdust or flyings.

Note: Fibers and flyings are not likely to be suspended in the air, but can collect around machinery or on lighting fixtures and where heat, a spark, or hot metal can ignite them.

www.ingramcontent.com/pod-product-compliance
Lightning Source LLC
Chambersburg PA
CBHW082028300426
44117CB00015B/2393